MW00748732

ELIJAH

NO ORDINARY HERO

PAULINE COMEAU

DOUGLAS & McINTYRE
Vancouver/Toronto

For Adrian Christopher Comeau and
Aliana Emilia Comeau, and future generations
with a chance to change the world

93 94 95 96 97 5 4 3 2 1

Douglas & McIntyre
1615 Venables Street
Vancouver, British Columbia V5L 2H1

CANADIAN CATALOGUING IN PUBLICATION DATA

Comeau, Pauline, 1956–
Elijah

ISBN 1-55054-082-3

1. Harper, Elijah. 2. Cabinet Ministers—Manitoba—Biography. 3. Politicians—Manitoba—Biography. 4. Indians of North America—Manitoba—Biography. 5. Cree Indians—Biography. I. Title.
FC3377.1H37C64 1993 972.27'03'092
F1063.H37C64 1993 C93-091606-9

Editing by Charis Wahl
Design by Barbara Hodgson
Front cover photograph by Wayne Glowacki, *Winnipeg Free Press*
Other photographs by Pauline Comeau or from Elijah Harper's personal collection. Every reasonable care has been taken to trace ownership of copyrighted material. Information that will enable the publishers to rectify any reference or credit is welcome.

Printed and bound in Canada by Best Gagné Book Manufacturers Inc.
Printed on acid-free paper ∞

CONTENTS

PREFACE

When the Meech Lake Accord came to its sudden halt in Manitoba in June 1990, I was privileged to be a legislative reporter for the *Winnipeg Free Press*. I say privileged because I knew the moment Elijah Harper said his first no that I was about to witness a fascinating part of Canadian history. For more than a year, most of my professional energies had been focussed on native issues, but this had been barely enough time to learn the basics. Still, it soon became apparent that even my limited knowledge of Canada's native people was greater than most of my journalistic colleagues could lay claim to.

As each day passed and the accord moved closer to its end, more perplexed scribes flew into Manitoba (many for the first time) and within hours were expected to explain what was happening. Some pointed to the white advisors hired by the Assembly of Manitoba Chiefs and declared that these men must be the "true brains" behind the strategy. Others looked at Harper and declared him either a pawn in a nasty political game or a solitary hero-prophet guided by some higher power.

But Elijah Harper was not simply a pawn or a prophet.

This is a book about how a status Indian from one of the country's most remote reserves came to be the sole aboriginal representative in the Manitoba legislature when his generation needed him. And it is the story of how he became part of a generation of native leaders who have changed the landscape of this country's politics.

The particular circumstances of every project may change, but no book can be written without the support of friends and family. First and foremost I wish to thank my dear friend Loreen Pindera, who always seemed to know what to say and when to say it and who, like me, still believes in miracles. I would also like to thank those who opened their homes and their hearts to me and who, through their generosity and patience, renewed my faith that the world can be a better place. My employer, Laurie Wiseberg and Human Rights Internet, must also be acknowledged for giving me time away.

Several people must be acknowledged for their technical and research help during the life of this book: Michael Robinson, Rob Ludlow and Michael Gort; Carleton journalism students Erin Anderssen, Kelly Martin and Katherine Martin; the Hudson's Bay Archives in Winnipeg; the Manitoba Legislative Library, and the Canadian Broadcasting Corporation, Television, (Ottawa). Special thanks must also be extended to my ever-calm editor, Charis Wahl, to my agent, Denise Bukowski, and to Scott McIntyre for his patience and enthusiasm about this project.

Finally, I must thank Elijah Harper for agreeing to work with me. He answered my endless, often repetitive questions with unswerving patience, introduced me to his family and friends, shared some of his personal papers and allowed me to share in some special moments of his life.

INTRODUCTION

In 1987, closed-door negotiations among Canada's provincial and territorial governments and the prime minister resulted in a proposal to amend the Canadian constitution—the Meech Lake Accord. The process that led to the accord was, as one constitutional expert describes it, "rushed, secret and elitist."

The gatherings clearly showed that little had changed since European settlers first came to our land. There was still no representation by or consultation with aboriginal peoples. Yet, the Meech Lake Accord touched on concerns critical to Canada's native people: reform of the Senate, Supreme Court of Canada appointments, future constitutional conferences, the amending formula, fisheries and immigration.

The main purpose of the accord was formally to embrace the province of Quebec. The document was based upon the valid concept of Quebec as a distinct society within Canada. Aboriginal people are not against the right of Quebec to their own distinct society. Quebec *is* a distinct society. The people of Quebec have their own language, culture and system of law; they have their own identity, history and vision of the future. Of course they are a distinct society. So are aboriginal people.

The accord totally ignored the integrity of aboriginal peoples as distinct societies. In referring to the "two founding nations," the architects of the accord neglected to acknowledge the equally legitimate place of aboriginal people within the Canadian federation.

This was just one example of the way politics has always been used to silence aboriginal people. The old style of politics has done more to damage this country than anything else I can think of.

Just before the accord died, the prime minister offered aboriginal people several things to get me to say yes instead of no to the accord: conferences on aboriginal issues, a future commitment to constitutional recognition, a joint definition of treaty rights and a royal commission. But such promises had been made—and broken—before. Besides, it was too little and too late.

These were days of immense pressure on me and on all legislators. It is not easy to stand apart from one's colleagues in the legislature. It is not easy to bear the consequences of a failed constitutional proposal.

But we are the First Nations of this country. We need to be recognized for the great contributions we have made. We shared our land and our resources with those who came here. We cared about these people and helped them to survive. Yet our contribution and our role as the original peoples of this land are not even recognized in the constitution. As a Canadian and an aboriginal person, I could not support an amendment to the supreme law of the country that failed to recognize the place of all the founding cultures of the federation. The suffering of native people is too great.

Aboriginal people in Canada die on average ten years younger than other Canadians. Three out of ten aboriginal families have no furnaces or heat in their homes, yet Canada has one of the highest standards of living in the world. Thirty-four per cent have no indoor plumbing; our homes are overcrowded and in poor condition. About 45 per cent of aboriginal people are on social assistance. Few of our people are in secondary schools. Only 5 per cent graduate from secondary school. In my province, Manitoba, aboriginal people comprise 7 per cent of the population, yet they make up 45 per cent of the jail population. Family income on reserves is about $10,000, less than half the national average. Alcoholism, drunkenness and solvent abuse are epidemic on some reserves, and we suffer the negative stereotyping that naturally follows from that. Unemployment is about 66 per cent; on some reserves it is as high as 90 per cent.

Even our languages are in danger. Many have already become extinct. Our religions were forbidden for long enough that much has been forgotten.

But these are only statistics. I cannot bring to you the despair. I cannot bring to you the fifteen-year-old boy in Winnipeg who will never share a bright future because that child was so depressed by what he saw every day that he took his own belt and hanged himself.

As aboriginal people, we expect to be treated fairly. Meech Lake didn't do that, the Charlottetown Accord didn't do that, and that is why aboriginal people said no and will continue to say no until we are treated as equals in our own land. We are not interested in short-term solutions. We are fighting for our children, our culture, our heritage and what we believe in.

Some progress has been made. We have achieved much in the arts, in athletics, among our community leadership, and in business. While state action has often been misdirected or the product of dubious political will, we have also seen attempts by governments, often with good will, to make improvements.

Building the future is more than saying no to that which is wrong. It is also saying yes to that which is fair and just. It is shaping the days, years and centuries to come with our ideas and our aspirations. It is about building bonds and coalitions with others who share our conditions or seek our vision of the future.

Some things are going to have to change. First, we as aboriginal people are going to have to work together as we did before governments developed their policies of dividing and conquering. They almost worked. We have been kept weak by those tactics. We have been divided.

We must attack our problems on two levels. We must attack them as individual problems and we must work to eradicate their origins. We must change personal circumstances and the system. We must build houses for the homeless, but we must also build better communities around them. We must cure the sick, but we must also eliminate the poor water, inadequate sanitation, poor nutrition and poverty that make our people sick. If we don't solve all our problems on those two levels, we will be eternally fighting against a current over which we have no control.

Most important, we must regain control over our future. We must take back what we never gave up. We must become fully self-governing again. We must carry on the visions and dreams of our forefathers of what this country, our homeland, should be.

I have always said that it was an honour and a privilege to have been elected the first treaty Indian in the Manitoba legislature. After Meech Lake, three other aboriginal leaders in Manitoba were elected. We need many more aboriginal people elected across this country.

This is one part of the work we have ahead of us.

We must redefine our First Nations so that they reflect our traditional values in a modern context. It has been our own constitution, our principles and values that have kept us strong. We must keep our eye on the future by never losing sight of our past.

Those few weeks during Meech Lake were a difficult time for all of us. The pressures were great. I stood to represent the shame and anger felt by the majority of Canadians over the betrayal by the Canadian government of the fairness and justice on which our nation purports to be founded. Personally, I can never thank aboriginal people across the country enough for their support, for their show of solidarity. I did not act alone. Through them I found strength. I had the collective will and the prayers of my people behind me.

After enduring so many years of injustice, aboriginal people are working to redress the inequities imposed upon our nations and communities. My role in Meech Lake was one small contribution to the struggle of aboriginal people for recognition and rights. I was proud to be able to advance the cause from within the political structure.

On June 23, 1990, when hundreds of aboriginal people held candles aloft and sang a traditional Cree song of thanksgiving, they were celebrating the death of the Meech Lake Accord and a rebirth of our people. There was born a new pride and a knowledge that we can make a difference, that we can direct the future of our country.

During those days when I stood in the legislature to speak for aboriginal people, our voice was one. I could feel the strength of all our people, a generation of our people, giving strength to my voice. In unity there is strength, in unity there is power, in unity there is hope. It is a feeling I never want to lose. It is a feeling I know our people felt every day hundreds of years ago, and it is a feeling I want all aboriginal people to share again.

Elijah Harper

Prologue

A GREAT DAY FOR CANADA

The security guards looked carefully at the crumpled white pass in the visitor's hand, then let him through the door. Head bowed, voice barely a whisper, the man canvassed the room before approaching a federal New Democratic Party staff member standing in the crowd. After cursory salutations, the visitor got to the point. "We need one like the one you have," said Ovide Mercredi, vice-chief of the Assembly of First Nations, pointing to a peach-coloured tag hanging amidst an assortment of passes around the staffer's neck.

It was June 1990 in the observers' lounge of the Ottawa Convention Centre, a time and a place where coloured tags defined one's status. White passes were the least desirable, allowing one little more than access to the ground floor of the building in which the heads of government had gathered to redraft the country's constitution. It gave one only fleeting opportunities to flag down key people in the convention centre foyer as they came and went. "Ovide was cowed, barely mumbling, like he had no confidence," the staffer recalls. "I kept thinking, this can't be the guy I think it is. Everyone was intimidated by the place."

What Mercredi and others from the Assembly of First Nations were desperately seeking was access to the premiers and their bureaucrats, who had been holed up for days in conference rooms upstairs. Mercredi's white pass was one of two shared among the handful of native leaders in town that week. What he needed was a delegate pass that would move him and the other native leaders one or two floors closer to the premiers' fifth-floor closed-door meeting. It would give them a chance to mingle with political officials and the media, who convened daily in a second-floor lounge to exchange rumours and information filtering out of the premiers' gathering.

But the NDP staffer did not have enough delegate tags for his own people and reluctantly turned down Mercredi's request. All he could offer was another observer's card. "Ovide was looking very small and unimportant in a place where importance was measured in the colour of your tag," remembers the staffer. "Ovide did not rank. He was stuck in a room and could not go beyond."

Being reduced to little more than beggars by the surroundings and the politics of the Meech Lake Accord was a situation that was becoming painfully familiar to Mercredi and Canada's other native leaders. While Mercredi was searching for a pass, Georges Erasmus, head of the Assembly of First Nations, was about to start another day of eighteen-hour lobbying at the back door of the convention centre. As he drove, a news item came on the radio detailing how the native leaders were struggling to gain access to the building. "I turned the car around and went back home," says Erasmus. "It was just too demeaning. I could not face it."

As they had been for centuries, the leaders of Canada's original people were relegated to the sidelines throughout the entire three-year Meech Lake process. The week in Ottawa was the culmination of that exclusion.

"We had problems with almost all the five points in Meech," says Konrad Sioui, former director of international programs for the Assembly of First Nations (AFN). Day after day, the French-speaking Sioui and his English-speaking leader, Georges Erasmus, approached the media, the premiers and any bureaucrats they could find as an English-French SWAT team. "We were arguing that we needed to be there to speak for ourselves," says Sioui of the pair's main message. Native leaders spent the week trying to arrange meetings with the provincial leaders to make their case.

They particularly wanted a chance to speak with Quebec. They wanted and needed Quebec to see that native people, also discriminated against and left in the political wilderness for much of the country's history, shared much with Quebec when it came to their relationship with the rest of Canada. Native leaders hoped at least to convince Quebec to ease the unanimity requirement under the accord for the creation of new provinces. The majority of the residents in the Northwest Territories and Yukon—the regions that might ask for provincial status—are aboriginal.

But no one was paying any attention. Even the media, starved for every new angle in a week with little to report, gave only superficial attention to native concerns.

"We needed allies," says Sioui of the native lobby effort. "But we were treated so badly and our role became so passive, it was frustrating."

Eventually, late-night meetings were held with representatives from Quebec and with the premiers of Newfoundland and Ontario, but little resulted.

Konrad Sioui sat in Georges Erasmus's office late in the evening on June 9, 1990, preparing to watch the Meech Lake signing ceremony on television. He felt the tremendous weight of defeat. In hotels, offices and homes across the country, native leaders sat in front of television sets to watch the premiers and the prime minister put their names to the latest document that would alter the course of natives' lives. The four chairs inside the convention centre assigned to native representatives to watch the official signing ceremony remained empty, a silent protest.

Native leaders had worked day and night, strategizing, holding press conferences and rallies, carrying their placards at the back entrance, cornering officials. And all for nothing.

"We were exhausted," says Sioui. He pauses a long time, struggling for more words to describe his emotions. Finally: "I was defeated in my heart because I knew that our aspirations to access a degree of self-determination and to become self-sufficient would never more be a reality."

Once the accord and the companion resolution made it through the legislatures, entrenching self-government in the Canadian constitution or creating new provinces would require the unanimous consent of all provinces. This, native leaders argued, would make either aspiration next to impossible. "I also felt very insecure for our first nations in Quebec," says Sioui, a Huron-Wyandot from a reserve north of Quebec City. Provincial politicians regarding native people as their enemies did not bode well for future relations. An overwhelming sense of frustration enveloped him.

"I believe in ourselves so much—our leaders, our cause, that we will always be able to bring people to understand our point of view and to support it," says Sioui. "I thought that Quebec would have a better ear, that they would understand us better. That they would see that Quebec and the First Nations were the two who have been left out, and we would give a hand to those guys and try to be their true allies."

But the premiers were signing final documents that did not address native concerns. The companion amendment put native issues on an agenda yet to be negotiated and discussed.

We are now at the mercy of these governments forever, thought Sioui as he sat in Erasmus's office. "They had full control. They all gave themselves the veto over our lives. I was feeling pretty sad."

At 10:30 P.M. on June 9, 1990, the prime minister, the premiers and their aides entered the convention centre room set aside for the official signing ceremony amid a standing ovation from several hundred staff and observers. Hovering near the prime minister was his wife, Mila, standing out in a strangely festive red and yellow dress, along with Senator Lowell Murray and Mulroney's chief of staff, Stanley Hartt, the advisors who had been central to the week's events. The men taking their places in the high-backed red leather chairs circling the conference table were an almost uninterrupted sea of dark blue suits and discreet ties.

The signing ceremony marked the opening of the only public session of the gruelling, seven-day first ministers' "supper meeting." This was "a new beginning," declared Quebec Premier Robert Bourassa. "A proud day for Canada," said another premier. "The people of Canada are the winners," declared a third. The leaders had gathered to sign the Meech Lake Accord and a companion resolution that contained promises about future negotiations for others standing in the constitutional queue—Senate reformers, territorial leaders and aboriginal people. Together, the two documents had enticed Quebec to officially join the Canadian constitutional family while calming the fears of the other provinces.

Norman Spector, Ottawa's leading bureaucrat on constitutional affairs, presented a fountain pen and the agreement to Brian Mulroney. There was applause as the prime minister put pen to paper. The binder was then presented to Robert Bourassa. There was another standing ovation.

New Brunswick Premier Frank McKenna, British Columbia's Bill Vander Zalm and Grant Devine, from Saskatchewan, all affixed their signatures to the document amidst silence. McKenna's official support for the accord had come somewhat late in the game.

The binder was then carried to Newfoundland Premier Clyde Wells.

There was a pause as Wells picked up the pen and then applause as he, too, signed. A standing ovation followed. Wells's face was pale and blotchy. He was not happy with the deal but had agreed to let the legislators and the people of Newfoundland and Labrador decide.

Following Manitoba Premier Gary Filmon's endorsement of the document, his standing ovation is interrupted by a burst of laughter. Filmon had absent-mindedly put the official signing pen in his jacket pocket. The moment of levity came, as in all good theatre, when the tension was highest.

The pen recovered, the signing continued.

"Ladies and gentleman. *Chers amis*. This is a happy day for Canada," began Prime Minister Brian Mulroney after the signing was complete. It was obvious from his demeanour that he actually believed it was.

"We have made it possible for one of the founding nations to reenter the family . . . through the front door," said Mulroney as the session neared an end. "Now, let us adjourn this meeting to June 23, proclamation day of the Meech Lake Accord!"

The deal appeared to be done. As the media moved in to talk to the participants, premiers brushed off suggestions that with two weeks and three legislatures to go, their celebrating might be premature.

The legislatures of Manitoba, Newfoundland and New Brunswick still had to pass the package. New Brunswick was a mere formality: McKenna controlled all the seats. The premiers and prime minister hinted that approval by Manitoba and Newfoundland was also little cause for concern. No one emphasized the obstacles. Ontario's David Peterson spoke of momentum. Filmon, who headed a minority government, pointedly noted that his two opposition leaders were on side. "We believe we can do it in the time that is allotted," he said. McKenna said Canada must "rely on the good will of Newfoundlanders to act in the national interest."

From the spectators' gallery, Manitoba Liberal leader Sharon Carstairs had watched the proceedings with bitterness. Worn down by a week of crass back-room manoeuvring, she had barely slept. She had missed her daughter's graduation from Harvard University, which she had vowed repeatedly she would never do.

After two years as the country's most vocal Meech Lake Accord opponent, Sharon Carstairs had folded. "They came in and I clapped for Filmon and Wells," says Carstairs. "And I clapped when Clyde signed it, and I clapped when Filmon signed it." But there was no applause from Carstairs for Mulroney. "When that scumbag opened his mouth and said, 'This is a happy day for Canada,' my whole stomach went up. I had to get out of there. I felt physically ill."

Carstairs had begun the process clear in her views, comfortable in her love for Canada and in her conviction that the Meech Lake Accord had to be defeated. But after a week in Ottawa she had grown terrified for the country. Carstairs believed the "crisis" had been precipitated almost solely by the prime minister's manipulative style of politics, but by the end of the marathon dinner, she believed the only two choices were doing Mulroney's bidding or allowing the country to disintegrate.

Carstairs fled before the prime minister finished his final comments and the premiers stood for the national anthem.

The statement that revolted Carstairs launched Phil Fontaine, the silver-haired leader of the Assembly of Manitoba Chiefs, out of his living room chair in Winnipeg.

"Bastards!" shouted this usually soft-spoken man, glaring at the smiling premiers on the television screen. He was disgusted. "They spent all this time congratulating each other and sort of slapping each others' backs. Great statesmen," he recalls. The sarcasm in his voice is biting and pained.

Mulroney's comments after the signing ceremony had Fontaine beside himself with rage. "History will show," intoned Mulroney in the sepulchral voice he invoked for particularly important occasions, "that Canada's first ministers persevered for seven days to find a way for Quebec to feel truly a part of a united Canada. No one loses in the agreement before us."

How could the premiers write an absolute lie into the country's defining document? Fontaine thought angrily. The accord would forever entrench the notion that Canada was the product of two founding nations—the French and the English. Canada's aboriginal people didn't even merit a mention. They were supposed to be appeased by a "promise" in the companion resolution of future discussions to determine their place within Canada. Fontaine was not appeased.

Just a few weeks earlier, Fontaine and other determined Meech Lake opponents had been invited to Conservative MP Jake Epp's Winnipeg office to meet with senior officials from the federal government, including Senator Lowell Murray and Norman Spector. The officials assured everyone that the final package would have something in it for all of them. Now the accord and the companion document were signed. They offered only first ministers' conferences on aboriginal issues every three years and a promise to discuss outstanding concerns at some undetermined point in the future. Fontaine was fuming. "It was the ultimate insult," he says. "It was humiliating."

Fontaine had originally asked to be part of the Manitoba delegation, but Filmon offered only observer status—less than Manitoba natives had enjoyed under the previous NDP government. If he had gone to Ottawa as a powerless observer, Fontaine would have been implicated in the outcome. Instead, the head of the Assembly of Manitoba Chiefs had decided to spend the week in Winnipeg, keeping in touch with Montreal lawyer Paul Joffe and two Manitoba native leaders sent to Ottawa to keep an eye on events. They would be in touch with the Assembly of First Nations' delegation of Erasmus, Mercredi and Sioui, but their strategy was their own, guided out of Manitoba.

There were other reasons Fontaine preferred to work alone. Phil Fontaine is an Ojibwa from the Fort Alexander reserve, an hour and a quarter's drive north of Winnipeg. He had served as chief of his home reserve and as vice-chief (Manitoba) with the Assembly of First Nations, and he was considered a leading candidate to take over as head of the national body when Georges Erasmus, a Dene from the Northwest Territories, stepped down the following year. Fontaine respected Erasmus as his national leader, but their relationship had been marked by some philosophical disagreements.

There was also some strain between the often caustic Ovide Mercredi and the usually composed Fontaine. The source of this tension is hard to track, says Fontaine. Some suggest it began when the two squared off in an election for AFN vice-chief years ago. Fontaine won, but he denies there was any ongoing strain between the two men as a result. "We were friends, then," he says. "We would see each other and talk."

(In 1991, Fontaine would run against Mercredi again, this time for the leadership of the Assembly of First Nations. Mercredi won after a bitter and divisive "anybody but Fontaine" campaign spearheaded by Mercredi's supporters. Fontaine remains incredulous that the campaign turned so bitter. All references to a friendship with Mercredi are in the past tense.)

During the week in Ottawa, there were other strains among native delegates from the Assembly of First Nations and the Assembly of Manitoba Chiefs. In the Assembly of First Nations contingent, Erasmus and Sioui worked together and used the AFN offices as their primary base. Mercredi, often sighted with Liberal MP Ethel Blondin, was more closely aligned with the Manitoba native contingent, which used a restaurant booth at the Château Laurier as home port. It was here, in this busy restaurant, that the Manitoba group and Mercredi would meet with interested politicians such as Manitoba NDP leader Gary Doer, Liberal leader Sharon Carstairs and anyone else who dropped in. Paul Joffe, working on behalf of the Manitoba chiefs, was an almost permanent fixture, taking calls and directing information traffic.

The division within the AFN can be traced to the initial agreement on the accord in 1987 and frustrations with what some viewed as Georges Erasmus's lukewarm response to the threat of Meech. "He said he was reacting," says one insider, "but the feeling was that it wasn't sufficient, that there needed to be a greater sense of outrage expressed." Others suggest that Erasmus was simply tired as he neared the end of his five-year mandate as AFN leader, but Erasmus denies the suggestion.

Regardless of the reasons, the constitutional game was moving away from Erasmus. Not long after the premiers emerged from the Langevin Block in June 1987, Ovide Mercredi and other western-based native leaders decided to fight against the accord through Manitoba.

This hidden division in the AFN ranks, coupled with the profound sense of defeat on the part of the key native players, would first confuse the prime minister and premiers, and later lead to an assumption and miscalculation that would help sink the accord. The premiers left the June 1990 signing ceremony believing that Erasmus would rail against the lack of fundamental recognition of aboriginal peoples but would accept the promise of a future aboriginal process. One Manitoba insider was told the morning after the signing ceremony: "Erasmus is going to kick and yell and scream but allow it to go through. . . ."

But native activists and those working with them in Ottawa that week say now that their overriding feeling was devastation. Paul Joffe stood outside the convention centre to hear the premiers' post-signing comments. "I felt such frustration and helplessness that there was absolutely nothing we could do," he says. Perhaps, suggest both Erasmus and Sioui, this sense of resignation was interpreted by the white leaders as acceptance. It would not take long, however, for it to become apparent that even if Erasmus had conceded this round, other native leaders had not.

As the premiers left the convention centre that night, the media focussed not on Carstairs's empty chair, nor on the four seats left vacant by the native protest, but on Wells's conditional signature and the logistical hurdles Filmon still faced in Manitoba.

Wells, a passionate student of constitutional issues and a fiercely pragmatic lawyer, could not reconcile the decentralizing Meech Lake view of the country with his own, but by the end of the week he was also not convinced that he had the right to stop Newfoundlanders from deciding for themselves. His preference was a referendum; but if there was not enough time, the Newfoundland legislators would vote on it after consulting with their constituents.

In Manitoba, Sharon Carstairs and her twenty Liberals had been publicly against the accord. Gary Doer's NDP dozen, who held the balance of power in Manitoba, were strategically undeclared. Together, the Liberals and the NDP could defeat anything Filmon put to them. (The Meech Lake Accord had been signed by NDP Premier Howard Pawley but not presented for ratification before the Pawley government unexpectedly fell in March 1988.)

Filmon had no choice but to try to forge an all-party consensus on the deal. Manitoba's history is scarred by painful constitutional wars and finicky laws that emerged from those battles. Filmon needed the opposition with him. If he suffered politically, Carstairs and Doer too would suffer. If Manitoba won concessions, then all three leaders would gain without disproportionate benefit. Moreover, a united Manitoba would have more clout at the constitutional table.

Unlike Wells, Filmon could not respond quickly on constitutional matters. He depended heavily on experts for advice and would always seek their counsel before commenting. It was Carstairs who could quickly judge the ramifications of new suggestions. Filmon signed the Ottawa package believing he had gained as much as he could for Manitoba. He, Doer and Carstairs returned home to face the logistical nightmare of mandatory public hearings with only thirteen days left before the accord deadline.

Fontaine barely slept after watching the signing ceremony, anger and frustration making his mind work furiously. He was to meet with several Manitoba chiefs that day. "We have to devise a strategy to block it," he prepared to tell them. At some point during the night Fontaine sensed, rather than reasoned, that Elijah Harper was a key. During the weeks leading up to the first ministers' meeting, a local reporter had asked Fontaine about the accord and noted that public hearings on the package were obligatory. It was at that point that Fontaine began to think about Harper.

Fontaine had had almost twenty years' experience in native politics. As head of the Assembly of Manitoba Chiefs, he represented 60,000 Indians in the province. He had a reputation as a talented consensus builder within the aboriginal community and was well respected among white political leaders for being both tough and fair. In short, Fontaine had influence in the native community. (When the word went out that Erasmus would support the deal after a show of protest, one insider advised: "You better phone Phil, because Manitoba is the tail that wags the dog. And if you cut a deal with Erasmus it may not necessarily cut it in Manitoba.")

Yet Fontaine's understanding of the often confining rules of the Manitoba legislature was practically nonexistent. He knew only that "one could be very creative in the legislature and in the House. We had seen the Tory tactics when they charged the speaker, and the bell-ringing, and filibusters."

As the premiers and bureaucrats were flying home from Ottawa, Fontaine, unshaven and haggard, was interviewed on CBC television. Manitoba's native leaders, he said, were examining their options. "We had expected that the first ministers would be as generous and fair with us as they obviously have been with Quebec," Fontaine told the interviewer. "But that fairness and generosity did not materialize for the first peoples of this country. We don't represent a significant force in this country, so in the end it is a lot easier to bargain away aboriginal people."

Fontaine said nothing about the calls he would make to the executive of the Assembly of Manitoba Chiefs or his plan to contact Elijah Harper. Nor did he mention the telephone conversation he had had with Assembly advisor Paul Joffe.

Joffe had left Ottawa at 5:30 that Sunday morning, anxious to get home to Montreal—and far away from the Ottawa experience. He was dreading the inevitable call to Fontaine.

"Phil, I'm sorry. We tried everything."

"Don't worry, Paul," replied Fontaine. "We'll take it from here. We'll block it in the Manitoba legislature."

Joffe was surprised by Fontaine's upbeat tone. "We knew there had to be public hearings, because Filmon kept saying so," says Joffe, but Filmon kept changing his mind about the deadline, leading Joffe to conclude that Filmon would be amenable to whatever was necessary to facilitate the accord's passage. Fontaine outlined his plan, then hung up so he could pass the message on.

As Joffe and Fontaine talked, many of Manitoba's sixty-one chiefs were en route to Winnipeg to attend a conference on native health sponsored by Health and Welfare Canada. The conference was to begin on Monday. A gathering on treaties and self-determination was scheduled for Sunday afternoon at the Assembly's Smith Street office in downtown Winnipeg. Fontaine decided to hijack the Sunday meeting for a discussion of the AMC's strategy on the accord and to prepare for further discussions on Monday with the province's chiefs.

As Norman Spector handed the red binder to the premiers for their signatures, Elijah Harper was sitting in Red Sucker Lake, seven hundred kilometres northeast of Winnipeg. He glanced periodically at the television in his parents' house to see the premiers signing and applauding, and he thought about the two-hour flight to Winnipeg. If he wanted out before the regularly scheduled Monday flight, he would have to call and arrange a charter.

Harper pondered what would likely happen in the coming days. The Manitoba legislature would be recalled and Harper would have to be there with every other MLA.

Elijah Harper had spent the last several days travelling to some of the larger communities in the northern part of his vast Rupertsland riding, trying to sell party memberships and feeling out the mood: in just a few weeks, he would face his third nomination meeting. Since the fall of the NDP government in 1988, Elijah, like many others in the party, had found it difficult to rebound. In fact, Elijah was in many ways adrift. His stormy marriage was turning messy again, his finances were in a shambles, and his nomination was in jeopardy.

Manitoba's only native MLA was exhausted. He had been in white politics since 1981; he had served as a cabinet minister, been involved in four first ministers' conferences on native issues as well as many other federal-provincial events, and in countless other ways worked hard for his constituents. Throughout it all, he had felt like an outsider. No matter how long he stayed, white politics did not become a comfortable fit. The fall of the Manitoba government in 1988 had exacerbated his sense of isolation. "Everybody was depressed," says Harper. "After a thing like that, nobody cares about anything. I felt the same way. There were days when I wanted to pack it up and leave."

Several people in the NDP and in the native community had been trying to make Elijah's decision for him. In the months before the week-long Meech Lake meeting, George Hickes, an Inuit born in the

Northwest Territories and living in Churchill since the age of two, had signed up more than four hundred new party members, giving him a hefty advantage in nomination support. Churchill was new territory for Harper, added to his already enormous riding in a realignment of the province's electoral map since the last election. NDP insiders believed Hickes was about to take the Rupertsland nomination.

Years earlier, Elijah's second nomination campaign had also been contested. "Don't worry about it," Peter Cox, a fellow MLA and friend had told the nervous candidate at the time. "What you have to do is go to the community, go to the grassroots, talk to the people. Go door to door. Then you will have nothing to worry about."

Elijah had always followed that advice. He had been in the towns of Gillam and Churchill visiting the grassroots throughout the week of the first ministers' meeting, and he had caught only brief news reports. Gary Doer had canvassed the NDP MLAs but was vague about what might be in the final package. "I was asking him what's in the deal," says Harper, "and he is asking me, 'Can I proceed with a deal—whatever it is? If it is good, can I make a deal?' " Elijah had told Doer that he would remain noncommittal until he saw the offer.

Harper had always been opposed to the Meech Lake Accord. The entrenchment of the concept of two founding nations and its lack of acknowledgement of the fundamental place of aboriginal peoples is anathema to all aboriginal leaders. Elijah had informed Pawley (and then Doer, when he became leader) that he would have to vote against the accord. Unless several MLAs joined him, however, Harper's protest would be little more than an embarrassment for the Manitoba government.

Sitting in Red Sucker Lake, Harper was not sure whether the companion resolution would satisfy native people. He would need to hear from Doer, speak with his own confidants and discuss it with Manitoba native leaders. That meant returning to Winnipeg as soon as possible. Although he had not planned to leave so soon, after speaking briefly with Phil Fontaine, he decided to return to his Winnipeg apartment on Monday.

Leaving his constituency would not make things easier for his nomination—he had barely begun campaigning—but the accord overrode all other considerations. Yet he was not overly worried. "My feeling has always been, if it's meant to be, it will be," he says, a philosophy that has caused endless frustration for many colleagues over the years. "I don't worry. Things will fall into place if you work at it." Perhaps he would get yet another extension on the nomination meeting. In any event, he would deal with it from Winnipeg.

A few week's earlier, Harper had sat in a sparsely furnished downtown Winnipeg office with a longtime advisor and friend, Lloyd Girman. It is Harper's habit to canvass his friends when facing serious questions. The talk with Girman was one of many such discussions Elijah had had throughout that year in an attempt to sort out his life.

Girman, Harper's deputy minister of northern affairs during Elijah's cabinet posting in the 1980s, is a blunt man, his vernacular loaded with expletives. His assessment of Harper's financial and political situation had been brutal. "You have two choices," Girman had told Harper at their last meeting. "One: you can resign, take your settlement and pay your debts, and you stay out of fucking jail. Or option two: pray for a fucking miracle."

Harper listened to his friend, as always; but panic and a sense of urgency are foreign to him, as they are to many native people. "Patience is the virtue," explained one Manitoba native leader. "Urgency is not a concept. I don't know of any tribe that has a word for it. The time in which things get done is less relevant than the doing. Inherently, there is a faith in our culture, in the outcome of life."

Elijah Harper heard Girman out, arms folded over his rounded stomach in what Girman calls Elijah's "Buddha pose." Finally, Elijah spoke.

"Something will happen," Elijah said slowly. "Something will happen."

PART ONE

The Old and the New

Chapter One

TWO WORLDS COLLIDING

A small heap of animal entrails sits on the unpainted wood porch. Black hooves and some dirty-brown fur beside the pile are the only hint to the untrained eye that these are the remains of a caramel-coloured moose.

Traffic through the single-storey, brown clapboard house of Elijah Harper's parents is heavy. Four girls race out of the white door and leap on two bicycles, circa 1970. The younger, lighter ones balance on the butterfly handlebars while the older girls navigate. One bike is labelled "Outlaw"; its passenger wears New Kids on the Block sweat pants. The girls giggle as they struggle over the scraggly grass and rough, hardened grey mud of a typical northern Manitoba landscape.

This is Red Sucker Lake reserve on a sunny August afternoon in 1992, a place where, every day, ancient history and modernity collide.

The Harper house sits with a handful of others on the eastern edge of the 255-acre reserve, home to about four hundred Ojibwa-Cree. The reserve's main road begins here, a rutted clay pathway that curves through the community and ends at the shore of Red Sucker Lake, perhaps a twenty-minute drive if one navigates around the potholes. About midway, the road curls past the site of the Harper family's original one-room log cabin, where Elijah was born and placed on a bed of spruce boughs forty-three years ago.

Inside the 'new' house, the Red Sucker Lake airport manager sits on a well-worn couch. Ethel Harper is feeling a little under the weather, but she remains patient as yet another grandchild scrambles up to cuddle with her. Ethel, sixty-one, doesn't really run the Red Sucker Lake airport, but her house sits so close to the nine-hundred-metre gravel runway that people on the reserve like to say that she does.

The runway has been declared unfit for larger aircraft, so the three weekly flights in and out of the reserve will be more erratic than usual. Elijah has chartered a small prop plane to fly in today and out in two days' time. In the summer, the only way into Red Sucker Lake is by plane. In February, you can drive to the community from Winnipeg on a road built of ice and snow, a twelve- to fourteen-hour journey depending on the weather.

On the wall above Ethel's head hangs a large wool tapestry. A wavy-haired, doe-eyed Jesus Christ stands by a small blue river, a flock of sheep nearby. He is holding a rough, wooden staff in one hand, a lamb in the other. A blood-red sky sets Christ's haloed head in sharp relief. A second picture of Jesus shares a wall with a framed certificate. "This is to certify that Allan B. Harper . . . an Ordained Minister. . . ." It is signed by officials of the Full Gospel Chapel in Steinbach, Manitoba, and is dated March 10, 1985.

Allan B. Harper, sixty-seven, walks into the living room with a pail of clean water from the water shed a couple of minutes' walk from the house. The water travels from the nearby lake through pipes installed by the federal government to a handful of small, wooden shacks scattered throughout the community; residents draw water from the exposed (and often leaking) taps. When the system fails, residents get their water directly from the lake. There is a single outhouse about thirty paces downhill from the Harper home. Only the school, the teachers' apartment complex and the nursing station have hot and cold running water and flush toilets.

This is a busy day for Reverend Harper. Visitors from Ontario and Manitoba are arriving for the annual five-day conference of prayer and Evangelical church services. A huge yellow-and-white striped tent has been erected in front of the small Red Sucker Lake Full Gospel Church, where Allan B. Harper serves as pastor.

The "B" doesn't stand for a name. The moniker is a remnant of the days when the Hudson's Bay Company governed the North and the managers of the posts logged the debts and credits of the area trappers. The company men were not very imaginative when handing out English names and often reused them. To differentiate among those with the same name, letters were added. Thus, Allan Harper became Allan

Harper "B", now modernized to Allan B. Harper.

English names were also doled out by the missionaries, with little explanation. This resulted in substantial cultural confusion. "This elder wanted to give the name Jonah to his daughter," says Elijah, recalling an old tale. "But the priest said, 'You can't have that name. It's a boy's name.' " The elder forever remained perplexed by this religion so bizarre that it determined names by gender.

From the moment his father enters the house, it is obvious that Elijah has a deep-seated respect for the man. Elijah explains that the church has been the centre of his dad's life for years. His father beams with pride.

There is a hint of grey in Allan Harper's black, collar-length hair. His smile reveals some bottom teeth, but only gum on the top. He speaks quietly, ponders questions for several moments before answering almost shyly. When thinking, Reverend Harper crosses his arms over a well-rounded stomach in a manner strikingly similar to that of his oldest son's.

There is a movie on television. The language of the actors is English. The language spoken in the room by children and adults alike is a Cree-Ojibwa dialect, evidence of a northwest flow of indigenous traffic through the primarily Cree area hundreds of years ago. It is a language spoken up in the back of the throat. To the untrained ear, one sound—Kah—punctuates the air over and over, usually at the end of sentences like the "eh" in Canadian English. Elijah explains that it can mean different things depending on where it is used, but most often it serves as a signal that the message has been received or as a bridge between thoughts.

Ethel and Allan understand a little English but do not speak it. Their children and grandchildren, however, switch easily back and forth.

Behind a wall, raw slabs of moose meat, stewing in blood, almost overflow a turquoise plastic bowl on a wooden kitchen table. There is cold tea on the propane-powered stove. Against another wall, a cold black wood stove sits on an unpainted skid. Later, under Ethel Harper's practiced touch, the moose meat will be cubed and transformed into a delicious, hearty stew accompanied by bannock, a flour- and water-based bread, reminiscent of hot biscuits, that can be baked in an oven or fried over an open fire. The food will be shared with relatives and friends, echoing an earlier era when Ethel and Allan were newly married and travelled through the Island Lake area in a rhythm dictated primarily by the seasons. Then, when a family caught a moose, it was shared with the three or four other families gathered in a winter hunting area.

This night, bannock and a pot of the stew will be delivered by truck down the dusty, busy road to Saul Harper's house. Saul, Elijah's brother, is the school principal, overseeing the educational needs of 170 children, from kindergarten to Grade 8. The Red Sucker Lake School term is supposed to begin in a few weeks, but the building has been closed by federal authorities because of ongoing flooding. Inside, the musty air catches in the lungs. The politics surrounding the closing of the thirty-five-year-old school are complex, says Elijah, typical of the centuries-old relation of federal overseers to their native wards. The government has declared that a new school cannot be built until 1996. Until then, the green mould growing on the walls and the mushrooms pushing up between wooden baseboards will simply make the building uninhabitable.

Saul's apartment is in a motel-style dwelling that houses the school's teachers during the school year. Tidy and modern, it has running water, a propane-powered stove (currently out of order) and a well-equipped entertainment centre. There is not much else to spend your money on, says Saul, and not much else to do in Red Sucker.

The reserve's electrical power is provided by a diesel-powered generating plant plunked down by government workers. Its placement in the middle of the school playground is a monument to bureaucrats' failure to confer with residents.

Elijah has a house on the reserve but is home too rarely to keep it open year round. Sometimes, when an emergency arises, the band chief, Elijah's brother Fred, will place a family there.

On this visit in August 1992, more than two years after the Meech Lake saga, laughter and many exclamations of "kah" punctuate Elijah's conversations with his family; the biggest laugh comes when he tells them that there will be a book written about his life. His mother finds the idea especially humorous, laughing behind her hands, a common gesture among native women.

A few months after this visit, Ethel will tell her husband that she is not feeling well and will go to rest in an adjoining room. She will not wake up. She will not be there when this book about her now-famous son is published.

Red Sucker Lake, its odd name derived from the bottom-feeding fish found in vast quantities during the spring in the area's waterways, lies amidst a dizzying collection of lakes and islands sculpted by the last ice age. Not the trees, mostly spruce and jack pine, nor the land's wild grasses hide the jagged underpad of the Canadian Shield, which was all but stripped of its topsoil by the advancing glaciers fifty thousand years ago. The flat, seemingly endless prairie so familiar in the south might as well be on a different planet: there is not a hint of it here.

This is Elijah Harper's home and his retreat; this is where he rediscovers himself. For at least ten days every fall, no matter what, he sleeps in the bush, canoes the lakes and tracks the moose. This is where Elijah Harper comes to confront the history stolen from Canada's first Canadians, a history that still echoes in his soul.

Elijah Harper was born on March 3, 1949, on a peninsula on the lake's northeast shore, just shy of the Ontario border. The name Elijah, pronounced with a hard "j", was a popular one in northern native communities at the time. It was given to him by his maternal grandmother, Emily Taylor, who was present at his birth along with midwives Maggie Harper and Harriet Little. Elijah's mother says her first-born son was an easy baby. "He never cried, and he slept all night," she says in Cree, her son Saul interpreting. "He was quiet."

Two weeks after his birth, Elijah was bundled up and taken by dog sled with his year-old sister Mary Jane about ninety kilometres east to his father's trapping territory. The young family stopped often en route, says Reverend Harper, to let Ethel rest.

(Elijah was the last of the Harper's thirteen children to be born in the log cabin. All the others would be born in a nursing station eighty kilometres inland and south, in Garden Hill, where the family maintained a permanent home. "They just decided it was more convenient," says Saul, translating his parents' story. Ethel travelled to Garden Hill weeks before her third child, Fred, was due and did not return to the bush that season, leaving Allan to travel alone. "There would have been no one to look after my mom," Saul explains.)

When the winter trapping season ended several weeks later, the family travelled back to Red Sucker, regrouped with other hunting families and continued on to Garden Hill. Here the furs caught over the winter were taken to the Hudson's Bay Company.

The place of birth for all the Harper children is listed as Island Lake Reserve, which was replaced by several smaller, independent reserves during the late 1960s and 1970s. Red Sucker Lake received reserve status in 1976, almost twenty-six years after families led by John McDougall decided to stay in Red Sucker permanently.

The Island Lake band had included the five thousand residents of Garden Hill, Wasagamack, St. Theresa Point (called Maria—pronounced Ma-rye-ah—Portage) and Red Sucker Lake, all permanent or semipermanent settlements that grew out of the ancient nomadic dictates of the trapping seasons. Life for Allan and Ethel's generation followed traditional patterns, although serious interventions by whites had begun to have an impact.

Ethel and Allan were both born at Garden Hill, or Smooth Rock, as it was called long, long ago. "Most of our ancestors come from Sandy Lake," says Elijah, naming a community on the Ontario side of the border. "The roots in Island Lake would be more with the Ontario people rather than the Cree, which is why we speak a different dialect than the Cree. We are more Ojibwa than Cree."

Canada's original residents arrived during the ice age when big game hunters crossed the land bridge between Siberia and Alaska. The first migrations to the Island Lake area likely came from the south and northwest when the last ice age receded between six and twelve thousand years ago. Excavations in the God's Lake area, just north of Red Sucker Lake, have placed civilizations there in 1000 BC.

Fifty native languages, classified into twelve families, were spoken across the country in those early times. The most widespread geographically were the communities within the Algonkian language groups, spreading from the Rocky Mountains to the Atlantic. They included the Blackfoot, Blood and Plains Cree of the prairies; the Ojibwa, Odawa and Huron of southern Ontario; the Swampy, Woodland and James Bay Cree of northern Manitoba, Ontario and Quebec, and the Mi'kmaq and Maiseet of the Atlantic.

It was the Swampy and Woodland Cree, and their Ojibwa cousins to the south in what is now Ontario, who gave birth to Elijah Harper's ancestors. The Swampy Cree are now defined as those who lived north of Winnipeg and in the low-lying areas of Hudson Bay. The Swampy and Woodland Cree, who populated the Shield a little farther east, were known for their mastery of the birchbark canoe and the snowshoe, masters of spears, bow and arrows, snares and clubs. Much of the year was spent in small family bands in which co-operation was as essential to survival as the hunt itself. Even the children were put to work.

It is not unusual for the first snow to fall in early October in Island Lake and for mid-May or early June to arrive before the ice sheets leave the rivers and lakes. In spring and fall, the bands would move from their base to favourite fishing spots or caribou migration corridors.

This nomadic way of life did not lend itself to complex community organizations. The basic social unit of these Ojibwa-Cree was the extended family: the care and teaching of children was a community responsibility rather than that of the "nuclear" family familiar to most Canadians today. The basic ethic of non-interference—advice not sought is not offered—extended to everyone in the community, including children. For example, children would learn through observation how to canoe, but would carry out this task in a time frame of their own choosing.

Grandparents had the honour of naming a newborn, and the children would often stay with grandparents for major portions of their lives. A child's chosen name would often relate to an event on the day of his or her birth. Men were expected to stay with or close by their parents throughout their lives, caring for them in old age. Marriages were usually arranged, often between first cousins. Men were allowed more than one wife if they could provide for them.

Families belonged to different clans guided by elders and medicine men. (The notion of a chief as leader was a later invention of the white man.) In the fall, before the seasonal bands scattered for the winter hunts, people met in council to readjust the winter hunting areas to ensure animal populations for the hunts to come. This centuries-old balancing act would be just one tradition irrevocably disrupted by the fur trade.

The people followed the rules of the earth itself—of winter, summer, spring and fall—dictated by the unalterable rhythms of animals moving through the land. Traditional Cree religion is an extension of this life. Humans were not separate or superior to their environment or the animals they killed in order to survive. Intense bonds existed between the earth and all its creatures, including people.

Manitou was the supreme universal power responsible for putting the universe in order and giving life. (The word Manitoba is believed to be a derivative of the word Manitou.) When the missionaries came and spoke of one "God," the Cree felt they understood. The Bible, for many, including Elijah's father, was the "word" of the creator. Such words did nothing to disrupt their understanding of the essential balance in the world. In fact, a close examination of the Bible, say Cree believers, supports this teaching.

Leadership was traditionally entrusted to the eldest male or the most competent, charismatic elder. (Age is not key to being an elder, explains Elijah; rather it is wisdom and insight.) Only one member of the community garnered more respect than the elder: the medicine man or woman, the shaman. Sickness was often believed to be the result of evil spirits having taken over the body and mind. Shamans like Elijah's great-grandfather, Barefoot, were revered and feared for having the powers to expel these spirits.

Not all power was good. Windigo was a giant, man-eating demon with the power to take over people's minds, making them deranged and a danger to the community. If a possessed person could not be cured, he or she would be killed by the shaman.

Spiritual wars, in which the shamans called upon such forces as Windigo, were renowned in the Island Lake area. These powers could cast storms, raise winds and cause accidents. Elijah Harper's great-grandmother, one of Barefoot's four wives, was killed in such a skirmish—scalped by competing powers, according to the tales passed down to Elijah's generation. The fear instilled by these "wars" was enough to discourage invasion by other tribes, enhancing the remoteness of the Swampy Cree.

In general, decision-making was by consensus among responsible adults and reflected the main goal of life—a spiritual harmony between nature and humans. Resolutions emerged from the various opinions expressed in discussions that might take days. Votes were not needed, and force as a method of governing was almost unheard of.

Every man was his own boss, given the understanding that decisions depended on maintaining the overall harmony and survival of the group. The modern concept of majority rule was alien to the Cree. Their approach was far more complex and required a deft touch by the leaders and decision-makers to maintain balance within their communities. Ostracism was the worst form of punishment in ancient native communities because it was the essence of disharmony. When a man or women was sent out of the fold, the impact was devastating. Crime was rare.

This is the history of Elijah's ancestors, a history that largely dictated the early lives of Elijah's parents and that filtered down to Elijah's generation. It is a history that was forever altered by the insensitive intervention of non-natives. And this, too, is the legacy of Elijah Harper's generation.

It was British explorer Henry Hudson's search for the elusive northwest passage to Asia that first brought white men into the inner sanctum of Canada's middle north. Sixty years later England discovered that

James Bay and Hudson Bay offered a direct water route to the interior of the Canadian Shield and to the rich furs that lay therein. On May 2, 1670, Britain gave control over the claimed area to the "honourable Company," giving the Hudson's Bay Company (HBC) a trading monopoly and absolute power over Rupert's Land, named after the governor of the company and King Charles II's cousin—Prince Rupert of the Rhine. The HBC was given sole control over the fur trade in the area, law and order, and war and peace; it became the first government body to rule the land of the Crees, an arrangement that would make the company an integral part of the North for more than three centuries.

The first trading posts were built thirty years later at the mouths of several rivers flowing into the waterway, including York Factory on the Nelson River, the main post leading into what is now northern Manitoba. It would be another twenty years before the interior was seriously explored, and then only after the North West Company began infiltrating from the southeast. Fur trading competition had many long-term effects, the most serious being a perilous depletion of pelts. In 1821, the two fur trading companies amalgamated, with HBC rules applied to the areas again, including serious restrictions on liquor distribution. (Island Lake has been an officially dry community ever since, a fact that would save Island Lake from some of the liquor-related destruction of many of Canada's other native communities.)

With few furs available, many of the HBC's inland posts were abandoned. Island Lake was closed in 1824 and moved to God's Lake, about eighty kilometres to the north. Merry's House Post, the closest to what is now Red Sucker Lake, was closed the same year. Hudson's Bay did not return with a post to Red Sucker Lake until 1947, about the same time the winter seasonal band established a permanent settlement.

The impact of Europeans on the people in Island Lake came relatively late. Still, by the 1840s, almost all the people living there were getting the bulk of their clothing from the Hudson's Bay or missionaries, in part because of a scarcity of hides but also because of the convenience. As well, teepees were being covered with imported canvas instead of hides and the winter task bands were building log cabins for lodgings on annual treks.

While the Island Lake people could see these changes all around them, they knew and cared little about the events that were responsible. Still, their lives were altered by what was going on far away. Between 1650 and 1765, when France and England were at war, control of the HBC posts switched hands many times. Both sides formed alliances with various Indian nations as they fought for control of North America. The Cree, for the most part, stayed out of the fighting.

The 1763 Peace of Paris marked the end of fighting in Europe. But a drop in fur prices and an influx of English settlers led to a revolt among Indian tribes south of the Great Lakes and east of the Mississippi. King George III's response was the Royal Proclamation of 1763, which, among other things, aimed to ease tensions over land claim disputes with incoming settlers through the introduction of land settlements called treaties.

The purpose of the treaties was to extinguish Indian title to the land in order to open up the country "for settlement, immigration, and such other purposes." They were a clever mechanism to replace military rule with civilian government and to prevent land settlements with Canada's original people until official agreements were negotiated between the British Crown and the Indian communities.

The 1763 proclamation included a provision that all of British North American lands not ceded to or purchased by Britain were to be "reserve lands" for the natives. The Crown retained the right to extinguish Indian title, defined at the time as right of occupancy and use, on the assumption that Britain held underlying sovereign title. The proclamation referred to "our" lands being reserved for native people to whom the Crown was extending its protection. The 1763 proclamation was, and is, regarded by Indian people as one of the most important documents to recognize the sovereignty of First Nations and title to land.

By 1830, the British—motivated by a notion that native people should either be separated from whites or assimilated into white society—had introduced the reserve system as part of the treaty-making process. (The first recorded "reserve" in Canada was created in 1637 near Quebec City. The French, borrowing from a Jesuit model used in Brazil, set aside land for use by the natives.) All Indians were placed in the wardship of Indian agents.

While other communities were being brought under the rules of the proclamation or new reserve policy, Elijah's ancestors remained under the administration of the HBC. Their transfer into the Dominion was interrupted by the 1869 Riel rebellion. By July 1870, Riel's attempt to establish a Metis government had failed and he was in exile in the U.S. On July 15, the administration of Rupert's Land was handed over to the Crown, and the province of Manitoba came into being. While the HBC was no longer the feudal lord, its posts and its employees remained an integral part of the North.

Despite being affected by the Riel clashes (Riel made a second run at Metis self-determination, only to be hanged for his efforts in 1885), the treaty-writing process established under the 1763 proclamation continued. Treaty One was signed in what is now southern Manitoba in 1871, Treaty Eleven in the Northwest Territories in 1921. Adhesions to these original contracts continued to be signed until 1930. Within this fifty-year period, more than half of Canada's aboriginal people came under agreements, says Elijah, made between two sovereign nations. The Island Lake band signed what is called Adhesion to Treaty Five. An "X" marked acceptance by Island Lake Chief George Nott, councillors Joseph Linklater and John Mason, and Ottawa Commissioner John Semmens on August 13, 1909.

While carried out with great pomp and ceremony, the treaties were regarded as little more than a formality by the English. The native people, however, whose word had always been law, viewed them with solemn reverence. "Treaties were understood by our forefathers as agreements to live with each other in friendship and respect while sharing the land and resources," Harper says. Elijah grew up respecting the treaties as the physical embodiment of the special bond between Canada's First Nations and the Queen of England, a towering figure in native lore. The bond remains profound, as governments discovered more than 120 years after the first treaty was signed, when Canada's aboriginal people voted overwhelmingly to reject the Charlottetown Accord partly because it might jeopardize the original, sacred treaty documents by altering the fundamental relationship between First Nations and Canada.

By signing a treaty, Indians agreed to "cede, release, surrender and yield up to the Dominion of Canada" the land, to obey the country's laws, maintain the peace and not interfere with settlements or people moving onto the land. In exchange, the Crown promised to establish reserves, their size based on population (160 acres for each family). Five dollars was given to each person upon signing, and annually in perpetuity. Other government undertakings included annual payments of $25 to band chiefs and $15 to councillors (three maximum), as well as a "suitable suit" of clothing for each chief and councillor. In addition, $500 a year would be provided for the purchase of ammunition and twine to be distributed among the Indians, and farming equipment would be supplied on a one-time-only basis. Schools would be maintained on the reserves. The sale of liquor would be monitored, and the

Indians' right to hunt and fish throughout the ceded territories (subject to regulations made from time to time by Canada, and excluding tracts required or taken up for settlement, mining, lumbering or other purposes) would be maintained. As well, the Crown was given the right to sell, lease or otherwise dispose of reserve land for the use and benefit of the band, provided the band gave consent.

What exactly native people in Canada understood of what they were signing has been long debated. There are the issues of language and translation, and of whether natives truly understood the European concept of giving up ownership of land: aboriginal people's connection to the land was so intimate that handing it off as one might a possession would have been inconceivable. "It is part of us," says Elijah. "Every thing is a living thing; the water, the land."

In 1876, in an attempt to consolidate the numerous laws governing Indians, the Canadian Parliament passed the first nationwide Indian Act. The aim of the act was to encourage the "civilization" of the Indian people into full-fledged Canadians. For several years, Indians were offered individual ownership of plots of land carved from reserves. They were also offered the right to vote in federal elections if they gave up their treaty status. But Indians resisted "enfranchisement," seeing it as an attempt to destroy their communities by slowly breaking their vital bond with the land.

While growing up, Elijah listened to the adults talking about giving up their status. He recalls his uncle, Robinson Harper, an Island Lake councillor, in particular. "I never used to understand what he was talking about, but one day he enfranchised himself. He used to say that if you did, you could vote, and he would also have a job forever. That is what he was told." His uncle also talked about getting unemployment insurance. "He said he had money coming in all the time."

It was in the original Indian Act that the concept of elected band chiefs and a band council was imposed in an attempt to destroy traditional native government systems. The Indian Act also defined 'Indians' for the first time: one must be one-quarter Indian blood to qualify under the act. The law also declared that Indians on reserves could not be taxed, or own their own homes or land. Chiefs and councils could pass bylaws on issues such as policing and health, but the Indian agent controlled band funds and could override any decisions made by local governments.

Suppression of Indian cultural traditions, dances, religious ceremonies and traditional dress were also part of the Europeans' "civilization" efforts. In 1884, rituals such as those of the west-coast potlatch were outlawed. In 1885, Indians were banned from performing traditional dances or wearing ancestral outfits at fairs and other public events; and still later, Indians needed written government permission before donning traditional dress. By 1920, with the missionaries upset because the ceremonies continued despite the restrictions, the RCMP began conducting raids and confiscating ceremonial artifacts.

Allan B. Harper was born on April 13, 1925, in Island Lake, Ethel Taylor (Elijah's mother) on December 17, 1930. Hunting still dominated much of the northern landscape. At the age of eight, Allan started making trips through the Red Sucker Lake area for the winter hunt with his family. Summers were spent hunting and fishing closer to Garden Hill. But while this part of Cree life survived, many traditional ceremonies were being forced underground. By the time Elijah was born, most had disappeared.

Not all can be blamed on misguided bureaucrats. The introduction of faster and more effective modes of transportation also played a significant role in the destruction of traditional customs by ending the isolation of the North. By the turn of the century, ships were making regular trips to the North via Lake Winnipeg. By the early 1920s, airplanes were calling regularly at Island Lake, bringing mail and other supplies. "I remember my grandfather telling me about the first time a plane came to our lake," says Elijah. "Everyone said that when this plane comes, it's going to make a lot of noise. A lot of people got scared. Some people were fainting. There was this old man who was sick, and they thought something might happen to him. When they heard something coming, they threw blankets over him so he wouldn't hear anything."

Despite all this, however, the government's "civilizing" policy was still meeting with only limited success, and in 1927 it moved again to try to speed up the process. The Indian Act was revised to prohibit Indians from soliciting any but government funds. This legislation made it impossible for native people to organize politically, as Indian agents controlled all band finances.

Between 1929 and 1944, while the outside world was dealing with the Great Depression and the Second World War, modern technology—transportation, medical advances, communications—continued to be introduced throughout the North. Few mourned the end of the physical hardships, but other links with their Cree past were also growing more tenuous.

The war had what some believe was a positive impact on Canadian native policy. More than six thousand native people entered military service, placing them in more intimate and sympathetic contact with white society than ever before. When the war ended, the first white effort was launched to improve the lives of the country's original residents by changing the restricting laws governing their lives.

Despite being born decades after the traditional ways of life had been pilloried by the modern world, and just a few years after the Indian Act was finally relaxed, Elijah Harper and others of his generation embody many of the mores of those who came before.

To understand Elijah and his generation, one must understand their almost unshakeable belief in the inevitability that life will work out. This single concept would cause both the most frustration and the greatest awe during Harper's tenure in white politics. "Sometimes, he just doesn't give a shit," says a former staffer with the Manitoba government. "He is the most spiritual person I know," says another political associate. "I watch miracles happen around the guy."

"I married one of the Innu people," says Konrad Sioui, who has crossed paths with Harper many times. "The Cree or Montagnais, they are all the same, the people of the North. They are quiet people. They do not express themselves as the Iroquoian would do or others do. But they don't miss anything. They see everything, they feel everything, and they understand a lot more than we would believe they do. One of these days, you won't know that they are there, but they will suddenly appear when you fall into a lake. They will come and save your life."

Chapter Two

LEAVING

It was September 5, 1954, and a festive air hung over the four Island Lake communities, as it did every Treaty Day. There were speeches, solemn ceremonies, lavish traditional food, canoe races, tugs-of-war and white visitors from the south. Bright colours seemed to dominate the normally subdued northern Manitoba landscape and pieces of orange plastic littered the ground.

The government of Canada has been hosting annual treaty days on the country's Indian reserves in mid to late summer since 1763. This is the day bureaucrats hand out the $5-per-treaty-Indian annuity. Medical personnel, police and census gatherers also take advantage of the community-wide gatherings to conduct surveys and annual medical and dental checks.

By 1949, when Elijah was born, much of the solemnity had been stripped from Treaty Day. As a toddler, Elijah says, he knew only that the $5 was important, that Treaty had something to do with the Queen and the past and that Indian Affairs and the Indian agents "controlled everything."

Allan Harper says that politics were not an important part of Treaty Day for most people. The Indian agent, called "Money Man," had been a fixture in the North for as long as Allan could recall, and was less feared than tolerated. Fear was reserved for the RCMP, whose officers would fly in and out of communities, enforcing discipline in their own ways. Their arrival always meant trouble and sparked a fear that lingers in many native people, including Elijah.

Overall, treaty days were a time to look forward to, says Allan Harper. And then, with a hearty laugh: "I liked getting some money once in a while."

This is a far cry from the view that treaties were written proof of centuries-old, sacrosanct promises between two sovereign nations to ensure their mutual survival with honesty and goodwill. The exalted agreements were sullied over time as rights to hunt and fish were ignored or overridden by new laws. During the post-war period, a growing public awareness of the restricted rights of Canada's aboriginal people began to create the atmosphere in which Elijah and his generation would later test their political wings. Joint Senate and House of Commons committee hearings were launched between 1946 and 1948 on the question of the treatment of the country's original residents.

In 1951, the Indian Act underwent extensive rewriting. Bands were given more autonomy, money could be spent more freely, Indian women were allowed to vote in band elections, alcohol could be sold to Indians (although they were not allowed to drink in public until 1970), and the power of the federal minister of Indian affairs and of Indian agents was greatly reduced. As well, the provisions outlawing traditional ceremonies and the wearing of ancestral clothing were repealed.

However, Indians were still not allowed to vote in federal elections unless they gave up their treaty rights, and native women who married non-aboriginal or non-status men immediately lost their hereditary status. And, of course, Ottawa would still be able to override even the most progressive legislation.

There are 633 bands across Canada, a number that has not changed appreciably since Elijah's birth, and more than 2300 reserves. About 125 bands are located in northern areas so remote they can be reached only by plane in the summer or by make-shift roads in winter. Even today, about twenty-five bands have no air service and can be accessed only by winter roads for about six weeks during the coldest part of the year.

For most of these isolated native communities, including Red Sucker Lake, the changes to the Indian Act in 1951 had little immediate impact. Life remained arduous. The trapping industry, which crashed around 1920, never returned as a major economic force. Government attempts to replace the fur trade with other industries met with little success. Island Lake, made up of hundreds of islands and waterways and isolated from all major transportation and population centres, held few job prospects apart from chief, band councillor and band support staff, and the few paid helpers in federally run institutions such as nursing stations and schools. Periodic mining ventures offered some opportunities, but they never lasted long.

By the 1950s, enforced idleness was fast replacing trapping as a way of life, and the standard of living began its steep and steady decline into poverty. Diseases associated with impoverishment, which first swept through native communities in the early 1900s, were exacting a particularly serious toll on Indian reserves. Red Sucker Lake would not be spared.

On Treaty Day in 1954, five-year-old Elijah was playing with friends. He had no inkling that he would be leaving home that day for the first time and that, by the time he returned, the fall hunting season would have passed and winter would have set in.

Even the orange sheets that fluttered across the coarse grasses seem to be part of the cheer of the day. The plastic squares were the backing of X-ray film. That year, like every year since the end of the Second World War, the doctor had been taking pictures of the residents' chests before the $5 treaty money was handed over. The doctor had given the children the plastic backings to play with.

There did not appear to be a problem with Elijah's chest, but something was wrong. For several months a lump had been growing under the boy's chin. "You could tell he was sick by just looking at him," Ethel remembered. "His neck was really swollen."

Elijah's parents were told the boy would be taken from the reserve that day. The plane was ordered to stand by. Explanations were translated, but never really made clear. Until her death in 1992, Elijah's mother would believe that the problem in Elijah's neck had something to do with his tonsils. She would also never be sure where he spent those six months or what happened to him there.

Such acquiescence may seem odd today, but it stems from two common native characteristics—a faith that other human beings will do what is right and an acceptance of new ways as necessary for survival.

When Elijah was young, it was not uncommon for children and adults to be removed by medical and Indian Affairs staff for months or years without any official reports on their whereabouts. Elijah's uncle, Isaac Taylor, was visiting the Gordon Hill reserve when a nurse spotted something troubling and had him flown out without time to pack or say good-bye. "He never came back," says Elijah. "We never heard anything about him again. People never questioned those things. They just went along with what they were told."

Elijah's first trip off the reserve, like all the others in his youth, embodied this history. Each leaving was dictated by bureaucrats, with little consultation, explanation or regard for the bush rhythms of Elijah's community. Each time Harper was yanked into an alien world, his isolation, helplessness and humiliation were mitigated only by the sense of powerlessness he shared with other natives in the same circumstances.

Later in life, Red Sucker Lake would remain Elijah's solace, the place where he could relive the memories of his childhood. For, despite the difficulties, Red Sucker Lake was filled with everything the white world lacked—warmth, acceptance, respect and connection with the land.

Elijah remembers little about the plane ride that day in 1954, except that "I was scared, terrified." A local woman, Marion Monias, was taken off the reserve with him. They landed in a place with roads and cars, neither of which Elijah had ever seen. After some time, he was taken "somewhere else."

Hospital records show that Harper's first stop was Norway House Hospital. A few days later, he was flown to a tuberculosis sanatorium on Clear Lake in The Pas, a Cree community near the Saskatchewan/Manitoba border. For the six months he was away, Elijah had no contact with his parents.

Elijah has only flashes of memory of The Pas. "I remember a nurse giving me a bath in a wooden tub, and getting candy from a nurse every day," he says. "And I remember chicken noodle soup and a sandwich made with white bread with butter and jam. They tasted really good."

Elijah also has a vivid recollection of being taken to visit Jonah Harper, an elderly resident of Red Sucker Lake who was also hospitalized. "He was sitting there in bed and he was really happy to see me." Jonah Harper never saw Red Sucker Lake again.

Elijah's clearest memory is of going home. "It was wintertime and the plane landed at the Hudson's Bay post," on the island named after the HBC by the residents. It is about a ten-minute boat ride from the Harpers' home, but an hour's walk across the frozen lake. "My uncle, Moses Monias, came and carried me on his shoulders all the way to Grandfather's house." His family was thrilled to have him home, and "I know I was happy to be back."

He did not look much different, but he had changed. He came home speaking Swampy-Cree, the language of The Pas, instead of his native Ojibwa-Cree, and there was an angry scar under his chin that remains to this day. For some time after his return, special food rations were delivered to help him stay healthy. He particularly remembers getting a box of butter, a rare treat in the North.

When asked, Elijah's mother described only the pain of her son's absence and the joy she felt when her quiet, obedient eldest boy returned. Did she feel any anger about not knowing where he was or why? Ethel Harper did not say. She just shrugged, grew quiet and looked down.

Elijah had never really known what his leaving was about. Perhaps they had to take his tonsils out, he suggested, repeating the story his mother told him. "I have a scar. They said I had a lump and they took it out. I guess they made a mess out of it." He sits silent for a long time when told that hospital records show he had tuberculosis. Forty years after the fact, Elijah becomes angry at being taken out of the reserve so peremptorily.

Tuberculosis is associated with the poverty and isolation still found on most reserves: overcrowded housing, poor or nonexistent sanitation and an inadequate diet. Highly infectious, TB is spread through the air by coughs and sneezes. In 1935, 41 per cent of the deaths recorded in native communities were due to TB. In 1953, the peak year for TB in Canada and the year before it struck Elijah, 3200 native Canadians were being treated for the disease, 2627 in TB institutions across Canada.

Aggressive campaigns to fight "consumption" had been launched at the turn of the century and were well entrenched by the early 1950s, so Elijah's chances of surviving the disease were good: the first anti-TB antibiotic had been discovered about five years before Harper was born, miniature X-ray film allowed early detection, and young patients had a better survival rate than did older people.

After 1953, the incidence of TB among natives began to decline. By 1964, only 639 Indians were sanatorium patients. In the ensuing years, however, the incidence remained higher in native communities than in the rest of the country. By the 1990s, there was a resurgence of TB worldwide: of the 1995 cases in Canada in 1991, 19 per cent were among native people.

Hospital records indicate that Harper was admitted to Norway House Hospital again for respiratory problems in February 1960.

However, despite these bouts, his childhood was so healthy that long-distance running became one of his favourite activities.

When Elijah returned home on his uncle's shoulders in January 1955, he had no difficulty slipping back into the old rhythms—hunting, fishing and the bush life.

Almost as soon as Elijah was weaned, he had gone to live with his paternal grandparents, John E. Harper and Juliette Wood. "I stayed at my grandmother's, just me," says Elijah. "I don't know why. My dad decided. My parents decided that I should be raised by my grandparents. Of course, I saw my parents every day."

Having children stay with grandparents is not unusual in native communities. When asked if the arrangement made him feel rejected or unloved, or even estranged from his parents, Harper finds the question bizarre. He reflects before answering, trying to bridge worlds and cultures. "You are part of the family, your grandmother is part of the family," he says with some incredulity at having to explain. "There is no separation."

His brothers and sisters would come over every day to play. Sometimes, some of them would stay at their grandmother's house or Elijah would sleep at his parents' home, whatever flowed naturally from the day's events.

From his paternal grandparents, Elijah began to learn the traditional tasks of hunting and fishing and the traditional philosophy of native life. John E. Harper was Juliette's second husband. (Her first, Thomas Harper, was Allan B.'s biological father; he died when Allan was very young.)

"I was very fortunate to be raised by my grandparents," says Elijah. "It was a very important part of my life, part of my culture and heritage to adopt and instill in me the values of my people. It is very important because your identity is instilled in you when you are very young. It has carried me through all my life."

Elijah's grandfather trapped in an area just a few kilometres east of Red Sucker, and the young Elijah would often go with him. Elijah's parents' winter hunting ground, near Echoing Lake, Ontario, was a two-day trip by dog sled. But, says Elijah, "My grandfather's trapline was so close that we could go most of the time in the spring. We would walk with a dog team. Most of the people had dog teams."

Elijah would be bundled into his grandparents' toboggan or canoe alongside the hunting supplies. On the trapline, everyone slept in three-yard-long canvas tents warmed by airtight wood burning heaters about the size of a small bar refrigerator. The men would hunt during the day; the women and children would take care of the camp. "When I was small," Elijah recalls, "I did a lot of chores—gathering wood, bringing in wood, hauling water. And I would do a lot of my own setting up of small snares for rabbits. I caught lots of rabbits. I used to have a slingshot and would shoot grouse. And then I would just wander in the bush, playing around."

Elijah would play with the children of the four or five other families trapping in the same area. Everyone relied on the food caught in the traps or shot by the hunters, supplemented by fish, bannock, some canned goods, and staples such as sugar, flour, lard and tea purchased from the Hudson's Bay store. Moose and beaver were major sources of food. "If we killed a moose, we all shared. Everybody shared if we were running out of supplies. We would run out of sugar sometimes."

Red suckers (mullets) were plentiful in the spring. Elijah recalls his maternal grandfather, Thomas Taylor, describing dropping a net into the Red Sucker Lake River one year and having it fill with fish before the weights hit bottom. (Elijah enjoys his mullet split in half, placed on a red willow branch and cooked over an open fire. He also has warm memories of his grandmother's boiled sucker heads.)

In his youth, the families trapped mostly beaver, lynx and muskrat. During the 1950s, there was still a market for these skins, as well as for fox and mink.

Native people have great admiration and respect for the creatures they hunt and depend on for survival. The fatty meat of the beaver provides extra calories needed by those who must survive in cold northern climates. Beavers subsist on trees believed by aboriginal people to have medicinal qualities. The animal's kidneys are therefore steeped in boiling water and the broth consumed to fight disease. Hunters also speak with admiration of the beaver's social order—it mates for life and lives in extended families.

Catching beaver and other animals in the wild demands intimate understanding of the creatures' habits. Beaver dams are scouted before freeze-up and revisited in the colder months when the beavers' fur is thick and luxurious. "In the fall, when the ice is not too thick and the snow is not so deep, you can walk over in the bush and you see these beaver houses," says Elijah, explaining the trapping lessons he learned as a child. "You can usually see where they go under the lodge, you can see the air bubbles locked in the ice. If you hit the ice with an axe, it sounds hollow. Usually the ice where they swim under is not as thick, so you usually stick your traps there, or else you use snares."

Elijah spent his childhood watching others trap, fish and hunt until he knew what to do. Then he did it for himself. "We used snares or these leg-hold traps with bait. The bait could be a green poplar branch planted near the trap or a dab of musk from the female beaver. You splash water on your trail as you canoe out to get rid of the human scent. With the muskrat in the spring and fall, you would come out, especially in the marshy area, and there would be these holes in the ice that the muskrat came out of." A long pole with a snare at the end would be placed near the opening. When the muskrat returned, he would be caught and drown. "In the springtime, you set these traps up along the shoreline, where it is marshy and grassy, and you use some bait or scent. In the leg-hold traps you use weights on the traps so that when the animal snaps and struggles, it takes it down right away and it drowns."

Elijah's first taste of a different kind of teaching would come from the missionaries of the Northern Canada Evangelical Church around the time he was six. The missionaries held classes in their log church on Desbrowe Island across the lake from the reserve. In winter, the children would walk across the ice to class. The classes were in English with English books, although everyone except Hudson's Bay employees and missionaries spoke Ojibwa-Cree. "I remember a whole bunch of us walking in the middle of a blizzard one time going to school. It was blowing hard on the lake, a total white-out, so we walked as a group." In the summer the children would paddle two or three canoes to school and back.

A favourite grade-school prank was to throw .22-calibre shells into the school's cast-iron stove. The unexpected "bang" during lessons was always good for a laugh.

Harper grew up knowing that the federal government wanted natives to go to school. "I remember someone saying we had to go to school or they would cut off the family allowance. I just heard that—I don't know if it was true or not." Such threats were indeed used, for a time, to encourage school attendance. Despite this intimidation, however, seasonal trapping would preempt school attendance for decades to come.

Elijah's paternal grandparents took care of his trapping education, but it was his mother's parents, particularly his grandfather Thomas

Taylor, who combined pragmatic hunting lessons with a spiritual education.

According to Hudson's Bay logbooks of the early 1900s, Thomas Taylor was a fine hunter. "Thos Taylor and John Little came in today. The former brought in a silver fox. That's the second one he has killed this winter," wrote the Hudson's Bay manager in March 1903. Although they lived in Garden Hill, almost a hundred kilometres to the south, Thomas and his wife, Emily, canoed up to visit their daughter's family in Red Sucker frequently. Elijah also recalls several trips to Garden Hill to visit his grandparents.

Elijah remembers his grandfather as always willing to play games, but it was the elder's stories of heroes and villains, good and evil, and the powers in the elements of the universe that made an indelible impression.

"I could sit there all day and listen," says Elijah. "It was just like going to a movie or something. You sit there and the way he would describe things, your mind would just wander off. I had a tremendous fantasy and imagination, and when he talked I could just see it, visualize in my mind everything he was talking about."

There were stories of the dreaded Windigo, which could turn people into cannibals, and myths about the powers of Windigo-fighting medicine men and about the animals that shared the earth.

There was also the story of the creation of the earth, a tale of a small, quiet creature accomplishing what the larger, more powerful animals could not. There are many variations of the story among northern aboriginal people. This version comes from Konrad Sioui, who says its lesson is of particular relevance to the story of Elijah Harper.

"The world was a world of water only. The bear, the chief of the animals, asked for a council of all the animals, which were all swimming at the time. The bear said, 'Down below is some earth. We need to find earth to put on the back of the turtle, and we will spread earth on its back and we will build an island on which we will live. We will have trees.'

"Each of the animals tried—the beaver and the otter, and the others—to go down to the depths to capture some earth. But each returned with nothing and finally they abandoned the effort. And then the muskrat stepped forward and said he would try. He was very small, very meek and very ugly, but he said he would try. All the other animals laughed. He left. Three days and three nights passed. And then he came back. He was dead, floating on his back, but in his mouth he had earth."

Says Konrad, "People think that it is always the eagle and the bear that can save your life, but sometimes it is the animal that you would never believe who will play a role to save us."

Asked to recall the legends and the characters he dreamed of at his grandfather's side, Elijah can summon only vague images and second-hand stories about powwows, shaking tent ceremonies and the other ceremonies forced underground when the government outlawed such practices.

"This old man in Red Sucker Lake told me that he knew a person who used to travel in the area doing the shaking tent ceremony," says Elijah, recalling one such story. "People would travel by canoe in the springtime to attend."

The shaking tent was a powerful tool, he explains, which allowed a medium to communicate with others over great distances and to reveal events. In his grandfather's stories the shaking tent let people know when enemies, particularly the Saulteaux from Little Grand Rapids, were heading their way.

"I remember this guy telling me he had asked this man to conduct a ceremony to see what was happening. This was right after freeze-up. The man said two people had died. He didn't know who. Later, someone came over and confirmed it."

Early missionaries had battled, sometimes using threats, to force the "savages" to abandon such rituals and beliefs. Sometimes they resorted to incentives, offering better prices for furs and free guns and ammunition to Christians. In some communities, guns would be given or sold only to those hunters who had converted. Some natives saw similarities in the two belief systems and had little difficulty adapting. Thus, Elijah's father became involved with the Northern Evangelical Mission of Canada, run out of Prince Albert, Saskatchewan, in 1957. Allan Harper lives his religion, yet he has never forcefully attempted to bring his children into the church "except through his love, teachings and prayer," says Elijah. "I have a great respect and faith in the work my dad does. I believe in God."

Elijah's beliefs do not fit into any church convention. Rather, his spiritual sense rests in a deep respect for the land, animals and people, and in a belief that one must give thanks to all.

"When you pray, you all pray to the same Creator," says Elijah.

"Whether you pray Christian or Buddhist. We may do things differently—Indian people may do things differently, like burning sweet grass or tobacco—but it is still about the Creator." Harper says he has watched remarkable things happen in the context of his father's Christianity, just as they occur under the direction of the medicine men and elders.

"I've seen a lot of things happen," says Harper. "I have a lot of experiences that, I guess, some people wouldn't believe. I remember, my nephew cut his foot really badly on some glass—blood was just pouring out. They wrapped a blanket as a bandage around his foot and my dad prayed for him. Then when he took the bandage off after, there was no scar. There was only blood on the bandage."

Various people speak of Elijah's uncanny sixth sense, a knowledge that something is about to happen or has recently come to pass. On August 21, 1990, Christine Robinson-Myron, a long-time friend who ran his constituency office, was killed in a car accident. When told the news the following day, Elijah did not appear surprised, says his friend Elaine Cowan. "He said he had seen her the night before and he thought that she was gone already. She had this blank look on her face . . . and she came and she talked to him and she was looking up at him and he said, 'I knew. I knew before anyone told me.' "

Elijah discusses this part of himself only after much prodding. "Ever since I was small I have felt something spiritual, something that can't be explained," he says reluctantly. "Often, when I was small, I used to feel that something was coming. I can't explain the feeling. It was just there and oftentimes it used to scare me. It is hard to explain Indian spirituality, that when you believe in something it actually happens. You actually have access to a lot of forces that are out there. The environment, the winds. . . ."

Native history is filled with stories of people seeing messages in the world all around them, and receiving them from the Great Spirit.

"I don't know what you call them—your spirits, your helpers," says Elijah. "A lot of that seemed very strong. When I was very small, I sensed it. I am sure that these things used to come to me at nighttime. They were in your mind and sometimes they were a presence. I don't know how to describe something like that. It was a throbbing thing, or a big heavy thing. It is hard to explain."

Such teachings were never given much time to take root, although Elijah visits a sweat lodge when he can. (In the sweat lodge ceremony, conducted in a squat tent heated by smouldering rocks, participants share their concerns and wishes, and ask for guidance while offering tobacco and cedar to the forces in the four directions—north, south, east and west—and to the heavenly powers.)

At the age of seven or eight—he is still not sure—Elijah was again removed from Red Sucker by plane and taken to Norway House. This time there was no medical emergency, although he would not return for ten months. Elijah was going to school.

For centuries, the federal government and the religious community had worked to eradicate Indian culture. But laws and religious edicts were harmless compared to the powerful tool of white education. Before the treaties, education was the exclusive jurisdiction of the missionaries. When the treaties gave the federal government the responsibility for educating native people, it decided to build on the missionary-school structure already in place.

Like most Indian policies of the era, education was seen as an opportunity to speed up the assimilation of native people into white society. The Indian Act authorized churches to remove children from their home environments and place them in church-run boarding schools or day schools. Boarding schools were preferred by the government because they removed children from their cultural environment, making assimilation easier. Ottawa built and financed the schools; the churches provided the teachers and the curriculum.

There were two basic residential-school models: boarding schools in larger communities housed students from ages eight to fourteen, and industrial schools located close to white communities ran elaborate programs and housed students up to the age of eighteen. In the latter, basic studies were combined with half days working on farms or in industry. Charges of abuse and high costs would force the phasing out of the industrial-school program by about 1920. Elijah, however, would find himself in a similar setting more than thirty years later.

In 1920, school attendance for Indian children aged seven to fifteen was made mandatory by law, but a lack of facilities in the far North exempted most of the Cree, and hunting seasons would interrupt attendance for the rest. (Allan B. Harper would eventually attend bible school as an adult, but Elijah's mother had no formal education.)

Elijah and his younger brother Fred left for school together, the first of the Harper clan to experience residential school. (Mary Jane, the first-born, stayed in Red Sucker and was educated by the Northern

Canada Mission.) In all, Elijah would attend residential schools run by the United Church in Norway House and Brandon, and the Birtle Residential School, run by the Presbyterian Church. Every August, the government plane landed at Red Sucker and gathered the children up. Decisions about where they were to be sent were made in Ottawa. They would not be returned until June. "It was hard to send them," recalled Ethel. "They were gone a long time and they were very small." Elijah remembers his dad telling him that he and Fred must go. "He told me that although he would miss us and everything, he knew that we had to get an education," says Elijah.

"I wanted them to have good job opportunities," says Elijah's father. "I wanted them to be able to bridge the gap between the Indian way of life and the white man's world so that they could survive. I knew that there would be a lot of white people around this area." While he did not exactly fear what would happen once whites came more frequently, he wanted to ensure that his children would still have a place in Red Sucker. After their schooling, he imagined his educated children would return to the reserve to live and work.

Not everyone thought sending the children away was a good idea, especially in the later years. Says Elijah, "The older people thought that when you went out and came back, it was bad for you, in terms of having a bad influence. You would come back alcoholics and drug addicts."

The plane that left the Red Sucker Lake airport Elijah's first year headed two hundred kilometres southwest to Norway House. Elijah recalls thinking that he was heading to a different country. "Like Norway, or something, you know? I felt like I was being sent far, far away and that I could never come back. I felt alone, detached from everyone." Such detachment would become a constant in Harper's life, eventually becoming a self-defence skill to be called upon when a situation was too stressful or too painful.

He remembers being reluctant to leave, but other Red Sucker Lake kids were on the plane, too, he says, so that made it easier. As the plane approached Norway House, Harper stared out the window. "I noticed the different environment, the water being a little different colour in the lake."

Elijah's feelings about his decade-long stay in Protestant-run residential schools are mixed. The schools he attended were not as restrictive as the Catholic-run institutions in the south, yet Harper shares the angst of others of his generation: no matter what the school, the overriding feelings of helplessness and humiliation in a foreign world of order and control were the same.

He recalls having his long hair shaved off "like in the army." All the children were deloused every time they returned to school from a visit home.

And he remembers rules and regulations. "You had to line up for everything. You even lined up to go for walks." He felt totally powerless. "You feel like you don't have any say, no rights, nothing." Every hour of the day was organized, except for "free time," a term that makes Elijah laugh to this day. "Free time" meant you could play in the fenced school yard. The bush was just beyond the fence but off limits.

Elijah still cannot fathom what school officials were so worried about. "Why should you be contained? I'm not going to run away. Where would I run away to? So you wander in the bush. There is no crime in that, it's natural."

"The dormitories, dining room and play rooms seemed to match a scene of an orphanage pictured in one of Charles Dickens's novels," says Bernard Lee, the principal at Norway House when Elijah was a student. There were about 150 boarded students and about 120 students who would travel to school from their reserve each day. The dazed look on young students' faces betrayed the culture shock. "The whole system seemed like a cross between an army barracks and a juvenile correctional school," Lee says. The food allowance, he adds, was less than that allocated to prison inmates.

Elijah recalls that his father visited him once at Norway House, a meeting that left Elijah feeling sad. "They only let us meet in the hallway," he says slowly. "I don't know why. But they wouldn't let us meet where everyone was."

Neither Elijah nor his parents recall him ever complaining. Yet it did not take long for him to quietly test the rules. He recalls an early attempt to make it to a bush just beyond the barbed-wire fence. He got caught. "I remember running fast from the bush back into the yard. I didn't see this barbed wire because it was low. I tripped over it and ripped my pants and cut my legs." Undeterred, he would keep trying. One day while outside the school boundaries, he saw a supervisor coming and hid. "I was stuck behind this big rock, but the supervisor saw me. He sent me to bed with no supper—and he was an Indian person."

In Birtle, he got the strap for sliding down a hill and knocking down some raspberry bushes, and was also hit several times on the hands with a broad leather belt for other misdemeanours. One supervisor had been in the army and treated the students like his regiment. They were forced to march everywhere and to stand at attention. One day Elijah failed to clean his room up to standard. "Do it right," came the order, "or I will bash your head against the wall."

Elijah's father would sometimes send money, which would be removed from the envelope by staff and doled out to Elijah and Fred a bit at a time to buy candy at the school's canteen. It was just one more example of the helplessness and lack of control, says Elijah, that characterized his life away from Red Sucker.

Yet Elijah escaped some of the more traumatic humiliations and abuse faced by many in his generation, especially in the Catholic-run schools. "It was our policy never to punish a child for speaking their mother tongue," says Lee. "It was taken for granted that they, and the way of life of their families, should be treated with respect." (By the time he reached Norway House Elijah had picked up a few English words from the missionary school. "We spoke Cree in the yard, but we were encouraged to speak English.")

Harper does, however, have a vivid and painful memory of a girl from Little Grand Rapids being berated at Birtle Residential School for writing a letter to her parents in Cree syllabics. It was dinnertime. The principal walked into the packed dining room. In his hands was the letter. He started talking about what a bad thing the girl had done. "You're here to learn English," he said.

"The girl was humiliated. Oh, the humiliation that she went through," recalls Harper, recounting the story with obvious distress. "And at the same time I was wishing that I could do that—write in syllabics and communicate with my parents. Here she was getting in trouble and I envied her because she could write in script. I wished I could write to my parents."

The students' incoming mail was also censored. "I remember this one girl, Donna Green, years after leaving school, was still really mad at the principal because her boyfriend was writing her letters but she wasn't getting them. Then, after a year, her principal came to her, gave her the letters and said, 'Here, I thought you might like to have these.' "

Elijah's next school was in Brandon. From the airplane Elijah watched as the landscape he knew gave way to an astonishing flatness. As far as the eye could see, there were squares of prairie farmland, uniform and ordered. The natural chaos of the North was gone.

Life at Brandon was the now familiar combination of humiliation and fear. "One time, we were all moving into the lunch room when a glass of milk spilt near me," says Elijah. "It wasn't my fault, but they made me stand up." He had to stand while everybody else ate. "Then everyone was going out—I never got to eat." The indignity was acute.

It was at Brandon Residential School that Elijah learned to play hockey. "I knew how to balance myself on skates and get in the way of the puck," he says. "I was the goalie." During this time he faced one of his first racist incidents. During an excursion with the hockey team to a nearby town, the coach, Norman Bird, decided to take his young players bowling before their hockey match. "We walked in, but the guy in the bowling alley kicked us out," says Elijah. "I didn't know why, but I saw the expression on Bird's face. He was mad."

Above all, those early years away from home were filled with a fear so overwhelming that it held him back even from asking for help when he needed it. In the summer of 1964, as Harper was about to enter his final year at Birtle, his family noticed that he had problems with his foot. A visit to the nurse in late August revealed a serious infection due to an ingrown toenail. Harper says the problem started during the previous school year but, "I was afraid to ask for scissors so I could cut my nails."

Elijah was flown out of Red Sucker to Norway House for a five-day hospital stay. When it ended, officials realized that it was time for him to head back to school. He was simply handed an envelope for his principal and given instructions on getting to the Birtle Residential School. He was fifteen years old.

"They put me on a plane to Cross Lake and told me that at Cross Lake you will pick up some students and we will fly you to Waboden; get on a train with them at twelve o'clock." His foot still too swollen to fit into a shoe, an embarrassed Harper left the hospital wearing fluffy turquoise slippers and carrying the clothes he had left home with. "I think I had seventy-five cents in my pocket." Instead of landing in Cross Lake, the plane flew directly to Waboden. Alone, he made his way to the train station. When the train came by at noon, Elijah got on.

Almost seven hours later, as the train pulled into The Pas, Harper realized he was way off course. "This train does not go to Birtle," some students finally told him, "it goes to Winnipeg." He had not eaten since morning, did not dare to leave his seat even for the washroom and did not know what to do. Things got worse after the conductor asked him for his ticket. Harper sat silent. "You Indians are all the same," said the conductor. "Every time he went by after that, he spoke to me," says Elijah, eventually insisting that the boy get off at the next stop. When the time came, Harper pretended to be asleep, but the conductor had been replaced by another who let Elijah be.

At seven in the morning, still without a trip to the washroom or any food, Harper left the train with some native students at Portage la Prairie and followed them to their school. From there he was finally rerouted by bus to Birtle Residential School. He later discovered that the train he was supposed to have taken from Waboden left at midnight, not noon.

Birtle combined classes with work on an adjacent farm that fed the students. Food at Norway House and Brandon had consisted mostly of porridge, macaroni and wieners, but at Birtle the students enjoyed fresh produce all the time.

"They had a manager and an assistant manager and all the rest of the work was done by students," says Elijah. Chores had to be done before school started at 8:00 A.M. "In the springtime we'd get up at 6:00 A.M. to milk the cows and feed the pigs and the chickens." Elijah learned to operate automated milking machines, when and how to spread manure on the fields, how to plant and harvest potatoes and other crops, and how to slaughter various animals. "We would do all the butchering and quartering and even the carving of the chickens. We'd even grind the beef up and make hamburger."

There were after-school chores as well, and on Saturdays the boys would be hired out to nearby farms. "I think they paid us maybe $4 for the day, but they didn't pay us directly. They paid it to the school." Students would have to ask for spending money out of their earnings.

Perhaps because he was older, Elijah's memories of control and humiliation during his years at Birtle are particularly acute.

Discipline on the farm was at least as strict as at the other schools. Once a boy was found hiding in the kitchen pantry in a bin of onions. "I don't know what he had done, but he was hiding in the winter storeroom of food," says Elijah. "The next morning, the principal came in with a bowl of raw onions and said, 'Eat this before you go to school.' " The boy ate them.

When two boys who had tried to run away were caught by the RCMP and returned, all the boys were brought into the play room and ordered to stand at attention. "They put a table in the middle of the room and they had this big strap," remembers Elijah, uncomfortably. "The boys had to bend over the table. Their pants were pulled down, then their shorts, and they were strapped a whole bunch of times. We just stood around the room, stood at attention and watched. It was to let you know not to break the rules."

Overall, says Elijah, the teachers were fine—it was the supervisors who were usually the problem. "They were institutions," says Elijah of the schools. "If you go to a federal penitentiary you probably have more access to things like television and a play room than we ever did."

Some believe that residential schools, despite their flaws, played an important role in the evolution of native Canadians. Bernard Lee, the former Norway House principal, wrote a newspaper article years later saying that the schools had helped Harper gain national prominence. "Without the residential schools, Elijah would not have got an education, and he likely would not be where he is today," says Lee. Sociologists also credit the much-despised system with providing native Canadians with their first grounds for unity. Through the 1960s and 1970s, native children of different cultures and aboriginal traditions shared an experience that left many of them scared and angry but allowed them to recognize their oppressors. In later years, they would come together again, this time to fight for change.

In 1965, at age sixteen, Elijah was to begin high school in Garden Hill, but his father had other plans. Instead of being flown out with the other students, Elijah headed into the bush to learn the traditional ways from his father, his father's brother Robinson and his paternal grandfather John Harper. Exactly why Allan Harper wanted Elijah to return to the bush is not something he can explain. "He just had to stay."

Things had changed since Elijah had followed his grandfather on the winter hunt as a child. Instead of a dog team, Elijah, his father and Elijah's uncle chartered a small plane to the Harper trapline, and they flew out of the bush again more than a month later. Over the winter months, Elijah travelled by dog sled to his grandfather's hunting grounds near Red Sucker.

Elijah spent his year in the bush perfecting his snaring techniques and setting up traplines along the fast-moving creeks. In retrospect, he is glad of his father's decision. "I was forced to be more appreciative of what the bush was really about," he says. "We ate muskrat and beaver and ducks, and I learned what to recognize, the dangers of the lakes." There was no time to get bored. "You get up early in the morning, walk around the bush. At nighttime you walk back to camp and you're tired. Every day is like that."

In the spring, Harper returned to his father's line near Echoing Lake to trap fisher, lynx, marten, fox and muskrat. It was on this trip that Harper became the first person from Red Sucker in a long, long time to kill a wolverine, an animal much despised by hunters because of its skill at raiding traps.

Elijah, his father and his uncle were scouting a shoreline when the young man spotted something cutting across the ice towards him. As it moved closer, he saw that it was about the size of a badger. Then he noticed the telltale white spot on the animal's broad back—it was a wolverine. "He is supposed to be a vicious animal, really strong. Anything that he kills he carries off. Anything that he does leave behind he pees on so nothing else can have it," says Elijah. (Legend has it that the wolverine's white patch of fur marks where it carried off a child.)

Elijah raised his .22-calibre rifle and fired a single shot. The wolverine fell, a pile of deep brown fur against the ice, and then grabbed at its injured leg. It tried to run towards the shoreline. Heart pounding, Elijah ran to cut it off, his moccasins slipping and sliding on the ice, his father and uncle laughing at his struggle. Elijah shot the wounded animal again, but the wolverine continued towards the shore. Finally, it just stopped and sat down. Elijah walked up, pulled out his axe and hit the animal over the head as it turned on him.

"And, that's how I killed a wolverine with an axe," says Elijah, laughing. "That's one of my tracking stories. It's a true story, not a fish story."

A few weeks later, Elijah flew out of Red Sucker Lake to Grade 9 classes in Garden Hill. It was there, at the age of seventeen, that he made his first foray into politics: he ran for Grade 9 student council president. The campaign involved going from classroom to classroom to talk to students. In the end, Elijah got all but two votes: one cast by his opponent, the other his own. "I think even the nominator of the guy that ran against me voted for me," laughs Harper. Why did he vote against himself? "I don't know. I just felt I shouldn't vote for myself," he laughs again. "I guess it was a part of some kind of ethic." While serving as president, Elijah remembers focussing on a simple political message for the young constituents: "I told them that you don't have to be elected to be a leader. You can do these things too. You can get involved."

To this point in his life, Elijah had been surrounded by native people. Although his residential school teachers and the missionaries were non-native, his fellow students came from small communities like his. But all that ended when Elijah flew out of Red Sucker Lake in the fall of 1967 for high school in Winnipeg. As usual, arrangements about where he would go, what courses he would take and where he would live had been made by Indian Affairs. More than anything, Harper wanted to go to school with his friends, who attended St. John's High School and Sisler High, Winnipeg schools in poorer neighbourhoods with large native populations. Elijah can't recall what he told the official who interviewed him for placement, but he was assigned to Dakota Collegiate in middle-income suburbia, a long bus ride away from where he was staying. His curriculum was made up of university entrance courses. "I saw only one other native student in my entire high school that first year. Her name was Cathy Sinclair. And then, later, I didn't see her. She left and I was the only one for a while." In Winnipeg, Elijah and several other native students were housed with a native couple named George and Irene Ross.

By this time, Elijah's English was passable but he did have a few problems understanding some of his early assignments and a curriculum in no way suited to a native student from the North. "This teacher asked me to do an essay on some television comedy series. I didn't know what to write. I'd never seen a TV series. I didn't even know what a television comedy series was at the time. So I went to the teacher and said, 'I don't know, really, what to write. I just came from up north and we don't have any TV. I know there are television programs, but I really don't know much about them.' He asked me to write another essay."

By Grade 11, Elijah was quite comfortable. His marks were not outstanding, but "I did well when I attended school," he says. He even grew accustomed to the racism of city life. Ask any native Canadian in western Canada to describe a walk through a mall, and the tale invariably turns on being followed and harassed by management. "One lunchtime a native friend and I dropped into a Safeway store. We were pulled over by the manager and hauled into his office where he searched our pockets. He said lots of cigarettes were being stolen." The manager found nothing. Elijah just shrugs. "You expected to be treated differently. You just put up with it."

Other irritants caused him more angst, such as the acute embarrassment of buying new clothes or class supplies with government vouchers. Registered Indian students living away from home were, as they are today, funded by the federal government. Their room and board was paid directly to the landlord. When they needed clothes and school supplies, they obtained vouchers from Indian Affairs and used them at designated stores. "You feel really awkward going through the process," says Elijah. "You're standing there filling in these vouchers and the line-up is getting longer and longer, and you had a specific amount that you could spend. It was demeaning."

Money for extras—movies or a game of pool—was rare. Entertainment wasn't free in the city like it had been in Red Sucker, so Elijah and his friends spent most of their spare time just hanging out.

Although he visited home every summer, he had very little regular contact with his family during the school year. But one day, a cousin, Wesley Harper, arrived in Winnipeg from the reserve. "Hey, Elijah. Congratulations," cried Wesley. "I hear you're getting married this summer!" Elijah was stunned. He had no idea what his cousin was talking about. "Your grandparents arranged a marriage for you."

"It was the first I'd heard about it," says Elijah.

While he respected his grandparents, Elijah's idea of how to live his life did not yet include getting married and settling down in Red Sucker. Terrified, he chose non-confrontation and decided not to go home for the summer. The high-school guidance counsellor, Frank Prouten, listened to his problem and found Elijah his first summer job, with the St. Vital School Board. Later that summer, Elijah visited his father at the Island Lake Northern Evangelical Mission bible school, but he did not go near Red Sucker. He never discussed the subject of marriage with his grandparents, and they never once raised it with him.

The next summer, back at the St. Vital School Board, Elijah became involved with the Manitoba Association of Native Youth. Through that organization, he came into contact with people who were emerging as the leaders of Canada's native movement. The U.S. was alive with the civil rights movement and Indians in Canada were organizing as they had never done before. The leaders, including a Manitoba chief named Dave Courchene, united to fight a federal government proposal to end natives' special status. Courchene would become the grandfather of native politics in Manitoba and have a profound influence on Harper and his generation.

Elijah finished high school a few credits short of university requirements. During the summer he worked during the day and went to night school to study mathematics. The University of Manitoba accepted his Cree-language skills for credit and, in September, Elijah arrived at the sprawling campus in Fort Garry.

He would stay in university for less than two years, but the experience would change his life.

Chapter Three

THE PIONEERS

Elijah entered the University of Manitoba in the fall of 1971. Twenty-two years old, he was one of about a dozen native students, almost all a little older than their non-native counterparts. These young men and women had beaten tremendous odds: according to the 1986 census, almost 40 per cent of adult Indians had less than a Grade 9 education; 5 per cent had graduated from high school; and only 1 per cent had made it through university. Elijah and his fellow students were the first generation of native Canadians to be schooled en masse in the white system. Neither traditional nor assimilated into white society, these pioneers would have a lifelong search for a balance between the two.

Life as a university student was quite different from the life Harper had known in residential schools and high school. Practically overnight, Elijah's support system was gone: he was given direct access to funds for food and housing and was left to fend for himself. After years of others controlling virtually every aspect of his life, "I found it hard to be disciplined," says Elijah.

Elijah rarely complains openly, but the word "hard" peppers many of his descriptions of his two years at university. "I didn't find university courses difficult, but it was a different world," he says, "and it was hard to adjust."

His first hurdle was to find a place to live. After a short stay at the YMCA, Elijah and friends Richard and Jennifer Linklater landed in an apartment block on Pembina Highway not far from the campus.

Jennifer eventually moved back home, and another friend, Stan Harper, moved in.

Elijah found himself drawn to courses about people, history and anthropology, but life outside the classroom captured most of his attention. Activities at the Manitoba Association of Native Youth, the Manitoba Indian Brotherhood and the various native friendship centres around Winnipeg were too exhilarating to pass up: all were offering opportunities to get politically involved.

The first decidedly political national Indian body was formed in Canada in 1954, three years after status Indians had been given the right to organize. The National Indian Council became the umbrella organization for the National Indian Brotherhood (NIB), which represented registered Indians, and the Canadian Metis Society (CMS).

In 1960, Canada gave registered Indians the right to vote in federal elections without giving up their Indian status; Yukon, Manitoba and Saskatchewan extended provincial voting privileges to the same group. (Status Indians already had provincial voting rights in British Columbia, Nova Scotia, Newfoundland, the Northwest Territories and Ontario.) All other provinces followed suit in the 1960s, with Quebec finally extending the right in 1969.

It was an exciting time: the civil rights movement in the United States was peaking, and it was hard not to see parallels between the treatment of blacks in the U.S. and native Canadians. "We followed it very intently and read all we could about it," Ovide Mercredi says of events south of the border. "There was a sense of relatedness to the American experience, with what the blacks were doing."

In 1968, the National Indian Council dissolved, and the partner organizations headed out in separate directions: the National Indian Brotherhood to restore to status Indians a sense of pride in Indian culture and identity, and the Metis Society to lobby on behalf of all landless natives, Metis and non-status Indians alike.

Before long, the groups had a chance to test their new mandates. On June 25, 1969, the NIB and the powerful provincial native bodies of Alberta and Manitoba were thrust into a high-profile campaign against a federal Liberal government document known as the 1969 White Paper, which proposed a far-reaching reorganization of native policy in Canada. The new goal of the government was to end all special status for Canadian Indians. Indian Affairs Minister Jean Chrétien stated that special status was racist and that it prevented Canada's native peoples from claiming their rightful place as equal citizens.

Native leaders were outraged. The government's position proved how ignorant Ottawa was of the country's history and the role of Canada's native people in it. Moreover, as they had done time and time again, the bureaucrats had failed to consult with native leaders before trying to restructure the lives of native people.

The native cause was led by three men who were to become the driving forces behind the modern native political movement. Walter Dieter of Saskatchewan was the first leader of the National Indian Brotherhood, Harold Cardinal was the brash twenty-three-year-old leader of the Indian Association of Alberta, and Dave Courchene was a tough-talking band chief and the founder and first president of the Manitoba Indian Brotherhood (MIB).

Courchene, whose Ojibwa name was Nee-Ghan-NiBi-Nah-Se (Leading Thunder) had been born on April 1, 1926, at Fort Alexander reserve in Manitoba. He was a large man with a big voice and a talent for inspiring his followers. He was also known to cause fear among those who dared to stand in his way. After serving as chief of his reserve, he led the MIB from 1967 to 1974 and was named the first Grand Chief of Manitoba in 1971.

It was the feisty, bombastic style and daring tactics of Courchene, Cardinal and Dieter that Elijah's generation watched and sought to emulate.

"We were going to meetings and holding many talks on native issues at the YMCA on Vaughn Street," says Elijah. As well, the student activists were invited several times to Courchene's home. "He was very influential," Elijah remembers. "He was supportive of aboriginal students, and talked to us about what could be done, what could be accomplished."

Native students at the University of Manitoba came from different regions and different traditions: Cree, Ojibwa, Inuit and Metis. For centuries, the segregating effect of federal policies had all but guaranteed that a united native voice would never emerge. However, several key elements began to unite native students in the 1970s. Most shared the experience of childhood in remote communities followed by the residential-school system, in which native children first saw beyond their traditional differences to commonalities: in particular, a deep-seated anger. From this starting point, Elijah's generation began the fight for change.

A few days after classes started, Elijah spotted a poster inviting native students to a meeting called by an articulate twenty-five-year-old student named Ovide Mercredi. That meeting inaugurated the Manitoba Indian and Eskimo Student Association, the first native student association in the country, according to its founders. Ovide was elected president of the group; Elijah helped behind the scenes.

The association decided on a multipurpose mandate. First, they would lobby for a native counsellor and support services for native students. The new association started with a "cubbyhole of an office" but graduated to larger digs in its second year as its credibility increased. "That first year we began a program of political action," says Harper. "We did a fair amount of lobbying with our professors and some of the university administrators," including the president of the university, Ernest Shirluk, and the board of governors.

Their other major goal was long-term. "The idea was to develop leadership," explains Mercredi. "We set up the organization for that purpose, to develop leadership." This resulted in the new organization's one and only rule: no one could serve more than one year as president.

Ovide Mercredi was what was known as a "non-treaty Indian." He had been born on January 30, 1946, on a trapline near Grand Rapids, Manitoba, a community of about three hundred on the northeast shore of Lake Winnipeg. "My mother was treaty but my father was not. That meant, because of the Indian Act, I didn't grow up on the reserve," says Mercredi.

Status or treaty Indians are those whose forefathers were registered as members of bands that had signed treaties with the Crown. The original registration lists were often incomplete, missing the names of inhabitants of less populated areas or those who were simply off hunting or fishing the day the census-takers happened to show up.

Until 1985, the government determined who was and was not a status Indian according to the bloodline of the father, regardless of traditional practice. (Among the Ojibwa, for example, the line of descent passes through the father; among the Huron it passes through the mother.) Thus, a non-native woman who married a status Indian (and any children of their union) would gain Indian status and the rights, benefits and restrictions attached to it. However, by marrying a non-status man, native or not, status women (and any children of the marriage) were automatically disenfranchised—all rights to live on reserves and to free education, health care and housing were cancelled.

This provision in the Indian Act was changed only after native women lobbied the United Nations Human Rights Committee. Ottawa finally buckled under international pressure and passed Bill C-31, under which women—and their children—whose status was lost could apply for reinstatement. Almost 100,000 Bill C-31 Indians had re-registered by 1992.

Ovide Mercredi is a Bill C-31 Indian, a designation that many bureaucrats consider equal to being non-native. "I was raised like everybody else in the community as a Cree," says Mercredi with impatience and a hint of anger. "At that time," he says of northern Manitoba in his youth, "there was no distinction in our community between Cree and Metis. It was either treaty or non-treaty, but you were an Indian. The word was Indian. The adjective was treaty or non-treaty."

The community may not have treated him differently, but the government certainly did. As a non-registered native person, Mercredi could not attend the reserve school, which he sees as no great loss. "There was a one-room classroom on the reserve, a federal school. It was just an old log building. The facilities were very poor in contrast to our facilities, which were not up to any great standards either, but at least it was constructed for the purpose of being a school."

When Mercredi was about ten years old, everything began to change. "Hydro moved into Grand Rapids in 1959. There was an influx of white labourers and engineers, and they demanded schools for their children." One of the results was construction of a new high school and a new elementary school. Mercredi spent a year in the high school before being transferred to a Catholic school in The Pas, a mixed native and white community almost six hundred kilometres northeast of Winnipeg. But by Grade 12, the lure of a job on a hydro project was powerful, and Mercredi left high school before graduation.

Mercredi worked with Manitoba Hydro in Grand Rapids and later in Great Falls. After a few years, he decided to take the summer off to become a part-time student at the University of Winnipeg. Like Elijah, Mercredi took Grade 12 mathematics in summer school. "That was the course I failed during high school," says Mercredi in the tight, uncomfortable voice that emerges whenever he speaks of failure.

It was during that summer in Winnipeg that Mercredi became, as he puts it, "politicized through contact with the emerging urban Indian movement in Manitoba." The native activists he met in Winnipeg "were associated with the Indian and Métis Friendship Centre and they had formed a group called Club 376," the street number of the building where the group met. Mercredi's involvement in native political action began, he says, by "just hanging out."

"We were just Indians discovering Indians in the city. We were also discovering the treatment of Indians for the first time and beginning to talk about it in a political context. And we began to do some organizing to change it." The unusual thing about the Friendship Centre group, says Mercredi, was that they all had high-school educations.

At the end of the summer, Mercredi returned to Grand Rapids and his hydro job. "I never did pass my mathematics or French," he says, with the slight stutter that strikes when he is particularly stressed. "I was too interested in what was happening in the Friendship Centre." But Mercredi came back with a heightened sense of the need to improve the desperate lives of native people. He became involved in community development projects, particularly those for non-treaty Indians, aimed at getting better housing and greater aboriginal control over education.

In 1971, at age twenty-five, Mercredi decided to quit his job and go back to university full-time, even though he lacked both high-school credits and money. "Don't forget, I am not treaty status, or registered, so I couldn't get money from Indian Affairs." Mercredi recalls that a "tough woman who used to smoke cigars" interviewed him for admission. "She was really good to me. She decided that it was worth the risk to spend some money on me, at least for a few courses."

Mecredi got a student loan and a scholarship from the university. He was admitted as a mature student for the summer session. He took biology and sociology and earned a B plus in both.

The Manitoba Indian and Eskimo Student Association was launched that fall. The group's lobby efforts were aided by a couple of unexpected, embarrassing episodes.

One involved the faculty of psychology, which advertised a study on racism and prejudice. Some Indian and Eskimo Association members volunteered for the study and then reported back to the group. In the experiment, electrodes were placed on white, black and Indian students, who were then asked a series of questions. The interviewer, at his or her own discretion, could administer a shock to the subjects based on the answers they gave. The aim, says Mercredi, was to determine if the shock levels administered varied according to the racial background of the subjects. (In fact, no shocks were administered. A light indicated the shock levels subjects had supposedly received, and the subjects had been directed to react accordingly.) "We decided we were going to sabotage this thing," says Mercredi. "So a number of us volunteered. We would exaggerate our behaviour, make it look like we were really getting jolted. In the end, the whole thing was just cancelled because the psychology department found out what we were doing."

By the early 1970s, native Canadians were tired of tests, studies, inquiries and commissions that led nowhere. "We thought it was a silly experiment," says Mercredi. "We thought the last thing you needed was proof of racism. We knew it existed."

The second incident got Mercredi and his association into the pages of Winnipeg's two daily newspapers. In fact, Mercredi says, the drive for more native services and, eventually, a native studies program at the university was successful not because there was "political will for those initiatives but because of what the engineering students did in the fall of that year."

The *Cursor*, the engineering students' newspaper, carried regular accounts of student pub crawls. The articles passed into university archives with barely a glance until the *Cursor* decided to tour the bars along Winnipeg's Main Street strip.

This was the "other" Main Street, a few square kilometres of rundown boarding homes, decrepit bars and social service drop-in centres where hundreds of off-reserve Indians live.

Elijah's generation was seeing a sharp rise in the number of Indians moving from their remote communities to the cities. Between 1966 and 1986, the number of off-reserve Indians (often called "bus refugees" by city planners), jumped 254 per cent, while reserve populations grew by only 24 per cent. During the same period, Manitoba's urban Indian population jumped 330 per cent, from about 4200 to more than 18,000. Some were students, but most were the poor and unemployed who came looking for a better life. Few found jobs, and they soon discovered that once off the reserve they were in political limbo. The federal government no longer accepted responsibility for their welfare, despite protests from the province and from native leaders. Ad hoc services were grudgingly provided by other levels of government, with little co-ordination or effect. Most natives from the remote north ended up on Main Street.

These were the Indians the engineering students highlighted. "They had gone on a pub crawl and taken pictures of the Indians in various stages of inebriation in bars and on streets," says Mercredi. "And they wrote about it in a very racist manner."

A young lawyer was hired to advise the Indian and Eskimo Association on their options. "We were going to take the university to court on the basis of discrimination and racism and seek compensation for damages against the reputation and integrity of Indian people," says Mercredi. "And then we organized a series of protests. We had a great big rally. We had prominent Indian elders come and make speeches about Indian aspirations." One of those leaders was Dave Courchene, who some say terrified the university president.

When the media picked up the story, the university found itself with a public relations nightmare. It was a perfect opportunity for the new native student association to test its political muscle. "This was our first plunge into political organization," says Mercredi. "We managed to meet and instruct our lawyer and organize symposiums at the Friendship Centre. We had the dean of engineering on the hot seat at the Friendship Centre, where he had to account for the behaviour of the students of his department to the urban Indians who came. The student body was very interested and so was the faculty.

"[The students] were very surprised that the Indian people were offended. They were just totally ignorant. They just didn't know any better, they said, and they were very apologetic."

Several face-to-face meetings were held with the students. "It was a real education for them, too," says Mercredi, "to talk to an Indian and have an Indian confront them about their attitudes and about changing their attitudes." The encounters led to negotiations for a settlement. Members of the association said they would be satisfied with a public apology printed in Winnipeg's daily newspapers, the *Free Press* and the *Tribune*. As well, authors of the offending article would be required to write a piece about the needs and aspirations of Canada's aboriginal people. "They would have to research it themselves," says Mercredi. "We would point them in the right direction, but we wouldn't write it for them."

Each article that was written was reviewed by members of the Indian and Eskimo Student Association. "And we'd send it back for more drafts. We did this for quite a while until finally they could produce articles that were a contrast to the pieces they had written previously," says Mercredi. "We used the idea of public education as a means of getting satisfaction."

Another major thrust of the new association's work was helping native students at other universities set up similar organizations. Elijah and Mercredi recall with great humour a trip for that purpose to Brandon University in the spring of 1972. Alan Ross, a non-native from Norway House, had asked for help in organizing an association for Brandon's large native student population.

The Manitoba Indian Brotherhood rented two cars for the students to drive to Brandon. Mercredi drove Elijah, Moses Okimaw, George Chingoose, Edwin Jebb and Harper's roommate Richard Linklater. A second car was driven by a student nicknamed "the Pope" because he was considered honest to a fault. "Once, he ran into a telephone pole and called the police," Harper says, laughing.

The meeting broke up in the late afternoon and everyone went for a couple of drinks before heading home. Richard and George, who had gone drinking earlier in the day, were discovered about 7:00 P.M. and poured into the back seat of Mercredi's car, says Elijah. For a reason that escapes them now, Harper and Mercredi were determined to get back home that night, but not long after they set out, they were foiled by a typical Manitoba spring snowstorm.

"We lost them," says Mercredi of the Pope's car. "We had no idea where they were." Mercredi's car reached Portage la Prairie by about 1:00 A.M.

"You couldn't even see anything," says Elijah, "so we decided to take turns running in front of the car. Of course, we were all skinny then—and younger." The idea was that the runner would follow the yellow centre line on the roadway and the car would follow the runner. "There were cars all over the ditch, and semi-tractor trailers," recalls Mercredi. "We made jokes about it as we went along." The roads were all but deserted. "Who's going to run first?" someone asked. "Send Richard and George out," came the answer.

The pair were awakened, told the plan and sent outside to lead the car onward. "There was this cold wind blowing. They didn't last very long," says Elijah, laughing again. Those in the warm car were hysterical with laughter as they watched the two stumble along. "George's sense of direction was not too good," says Elijah. By the time the pair got back in the car, they had almost sobered up. "What are we doing on the highway?" they asked. "Oh," came the reply, "about a mile an hour."

During that first summer after his university courses ended, Elijah took a job with the Manitoba Department of Education, doing research and writing papers on various native projects. His job included travelling to gather information and take pictures of various native cultural events. He was also sent to speak to native youth about the need for post-secondary education. Harper says he and many of the other native students would spend their spare time at the Manitoba Indian Brotherhood offices doing whatever was needed. (Unlike native organizations that followed, the MIB administered a variety of programs as well as driving the movement's political agenda.) "We never got paid for it," he says, "we just did it because we wanted to do it."

Early in Elijah's second year in university, he married Elizabeth Ann Ross, whom he had known since high school. The wedding took place in Saint Charles Church in downtown Winnipeg. Elijah's roommate Stan Harper was best man. Elizabeth is from God's Lake, about sixty kilometres northeast of Red Sucker Lake. She had attended school in Winnipeg for several years, and would travel back and forth between reserve and city life during her marriage. The couple's union would suffer many breakups and end in divorce in 1991.

Elijah and his new family (Elizabeth had an infant son, Marcel, whose father had died in a fire), moved into the Eden Roc Motel on Pembina Highway. Elijah continued to go to school and to work for the Manitoba Indian Brotherhood, this time analyzing a series of federal native policy papers. Indian Affairs was proposing the creation of tribal councils, native-run umbrella organizations that would make decisions on programs and services affecting several bands in one geographical area and eventually take over the administrative work of Indian Affairs.

Harper's report advised against the government scheme. True, the councils would give native people more administrative responsibilities, but ultimate control of spending and project approval would remain with Indian Affairs. "Basically what I saw was that they would establish a brown bureaucracy for Indian Affairs to administer all that misery. Over four or five years, the money that was coming in federally would be reduced, and eventually the bands would be supporting their tribal council." (Despite the negative analyses of Elijah and others, the council system was established in the late 1970s.)

It was during this assignment for the MIB that Harper first crossed paths with a man who would play a significant role in his life. Phil Fontaine is the eldest of the generation of Manitoba native leaders who would carry on the Dieter, Cardinal and Courchene legacy. Fontaine was born in 1945 on the Fort Alexander Reserve, home to the grandfather of Manitoba native politics, Dave Courchene. In 1968, Fontaine, an Ojibwa of the Sagkeeng Nation, became a band administrator for Courchene, the first such post in Manitoba. When Courchene became president of the newly established Manitoba Indian Brotherhood, Fontaine followed him to Winnipeg to serve on the provincial executive and work as the MIB office manager. In 1972 Fontaine returned to his reserve to run for chief. The position was open since Courchene had decided that being chief as well as head of the MIB was too taxing.

It was a tough decision for Fontaine. For years he had worked in the back rooms of the movement and imagined that he would remain there. "I could not speak in public," he says. "I was terrified to say even a few words." Fontaine credits Courchene with handing him situations that helped him get over his fear.

Fontaine served as chief of Fort Alexander for four years, during which time he worked with Elijah on the research project. "Our job was to review these policy papers, analyze them, and come up with appropriate recommendations for changes," says Fontaine. "We felt the policies were too restrictive and weren't going to result in the kinds of change we needed to effect self-government. We weren't talking about self-government, necessarily, but that was what we were striving for."

Phil Fontaine had met Harper a few years earlier. "One of my first impressions was, and it really hasn't changed although it is more pronounced now, is that he is a quiet individual, unassuming and a person with a real sense of humour."

The thinking of the new crop of Canadian native leaders was much influenced by events to the south of them. In 1972, Indian protestors from across the U.S. had occupied the headquarters of the Bureau of Indian Affairs in Washington, D.C. In February 1973, the occupation of the Pine River Reservation in Wounded Knee, South Dakota, led to the shooting deaths of two Indians and the wounding of a government agent. The ensuing standoff lasted until May. Such events ensured the attention of all politicians when native leaders made demands.

Despite the excitement and opportunity of such times, Elijah soon found the responsibilities of married life, activism and school too much. In the middle of his second year of university, he accepted a community development posting with the Manitoba Indian Brotherhood that allowed the family to return to Red Sucker Lake. In the winter of 1972, Elijah, Elizabeth and baby Marcel left Winnipeg to live with Elijah's parents. The couple eventually moved into an abandoned house on the reserve. They would have three more children by 1978—Bruce, Tanya and Holly.

In his new job Elijah could clearly see the immense needs within the native community. "There were all kinds of demands made on community development workers," says Elijah. "You were a jack of all trades. You would even have to help people figure out personal income tax forms."

The next few years would also be busy ones for the emerging leaders of this new native generation—Fontaine, Mercredi and others who had crossed Elijah's path in Winnipeg. In the fall of 1972, Moses Okimaw took over as the University of Manitoba's Indian and Eskimo Student Association president. During Okimaw's term the university made a commitment to establish a native studies program. "We had an ad hoc committee set up to begin to review what was needed and how it should be implemented," says Mercredi. "The department of native studies at the University of Manitoba [which began in 1975] is a direct result of the political lobbying of native students."

As Harper settled in at Red Sucker Lake, Ovide Mercredi headed into his third year of university and a position as a native peer counsellor for students. "We were talking about the academic concerns of students—literacy, writing papers, doing research, and reading and writing skills mostly," says Mercredi. "We were making sure that students felt that the support was there for them when they needed it." The counsellors determined what the students needed and then found help within the system.

Mercredi ended his university studies one credit short of a Bachelor of Arts degree. "I always swore I would go back to get that B.A.," he says. "Some professors told me, do it now or you never will—they were right." Instead, he entered law school.

In the summer of 1974, Mercredi, then a second-year law student, worked for the Manitoba Indian Brotherhood as executive assistant to the new president, Ahab Spence. It was here that Mercredi met Chief Phil Fontaine. The next summer, Fontaine offered Mercredi a job setting up a child welfare system on the Fort Alexander reserve.

That same year, Elijah's MIB job took him and his family to Thompson, Manitoba, for a short stint as area supervisor of community development initiatives in Churchill, The Pas, Shamattawa, Brochet, Nelson House, Oxford House and Thompson. Elijah says he moved around so much because there were many opportunities and often higher pay to be had. As well, the goal of several of his postings was to leave the community self-sufficient—in other words, to work himself out of a job.

One of the problems Harper and the northern MIB staff tried to tackle was the decades of alcohol abuse and gas sniffing in Shamattawa. "Everyone started to jump on the bandwagon," says Harper, "Indian Affairs, Social Services, the RCMP." Twenty years later, Harper shakes his head at the futile effort. "It is a tough one, but basically, it has to come from the community. It is like a person who refuses to be helped. It is the parents who are doing it to themselves, and then the child learns. Where is the hope of this generation? Still, we must never give up."

In 1975, Harper accepted a job with the Manitoba Department of Northern Affairs as a program analyst. The department is responsible for the 33,000 Metis residents of Manitoba but is also involved in matters affecting the province's almost 60,000 Indians and Inuit.

About the same time, Harper was offered a position with the federal department of Employment and Immigration. It would have paid more, but it required extensive travel, and Elijah did not feel that being away so much would be fair to Elizabeth or their children. In the end, he says, he made the right decision. "[Working with Northern Affairs] was good for me. That's how I became politically active. I got to know [Premier Edward] Schreyer. I came in with the crowd that was with him. If I hadn't done that, I don't think I would ever have become an MLA." While with Northern Affairs, Elijah earned a reputation as an excellent development officer. His foray into the inner workings of white bureaucracy and government had begun.

Elijah's career in provincial politics was interrupted in 1977 when Sterling Lyon's Conservatives took office. It was a government marked by austerity and severe cutbacks. "I left on March 31, 1978," says Elijah. "I didn't get fired. I just felt uncomfortable there. He was cutting back all these things."

Harper returned to the Manitoba Indian Brotherhood to help with research and other projects focussing on native self-government, which was emerging as a major national issue. A few months later, however, he heard that the Red Sucker Lake chief was about to step down. The idea of running for chief was appealing.

His view of what a chief should be—"a leader, the head of the community. People respect the chief, they listen to him."—was based on his memories of the chief who had been posted at Garden Hill while Elijah was growing up. (Red Sucker got its first chief, Angus Harper, in 1969.) Elijah had moved from job to job and wanted to settle his family. He decided to run, and he was elected chief of Red Sucker Lake in 1978. He was twenty-nine years old.

"It was a lot of work," he says of his first months on the job. Harper had campaigned on upgrading the community and, in particular, on creating jobs for the more than three hundred residents. The issues were the same as those plaguing Indian communities across the country—unemployment, poor housing, a lack of basic services and facilities, and enforced idleness. Historically, a chief's value had been his mystical connection to the wisdom of nature and the universe. The modern-day chief, Harper discovered, was as good as his insider knowledge of the complexities of federal and provincial politics and the programs that natives are forced to use—and sometimes abuse—to survive. "You have to know the system," says Elijah.

His work with the Manitoba Indian Brotherhood and Northern Affairs had taught him where money for programs could be found and had introduced him to many of the key players. "I was basically knowledgeable about the system, Ottawa's government and the programs that were taking place," says Elijah. "I knew some of the people and I had been to all the communities in the North. I knew the chiefs."

Not the least of his abilities was his talent for manoeuvring around cumbersome bureaucracy. Indeed, as chief, Harper honed one of his favourite skills—breaking the rules quietly and with a strange kind of passive aggression.

It was a style that resulted in several major changes in Red Sucker Lake during his three-year term as chief: a permanent nursing station was built and staffed; a new band hall was constructed; the government-funded winter road system was extended to the isolated outpost, the local road was upgraded and television made its debut.

How television and the winter road arrived in Red Sucker Lake are two of Elijah's favourite tales. Native humour often has a self-deprecating tone, but not when the tale pits one of their own against the big, bad Ottawa bureaucrats, especially when the bureaucrats are left in the dust.

Soon after his election as chief, Elijah considered introducing television to his remote community. At the time, a debate raged throughout native communities: would television do more harm than good, especially to the children? What would happen to native culture, language, traditions and values?

Harper sympathized with those who feared its effects but argued that not having television was simply one more example of Indians being have-nots. (In the back of his mind sat his high-school memory of being unable to write the same essay as the rest of his class.) Harper believed that, with some restrictions, television would be a good thing for the community.

Years later, as more children lost their native languages and frustrations grew over the inequities between Indian and non-Indian communities, Harper would wonder if he had made the right choice; but back in 1978, his biggest concern was a technical one: the reserve was too far from any major community to pick up the signal. It would not be a simple matter of ordering up a television set and plugging it in.

At the time, the Canadian Broadcasting Corporation was expanding television services via satellite dishes to remote areas with populations of five hundred people or more. Red Sucker had just over three hundred people. They tried padding the population figures, listing transient workers and other visitors, but could not get the numbers high enough. Arguing with the government to make an exception got them nowhere.

One day, a pamphlet advertising satellite dishes crossed Harper's desk. After determining that the band had the $60,000, Harper contacted the Vancouver supplier, who assured the chief that residents would be able to watch a number of channels and transmit locally produced programs. Moreover, Harper was told, the satellite's signal would not break federal laws governing communications. "We would only be transmitting half a watt," says Harper. "If we were transmitting over four watts, then we would fall under the jurisdiction of the CRTC. But it was only half a watt, and it wasn't interfering with anything.

"We checked out the airport and future plans for communications. And we checked out the frequency to ensure that we weren't interfering with anything. We decided to bring in a satellite." The unusual delivery would cause a stir in Ottawa, but Elijah knew that if he could just get the dish onto reserve land, Ottawa would have no jurisdiction to remove it.

The day finally came when the huge dish arrived tied under the belly of a DC-3. Elijah and several other men carefully loaded it onto the back of a pickup truck. It was planted on newly poured cement footings in the middle of the community. "It was a big dish and took a lot of people to move it," recalls one resident. "When you wanted to change channels you had to go outside and move the satellite manually. There were markers telling you which way to turn it, exactly, to get the channel you wanted."

In preparation for the satellite's arrival, the Hudson's Bay store had stocked up on televisions and cables, and they were sold out in days. "They made a lot of money off it," says Harper, laughing. "We put in four channels, one that we could unplug. I could come on TV any time. So I'd get on TV and talk and make reports about committee meetings. We even left the cameras on for live band meetings, so people at home could watch." The idea was to improve communications with the people, and it worked, he says.

The dish could pick up twenty-two American channels twenty-four hours a day, as well as Canadian programming; but it was the U.S. access that caught the attention of Ottawa bureaucrats. "What the community really liked was wrestling," says Elijah. "Every weekend from Madison Square Garden. Even people from across the Ontario border would travel sixty miles by ski-doo—four hours—to watch it." Elijah also recalls Mohammed Ali's fights causing quite a stir those first few days the satellite was set up, and residents also watched movies and the news.

Not long after the dish arrived, government officials wanted to know what was going on. "We got a call from the Department of Communications asking us what we were doing and what we were watching," says Elijah. In particular, they asked Harper if the community was watching foreign shows.

"Yes," answered Elijah.

"What about the CBC?"

"Well, that's what I meant," he replied.

"What they meant, of course," says Elijah, "was whether we were watching American programs." Tapping into American satellites breached international and Canadian laws, and the government called in the Canadian Radio and Telecommunications Commission (CRTC) to investigate. The only trouble was that the CRTC did not have jurisdiction—and Harper knew it. The CRTC called the Hudson's Bay store manager to find out what programs the community tuned in to. He refused to answer, saying that the caller had better check with the chief. Metis residents across the lake were also quizzed, but they too told the officials to call Harper.

As the issue heated up, the southern media caught on. One of the first items videotaped off the new satellite feed was the June 19, 1979, edition of "The National," in which a young-looking Knowlton Nash interviews a baby-faced Elijah Harper. The tape is still a favourite bit of entertainment in Red Sucker.

When an official from Ottawa flew into Red Sucker to inspect the equipment, his timing was bad. Elijah was in England with the native lobby against Ottawa's plans to patriate the Canadian constitution. "I guess the guy wanted to fiddle around with everything, but we had left saying no one could touch [the equipment] without permission of the chief and council," says Harper. The councillors said they had no authority and the officials would have to get the chief's permission. "The guy said 'I'll give him a call.' So they gave him my phone number—only I was in England. I never did get that call."

Ovide Mercredi was studying law, including communications, when the satellite episode made news. Mercredi says he could not help but admire the Red Sucker chief. "Elijah was challenging air space," says Mercredi. "He was saying, this is a reserve, this is our land, and we can do whatever we want on it. Right now we have no access to television and the CRTC is not going to tell me what is not good or good for my community. My community will decide what our needs are. We are going to put up this tower and bring satellite services to our community."

Mercredi remembered Elijah as a quiet, mostly unassuming person with a good sense of humour. "It was sort of uncharacteristic of Elijah for him to challenge authority in such a direct manner. That required, I would say, some tenacity. And he was doing it at a time when nobody was doing that kind of stuff, so that was a surprise to begin with. Not just that Elijah had done it, but that an Indian would stand up to a government agency, the CRTC."

Harper's actions may have seemed out of character to Mercredi, but such episodes pepper much of Elijah's political career. His manoeuvring to have the winter road extended to Red Sucker is another example. Every winter, the province would build a winter road that covered the seven hundred kilometres from Winnipeg to Garden Hill; the costs were shared with the federal government. And every winter, the residents of Red Sucker spent about two weeks packing snow and ice to extend this road one hundred kilometres northeast to their reserve. It was arduous and time-consuming work that provided just six weeks' driving access from Winnipeg.

Harper decided to get Red Sucker Lake permanently on the road-building program. Federal government officials said they would pay for the road extension only if the province also contributed; the provincial minister of roads and highways, Don Orchard, said the province would kick in only after Elijah had secured Indian Affairs funds. "I was put in a Catch-22 situation," explains Elijah, and January was approaching.

At the time, Harper was on a federal regional development committee funding make-work projects. "So I took a plan to build a winter road to the board and they approved it," says Elijah. "I got a contract signed that afternoon for about $13,000." Elijah then took the contract to Don Orchard's assistant, who was aware that Orchard had promised to match federal funds. "I explained to his assistant that all I needed was a letter saying that we'll match this $13,000. That's all I needed." The fact that the funds were from the federal government was stressed, but the exact department was not. "I got the letter," says Harper, laughing.

Armed with the province's promise, he went back to the federal government. "I took it to Indian Affairs and they matched it, too." Harper ended up with $39,000—$13,000 more than he had set out to get—and a promise that Red Sucker would get a winter road. "They found out about it later," says Elijah, "but they couldn't do anything about it."

Years later, on the day that Elijah made his maiden speech in the Manitoba legislature, Tory MLA Don Orchard sat across from Harper and recalled the episode with some humour. "I must tell the minister he's got a very industrious and very astute legislative assistant in the MLA from Rupertsland. The chief played a very excellent three-way game of chess between the provincial government, myself as minister, the federal minister of Indian Affairs and the Department of Regional Development. The chief very skillfully negotiated—I won't say manipulated—but he very skillfully negotiated the three of us around until one of us made a commitment. . . . I'm proud to say that it was myself and my Department of Highways that made the first commitment." Elijah took the opening to let Orchard know that, in fact, he had been second.

But while such assignments kept Harper busy enough, events unfolding on the national scene would divert much of his attention between 1978 and 1982. Native leaders had joined forces again, this time against Prime Minister Pierre Trudeau's dream to end Canada's status as a British colony through a constitution that could be amended in Canada rather than with the permission of the British Crown. Nothing since the 1969 White Paper so unified native organizations.

As usual, native leaders had not been consulted about the constitutional proposals. Native representation at the negotiating table was dismissed out of hand by Trudeau and the premiers. Canada's three main native organizations—the National Indian Brotherhood, the Native

Council of Canada (formerly the Canadian Metis Society) and the Inuit Committee on National Issues—argued that Trudeau had no right to change the terms of the constitution without input from the country's original citizens. Canada's aboriginal people had signed their treaties with the British Crown, and if their historic benefactor was to be written out of the country's fundamental document, native leaders wanted a say in the changes.

After much resistance, Trudeau finally agreed to a provision in the new constitution stating that nothing—even the equality provisions of the Charter of Rights—would erase natives' special rights granted in the Royal Proclamation of 1763. Trudeau also asked the three native organizations to be observers at the next first ministers' conference, planned for 1978. Later, with a province-wide referendum on Quebec sovereignty looming, Trudeau offered to include native issues as a general agenda item at a future first ministers' meeting.

Such initiatives were too little and too late. Native leaders launched a high-profile but ultimately unsuccessful lobby in Canada and abroad. In 1980, the National Indian Brotherhood opened an office in London, England, to co-ordinate their public awareness efforts. It was as part of this effort that Elijah travelled to London in the midst of the satellite-dish war, with Manitoban Joe Guy Wood, Dene leader Georges Erasmus and other native leaders. The group met with the Archbishop of Canterbury in the hope that he could convince the Queen to intervene on their behalf, but efforts to meet the Queen or her representative failed.

On November 5, 1981, "the night of the long knives," the final constitutional package was drawn up in an all-night session. That Quebec was not invited was seen by many as threatening national unity; but Canada's native people were as shocked as Quebeckers, for they too had been excluded.

For almost a year, Canada's native leaders had been led to believe that the final package would include this amendment: "The aboriginal and treaty rights of the aboriginal peoples of Canada are hereby recognized and affirmed. In this act, aboriginal people of Canada include the Indian, Inuit and Metis." As well, Trudeau had promised that the equality rights in the charter would not negate any special-status provisions. While disappointing, the general consensus was that these promises were the most native Canadians could hope for in the current political climate.

After the November 5, 1981 all-night meeting, however, the aboriginal rights clause had vanished. Fierce last-minute lobbying, coupled with a promise by federal New Democratic Party leader Ed Broadbent that his party would fight the constitutional package, led to the introduction of a watered-down amendment that merely recognized "existing aboriginal and treaty rights." By way of compensation, native Canadians were also promised four first ministers' conferences focussing exclusively on native issues.

Elijah Harper was not present when the Queen signed Canada's new constitution in Ottawa in 1992, despite an invitation. His absence was a quiet protest on behalf of native people.

After almost five years of fighting, native Canadians had gained little and the battle had cost them dearly. Some estimates put the cost to native organizations at more than $4.5 million, a burden that would force several native bodies to regroup and downsize.

One of the first casualties was the Manitoba Indian Brotherhood. It was replaced by the Four Nations Confederacy, divided between north and south, a "natural" division based on geography and the differing needs of two regions, says Elijah.

A few years later, the National Indian Brotherhood also crumbled under heavy debt and accusations of financial and other mismanagement. In its place rose the Assembly of First Nations, made up of the more than six hundred band chiefs across the country and headed by Georges Erasmus. The policies of the new organization were to be driven by the grassroots through the chiefs.

In 1980, a Manitoba election was on the horizon, and Ovide Mercredi heard that the New Democratic Party was looking for native candidates to run in northern ridings. Mercredi was president of the NDP association in The Pas at the time and, "they were wondering if I would be interested in running," says Mercredi. "I wasn't." Henry Wilson became a candidate but lost the nomination to a non-native. The search then moved to Rupertsland, a massive riding created in 1916 that covers almost half of Manitoba. First to be approached was Moses Okimaw. He wasn't interested, but he suggested Elijah might be.

Not long after, Mercredi received a call. "It was Moses to tell me that he was working for Elijah, and they wanted to know if I would be willing to do some work and contribute to the campaign." (Mercredi did not become directly involved, but he made a contribution.) Mercredi says he was not surprised to hear that Harper was interested. "Obviously, he is politically aware. And his experience with the CRTC would have trained him in terms of power politics and authority and how Indian leaders can work within the system or outside of it to meet their objectives. So my impression was that Elijah would have been a good candidate, and he was a good candidate."

Elijah says he had decided to run provincially about a year before he was approached by the NDP. In Manitoba the only choices were the Tories and the NDP (the Liberals rarely elected anyone), so his choice of party was easy. "I made my intentions known," he says, and he made contacts at a couple of NDP conventions.

"We were proud of the fact that we had Elijah as our candidate," says Howard Pawley. The NDP leader knew of Harper's work in the Department of Northern Affairs, and his first impressions of Elijah were lasting ones. "Very subdued, extremely quiet, very modest and a great sense of humour. He really liked to kibitz with me," says Pawley.

Being a native candidate in a northern riding presented several unique obstacles. Funding the campaign would be an ongoing difficulty, but there were even more basic problems. To vote at a nomination meeting, you have to be a party member; to be a member you have to pay a membership fee. It may be as little as ten dollars, but cash is a scarce commodity on reserves, most readily available the day government cheques arrive, says Elijah, before the money is spent on necessities or debts that accumulate between cheques. There are no banks. The Hudson's Bay stores cash cheques and sometimes hold welfare and pension funds—often without paying interest.

"Lots of people say they will support you for a nomination, but it is hard to generate the money," says Elijah. It is even harder to get people to come out to vote—less than 10 per cent of eligible natives vote in most elections.

Elijah's nomination meeting was scheduled for 7:00 P.M., but when Howard Pawley arrived, the meeting hall was empty. "There wasn't anyone there outside of Elijah, Elijah's wife and myself," recalls Pawley. "I was quite concerned that it was going to be a total washout."

"Don't worry," Elijah reassured him. "We've just hooked up this satellite and programming is being introduced to Red Sucker from Detroit. Tonight, there is a western—cowboys and Indians—and John Wayne is starring. Everyone in the community is watching."

And so, Howard Pawley got his first taste of "Indian time," as Elijah called it that night. "Indian time means it's the right time," says Elijah, laughing at the memory. While the phrase is often used by non-natives to indicate that someone is late, this is not how it is understood in native communities. "We're always on the right time," he says. "When you start, you start. There isn't anything else to do. Where are you going to take off for? Sunday shopping?"

Two hours later, the hall was filled and the community watched their chief, newly nominated to run in the provincial election, introduce them to the man who would soon be premier. In what would become typical of him, Elijah conjured up a story for the occasion, in this case a reminder that, in 1973, as attorney general, Pawley had landed in hot water for instructing his bureaucrats not to charge Indians for violations under the Migratory Birds Act. Pawley was roundly condemned at the time for interfering in the judicial process, but his stand was appreciated by the native people.

On the way to Red Sucker, Elijah had discovered a Pawley quirk: Pawley has an aversion to fowl and refuses to eat it. "It's against my principles," Pawley told him. Here was a man, Elijah says, who had protected the rights of native people to kill the fowl he hated.

"If you're going to survive up here," Elijah advised Pawley with just a hint of irony, "you'll have to learn to eat your principles."

PART TWO

Between Two Political Worlds

Chapter Four

WHITE POLITICS

"City slickers need not apply" could have been on the job posting for Elijah Harper's first campaign manager. Running an election in the remote communities of northern Manitoba requires a kind of thinking and organizing distinct from that applied to more urban election campaigns in the south.

Since realignment in 1990, Rupertsland constituency begins at the Fort Alexander reserve near the south end of Lake Winnipeg and fans out north, east and west to the province's borders with the Northwest Territories, Ontario and Saskatchewan. It is five hundred kilometres wide at its broadest point.

In 1981, when Elijah ran in his first campaign, the riding was only slightly smaller. The 13,000 or so residents were scattered throughout hundreds of square kilometres of lakes and rivers. In the 1981 census, about 10 per cent of the residents listed English as their first language, and just under 2 per cent listed French. The rest, more than 10,500, spoke a Cree or Ojibwa dialect.

Sea planes for landing on the lakes and single-engine craft for the miniature, rugged northern runways are a campaign staple despite their expense and unreliability in bad weather. "It isn't like in the south where you can drive up in a car with your pamphlets and drop one off," says Elijah. "You have to lug everything with you, all your brochures and posters. You have to put them in the plane, take them out, put them in the boat, carry them with you. There is a lot of physical work."

In the larger Rupertsland communities, southern campaign strategies are useful. Lists of voters' names and street addresses can be assembled; canvassers can go door-to-door along passable roads, put up lawn signs to mark supporters and try to gauge support from quick conversations on doorsteps. But almost 90 per cent of Rupertsland's population is scattered on remote reserves and in Metis communities, where there are few roads or neatly mapped out neighbourhoods.

Then there is the matter of language. In the North, speaking English only is a significant impediment: campaign literature in Cree, Saulteaux and Ojibwa is advantageous. Moreover, many residents simply do not understand the white political process.

"In the city, you are followed by the media and you know that people are being informed," says Elijah. "But people in the North don't have that. I have to explain to them that I am running for the NDP, and that there will be different colours on the ballot for each party. Parties don't mean much to them in a political or philosophical sense."

The New Democratic Party, which had held the Rupertsland riding since 1969, sat poised to return to power under their new leader Howard Pawley. After one term of austerity and cutbacks under Sterling Lyon's tough-minded Tories, the electorate was in the mood for change. Harper was hoping to replace retiring NDP MLA Harvey Bostrum, who had held Rupertsland since 1973.

As the election approached, Wilf Hudson, a steelworker in Regina, got a call from NDP organizers in Manitoba. Hudson had worked in several election campaigns in northern Manitoba, including Rod Murphy's successful bid for the federal riding of Churchill in 1979. Now Hudson was being called in to run the campaign for Elijah Harper, whom the party hoped would become the first treaty Indian to sit in the Manitoba legislature.

Hudson had never met Harper, but he was immediately impressed with the candidate. Elijah had a number of selling points, although being a treaty Indian was not necessarily the strongest—others were also fielding native candidates. A non-native, Liberal Alan Ross of Norway House, however, was considered the man to beat.

Elijah's advantages were, however, significant. The riding's NDP roots ran deep and there was little reason to doubt its loyalty. Moreover, Harper's years of work with the Manitoba Indian Brotherhood, the Department of Northern Affairs, and as Red Sucker Lake chief had given him a great deal of exposure in the riding. He could also communicate with Cree-speaking voters and was obviously comfortable with people. "I was really impressed with how articulate he was," says Hudson. "He spoke really well to a group." While hardly flamboyant, Elijah's speaking style was always sincere, says Hudson. "That was his greatest strength."

Hudson had learned several key lessons about northern campaigns. First, predicting the outcome before election night would not be easy. Northern communities took their politics seriously, but voters were polite and rather shy about who they supported. Many residents would allow signs to be posted in front of their houses even if they did not support the candidate. Moreover, candidates and canvassers could not just knock on doors with a quick request for support; residents in the North expect real conversation, according to Hudson. "It took more actual talking," he says, which also meant more of a candidate's time.

Hudson also recalls some tense moments for his candidate in the 1981 campaign. In Alan Ross's home community of Norway House, "Elijah went to a restaurant by himself to have a bite to eat," says Hudson, "and Maggie Balfour, the chief at the time, attacked him, not physically, but verbally. Elijah was really taken aback by it." Elijah recalls that Balfour commented that someone was looking into his finances. "I remember distinctly wondering why she would say that," says Elijah. "But I didn't take it seriously at the time. I figured it must be because Alan Ross was from Norway House."

Hudson was confronted during the campaign by the Tory candidate, Nelson Scribe, Sr., who demanded that Hudson stop Elijah from lying, although Hudson was never clear what Harper was supposed to be lying about. "To the best of my knowledge, Elijah has never lied about anything," says Hudson.

The long hours of campaigning took a toll on Elijah; he was obviously exhausted after a twenty-hour day. Still, he organized meetings throughout the campaign and he put together a sizeable conference during the final days. He also used his understanding of television, picked up as chief in Red Sucker Lake, for additional exposure. Elijah's wife, Elizabeth, also canvassed periodically. "She didn't go out a lot, but when she did she was good. And on election day she was really effective in getting the people out to vote," Hudson says.

During the final days, a plane was chartered full time to allow Elijah to crisscross the riding. On November 16, 1981, the day before the election, Elijah and Elizabeth headed out to God's Lake.

"We left around two in the afternoon from Norway House," recalls Elijah. "And it started snowing. We flew over the clouds, but we just hit a white-out." The plane was totally enveloped by icy sleet and snow. On the approach to God's Lake, "we couldn't find the airport," says Elijah with a tense laugh. "Something had happened to the instruments."

Darkness was falling. The pilot decided to head for the larger air strip at Island Lake, about fifty kilometres south, but bad weather and technical problems prevented the plane from landing. They then made a desperate dash more than two hundred kilometres north to the municipal airport in Thompson. "The pilot looked at his fuel gauge," says Elijah, "and it was empty." As the plane neared Thompson, the tower lost radio contact and feared the craft had gone down. "It was scary," says Elijah wryly, "but it wasn't my time yet. I didn't feel it was my time." Finally, the craft broke through the clouds and landed, running out of fuel partway down the runway.

The next day, Harper boarded another charter and headed to Garden Hill to await the election results. "By the last week you are just dragging your ass around," says Elijah. "By the end you are having mood swings. You go into a community feeling high and then you feel down. It's really stressful. But we did it—we visited every community except for the really small ones with only eight or nine people."

Elijah sat at his cousin Simon Monias's house waiting for the results to be announced on the local television. "I was nervous. I remember my palms were sweating. I was drinking lots of coffee," says Elijah.

Perhaps, but he sounded his usual calm self when Hudson called from Norway House later that night to get the Island Lake area results. The phone connection was so bad that when Hudson asked Elijah how the voting was going, all he could hear was "fifteen votes."

"What do you mean, fifteen votes?" cried Hudson, his stomach dropping. The Island Lake area was Harper's strongest community.

"No," came the reply. "*They* got fifteen votes."

The pattern held. "He wiped up clean in the Garden Hill area and the southeast corner of the riding," says Hudson. "He cleaned up in Island Lake." The final tally was Harper, 3032 votes; Ross, 1004, Nelson Scribe, Sr., 272; and Frances Thompson, of the Manitoba Progressive Party, 56. Harper had taken in just under 70 per cent of the vote.

Once his win was official, Harper headed over to the band office in Garden Hill. "Lots of people came over—well-wishers. Everybody was happy. Then this woman came over, this old woman named Harriet Little, and she told me that she had delivered me. I was happy to see her and thank her for that," says Harper, laughing.

Later that night, Harriet Little went on the local TV station to tell the story of Harper's birth. "I knew this man when he came into the world," Little told listeners in the North. "He had nothing on. He was born in a log cabin on the spruce boughs."

A small item the next day in Manitoba's daily newspapers announced that the first treaty Indian had been elected to the Manitoba legislature.

Two days later the new MLA made news again. Harper and friends had gathered in a downtown Winnipeg hotel to thank everyone who had worked on the historic campaign and to say good-bye to those who would be heading home. Elijah presented Wilf Hudson with a cowboy hat. "You must be a cowboy to work with all these Indians."

Hudson left the party hours later when the festivities seemed to have died down, but Elijah and some friends continued to party. At 8:30 A.M Hudson was awakened by the Winnipeg police and asked to come down to the hotel. "Someone grabbed the desk manager and accused him of discrimination and he called the police," recalls Hudson. "I had to act as peacemaker."

Harper says he had gone into the lobby looking for cigarettes and was told that the person at the front desk was being belligerent and calling the people in Harper's party names. "I went down there and said he shouldn't talk to people like that," says Harper. "And he punched me in the nose. I did not fight back." But others did. "The police came and were trying to take me to the station. I felt bad," said Harper. That was when Hudson was called.

"It wasn't a serious thing, but it marred his victory," says Ovide Mercredi. "And then from there, it was like a monkey on his back that he had to get rid of. It was a monkey that he didn't need . . . here was the first Indian MLA, he was having a celebration for his victory and sometime during the celebration he has a fight with someone. That, I think, hurt his image initially."

A few days later, newspapers reported that Indian Affairs was investigating the Red Sucker Lake band books. Someone had alleged that money advanced to build a new school had been used for other purposes, including the financing of Harper's election bid. According to one report, the band's books had not been kept up to date during the three-month campaign. To make matters worse, the man who had taken charge of the books was away hunting when the investigation was launched, making it difficult to determine what, if anything, had gone on.

Elijah says the rumours made him recall Norway House Chief

Maggie Balfour's comments during the election campaign. At the time, he had suspected that the Manitoba Liberals and their federal counterparts were up to typical election tricks. "There was someone in Indian Affairs leaking information to the *Winnipeg Free Press* about band audits," says Elijah. "That was a Liberal government [in Ottawa]. I have never forgiven them for that."

The RCMP investigation of the band's finances lasted about a year. "They checked all my cancelled cheques, everything," recalls Elijah. In the end, the RCMP found nothing and issued a press release saying so. A small news item clearing Harper's name was buried in the back pages of the newspapers. "It is like anything else," says Elijah wearily, years later. "When you are trying to make your way, there are always these ways of trying to bring you down."

Was the media hunger for scandal more than usually voracious when it came to Elijah? "As a public figure, right or wrong, the media will scrutinize your career," says Mercredi, who had to deal with negative press in connection with his personal life years later. "This is one of the risks you take."

However, Elijah did face unique obstacles as the first-ever Indian MLA, say friends and enemies alike. "The expectations of him initially were very high," says Mercredi. "The expectations were high because the needs of the Indian people—for economic development, for a better school system and a better fishing policy, something for trappers—were high. The needs are enormous."

Yet Harper did not have a power base within the political system or the jurisdiction to make the changes many native people sought. As a provincial backbencher, Elijah could do little concrete for native constituents, since Indian affairs—especially those dealing with on-reserve residents—are a federal responsibility. His efforts could affect only aboriginal people living in cities or within Metis communities.

Premier Pawley and his government were sympathetic, but they were determined that the province should not come to own projects that belonged under federal jurisdiction. Their position was especially important in light of a long-standing federal policy to shift responsibility and financing for native Canadians to the provinces. Such moves were resisted both by the cash-strapped provinces and by native leaders, who viewed the proposed devolution as an attempt to rid Ottawa of its legal guardianship of native people. (Indeed, the 1985 report of the Nielsen Task Force on government spending clearly stated that such devolution to the provinces was, and had been, the federal Tories' goal.)

Moreover, of course, the Manitoba legislature was a new environment for Elijah. "His experience in politics was as chief—community politics," says Mercredi. That world, says Elijah, functioned by respect for people; government, for the most part, was based on co-operation. "It's a little more diplomatic, more understanding. I mean, there's politics all the time in any community, but not attacks on you personally. In the communities, I think a lot of things are done because of frustrations with the government. You are frustrated by the things you need to be aggressive about, like housing and welfare."

In his new role, "he had to learn that system. Democracy as practised by the white man is a democracy of rules, like the legislative assembly," says Mercredi. "You can only function there if you know how to operate within the rules. If you don't, you're dead."

Elijah remembers his first months as an MLA as being frustrating and lonely. "My first time going into the chamber, I wondered what I had gotten myself into. It was a different kind of feeling than when you go into a chief's meeting—this was not my own. I didn't know if I had enough knowledge about parliament or anything." One of the greatest shocks was the adversarial nature of the debate in the House. "I felt sensitive and uncomfortable. You feel personally attacked, but after it went on you begin to understand." What he learned, he says, was that the opposition members throwing comments at him, barbed with racist overtones, "probably meant it," but he wasn't supposed to react to it. "After a certain point I didn't take them seriously," says Harper. "It was just like water off my back."

For several months, Harper stayed in Winnipeg with Vic Savino, a lawyer and friend. Elizabeth remained in Red Sucker Lake with the four children. (Throughout Elijah's two terms in office, family life was stressful. Elijah, always averse to speaking of his personal life, hinted only that Elizabeth wanted him to return to the North at various times during his political career.)

At the first caucus meeting, MLAS were given an overview of the Manitoba legislature, introduced to one another and assigned seats in the House. Beyond that, says Harper, he and the other rookies had to decipher the ins and outs of Canada's parliamentary system on their own. "You have a basic idea, but you never really knew what to do. And being a new government, people were busy."

Harper applied the learning techniques he had used as a child—watching and listening—but it was often a frustrating exercise. "I knew that as a member of the government there are things that you're expected to do and not to say. I wanted to say more, but at the same time I didn't know how government operated. Even in the committee meetings, I didn't know how or what I should ask. I didn't know how far you could go."

Elaine Ediger, an employee in the province's Northern Affairs department, became a researcher for the new Northern Affairs minister, Jay Cowan. (When the two married in 1986, Ediger would change her name to Cowan.) She had been raised in Waboden, about five hundred kilometres north of Winnipeg, surrounded by native people.

"On election night, everybody was ecstatic that Elijah had won," says Ediger. "The first time I saw him I saw this lonely person sauntering down the hallway and my heart went out to him. I could relate to how he was feeling, how he must be trying to adjust to it—this big brick-and-cement building and all the rules and regulations that go along with the position he had just been elected to." Little did she realize then that she would become one of the most important people in Elijah's political career and personal life.

One of Elijah's first tasks as an MLA was to prepare his maiden speech. All MLAs work especially hard on their first official statement to be recorded in *Hansard*. His moment came on March 5, 1982, four months after the election. "I was nervous," says Elijah. "I didn't know what the hell I had gotten into. I was awed by the whole thing."

In his speech, Elijah spoke of his riding, the Canadian constitution, and the needs and aspirations of native people. The most telling aspect of the speech was the sense that Elijah was an outsider speaking from within what had often been an enemy stronghold.

"I remember Elijah's first speech," says Gordon MacIntosh, deputy clerk of the Manitoba Legislature in 1981. "You could hear a pin drop. Never for a maiden speech—and maiden speeches are usually listened to—were all the members so attentive. They were respectful like to no other member. He spoke so well of the problems facing his people," says MacIntosh, obviously moved by the memory more than a decade later.

Harper began his speech by breaking with the tradition of paying homage to the various players within the legislative setting. "Mr. Speaker, before I acknowledge the members of this House, I would like to speak to and acknowledge my constituents, for they are the reason I am here. Nee-moon-en-dan ka kee woon akwin ni see-ache. Ewkwa me na hee koos sicks ka goon oo-way un-kwee-win. Me-quech ki din na wa. Miss-ta-hee wee-gee-gom ne da way-dan. Chi do da man kwhy-uck-dn-kwee-win," he said, and then translated for his non-Cree audience. "I am glad that you have elected me. I say that to you all. Also, this task has put a heavy burden on me. I need all the support to do my job properly." For the first time that anyone could recall, Cree had been spoken and recorded in the official records of the province.

He then spoke of the honour of being the first treaty Indian in the house, and described the wretched state of the lives of native people throughout Rupertsland, a region that had seen little development during the reign of previous NDP and Tory governments. "The communities still have poor housing; the health among native people is very poor; unemployment in these communities runs very high—70 to 90 per cent. As a result, there is a lot of social chaos," Elijah said.

Little of his information was new, but the enormity of it finally struck home for many that day as the words emerged from a soft-spoken man with a braid down his back. "The native people do not want to be a burden to the rest of society," Elijah told his hushed audience. "Native people do not want handouts. We have a great contribution to make."

He then took on the previous governments for the policy of "exporting" Indian children and demanded the practice be stopped immediately. Throughout the 1960s and 1970s, social services agencies often "saved" native children from the deplorable living conditions of their home communities by placing them in foster care or adopting them out, mainly to white families in United States and abroad. "It was a new issue just emerging," says Elijah. "Ninety-five per cent of the kids being sent to the States were aboriginal children." During the 1970s and 1980s, native groups were lobbying hard to regain control of their children by establishing native-run agencies.

"This is an emotional subject for me, Mr. Speaker," Elijah said, the tone displaying an uncharacteristic hint of anger. "And it is for every other native person in Manitoba, and Canada for that matter. I might add, maybe officials responsible for creating a black market for Indian children [should] themselves be considered for export."

Not long after the election, Harper was invited to talk with Premier Howard Pawley's aides to discuss how and when Elijah might become a cabinet minister. "First and foremost," says Pawley, "I certainly thought it was important not to appoint him to cabinet immediately because he didn't have the experience at that point." But Pawley need not have been concerned that the new MLA would be disappointed. "I'm not prepared for it at this time," Elijah told the aides. "I'd rather wait and get used to things."

"Elijah's strength was that he was not interested in grandstanding," says Pawley. "He was not interested in being a star; he was interested in gradually working his way up. I understood this. He knew I understood this, that he wanted to develop his strengths, develop confidence and not prematurely get into something that could certainly undo him."

Elijah's training began with an appointment as legislative assistant to Minister of Northern Affairs Jay Cowan. Cowan, first elected in 1977 as an MLA in Churchill, the enormous riding adjacent to Harper's, is a highly articulate man with an exceptional understanding of parliamentary house rules and strategy. (He would later serve as house leader in the Pawley government.) If there was anyone who could help Elijah with the rules of the game, it was Cowan. Yet, although they worked closely together, Harper would more often than not shy away from asking direct questions about procedures, preferring to deduce what he could from watching and listening.

"I never felt Elijah had a big ego," says Howard Pawley. "You had to encourage him to become actively involved in speaking out in the early period. He was shy and subdued—a strength, in my view."

Harper also became chairperson of a government task force that travelled throughout the remote communities of the North to consult with residents on future hydro developments. Elaine Ediger was the co-ordinator of the task force. "Elijah and I started working together on that," she says, "and we just hit it off. I related to him because he seemed to be this lonely person."

Elijah may have been uncomfortable within the confines of the Winnipeg legislative building, but he was a different man in the small communities that the task force visited. "When we went to a northern community, he just melded among the people," Ediger says, a touch of awe in her voice. "People adored him. People would come up and touch him because he was an elected treaty Indian. He was one of them. It was incredible to see. Other politicians who went into these remote communities would stick out like a sore thumb or feel uncomfortable. They couldn't mix with the people the way they probably wanted to."

Harper says the committee experience gave him new insights into the cumbersome bureaucracy surrounding federal training programs, which had often left aboriginal people on the outside of lucrative employment opportunities that should have flowed from hydro and other developments in the North.

Ediger and Harper spent many hours together during the two years the committee travelled around the province, and each grew to lean on the strengths of the other. Elijah would depend on Elaine for her organizing capabilities, and she would call on his warmth and talent with people. "He was a pure joy to travel with. He was well respected among so many people in the community. I mean he had enemies, but even his enemies would keep very quiet."

Yet she also found it hard not to be concerned about him. "He was such a quiet person and kept so much to himself that I used to worry about him. I couldn't understand how he could cope with all these pressures and all these demands and all these regulations. He would just go into his office and be by himself."

While he faced some difficulties adjusting, Harper did not stop seeking out new experiences. In 1983, he met the chief of the Mapuche Indians of Chile, Mellilan Painemal, at a World Council of Indigenous People conference in Regina. Months later, Harper accepted an invitation to attend a conference in Temuco, Chile. At the time, the Mapuche were fighting a Pinochet decree that abolished their identity and called for the breakup of their lands. Despite the different political landscapes and culture, Harper found much in common with Painemal. "The Mapuche people have their own languages, customs and characteristics, and have for centuries suffered the aggression of a society that tries to assimilate them," Painemal would tell his foreign audiences.

Always fascinated with the history of peoples, Harper could not resist the invitation, although he spoke not a word of Spanish and would be travelling alone in a country ruled by a particularly brutal military dictatorship.

He arrived at the Santiago airport and was immediately struck by the number of heavily armed guards. After much difficulty, he found the bus that would take him the six hundred kilometres south to Temuco. En route, the bus was pulled over by the military. As the soldiers approached the bus, Harper realized that he was carrying literature from the Chilean community in Winnipeg. One of the sheets called Pinochet a fascist. A sensation swept over him that he had not felt since he was first flown out of Red Sucker Lake to attend residential school.

"The feeling of distance and detachment and loneliness came back to me—like I could never go back home." Slowly, Harper ripped up the offending pamphlet, chewed the pieces and put them one by one into a Coke bottle. "I knew only one person in the whole country and he didn't know I was coming that day," says Elijah. "Nobody knew where I was. It was a time when people were disappearing."

But when the guards finally got to Harper, they passed without comment. He made his way to the conference and home again without further incident, but with a better understanding of how similar indigenous peoples' problems were around the world.

Elaine Ediger says she was determined to find a way to bridge Elijah's personal style with the demands of the legislative bureaucracy in Manitoba. It was a role that would become increasingly significant as Elijah's responsibilities grew, but in the beginning, it often meant accommodating Harper's—and his constituents'—particular needs.

"He had a number of friends that he had to go out of the building to meet," she says. "He always had difficulty getting his own friends to come to the building. He often had difficulty setting up meetings, getting members of the bands or whoever it was—who weren't accustomed to the system of meeting in government buildings—to come. So, what he had to do was to go out to meet them. He didn't mind doing it, he understood that so-and-so was uncomfortable coming into the legislature."

In these situations, Harper would often hold court at the St. Regis, a downtown hotel affectionately known by aboriginal people across the country as the "Indian Embassy."

"So the meeting would take place there," says Ediger, "and half the time there wouldn't be any notes taken about the issues and he'd come back and say, 'So and so said this and that, and this is what he agreed to.' We had to document this stuff. A lot of it never got documented because of those meetings, but Elijah remembers everything, absolutely everything. He has an amazing memory for appointments and dates."

It soon became apparent, however, that Elijah was less than amazing when it came to his personal finances. In later years, NDP leader Gary Doer would say, "Harper has an interesting way of dealing with finances—he doesn't."

"I remember him coming in with a clump of accounts," says Gordon MacIntosh. The province had just set up a new expense system for MLAs, and Harper was lost. "I helped him understand this new system."

"He is so honest," says Elaine, "that when he comes up to you with these chits and says, 'I don't know what to do with them,' he really doesn't know what to do with them. You just want to automatically say, 'Just give me those and I'll sort it all out.' I worked for him anyway, so it was very easy for me to do that."

Elijah's personal accounts caused Premier Pawley a few sleepless nights. "That was not Elijah's area of strength, to say the least," says Pawley, with a great laugh. "I was a nervous nelly for several years because the premier's office had to become involved, often being financial counsellor, balancing his accounts. Creditors would come directly to our offices, which I didn't think was right, in one way, because I thought it was a bit like blackmail. But, in another way, I guess I understood why they did."

"Elijah was naive," says Cliff Scotton, Pawley's principal secretary. "If he wanted to go somewhere, he would just slap his credit card down. I think Elijah felt that he wasn't doing anything outrageous or improper."

The opposition and the media were always looking for something that would embarrass the government, and Elijah's fouling up of his business affairs left the door wide open. "It wasn't because he didn't want to pay his bills," says Pawley. "The white man's commercial society was outside his line of thought and he was very generous to people who came in. He wasn't concerned about his daily budget."

Pawley and others saw much of Elijah's financial difficulty as related to native peoples' expectations of 'their' MLA, and to the stark circumstances of their lives. "As a member of the legislature he was consistently having folks come in from Rupertsland—and he's putting them up, feeding them, because they would be people without paper currency," says Pawley. "He had a big heart." Only half joking, Pawley adds, "He was redistributing wealth."

Pawley recalled a hotel bill that had to be paid. Four constituents had come to Winnipeg and, with nowhere to stay, turned to Elijah. Years later, Elijah was left with the bill for flying some constituents to a relative's funeral: they could not pay themselves and they had to be there. "Every community had an expectation of Elijah," says Pawley. "He couldn't meet all the demands."

Although she picked up many of the financial pieces, Elaine Ediger's admiration of Elijah through those years, good times and bad, never faltered. "He has that inner strength and that aura that only a few people have," she says. "He was born with it. He is the kind of person who only has to walk into a room and his presence is felt. You turn to look at him, you want to talk to him. That is the effect I've seen him have on people all the time I have known him—when he was a nobody to the time he was a cabinet minister."

Harper would learn much about balancing white political realities and the needs of native communities through his work on the task force and as Jay Cowan's legislative assistant. And, as promised, he was gradually given more responsibility.

To this point Elijah's contact with native leaders as an MLA had focussed on local issues. "The Indian leadership [usually] has little to do with the provinces because the relationship is with the federal government," says Ovide Mercredi. "Overall, Elijah wasn't relevant to what the chiefs' objectives were because they dealt primarily with the federal government."

However, an attempt to settle outstanding land claims in Manitoba and discussions on the constitution would change that. Elijah's stature within the native community began to grow. "Land claims and aboriginal self-government were two of the most critical issues confronting northern Manitoba, and Elijah was responsible for both," says Pawley.

The land claims issue would end in grave disappointment, says the former premier, when the Trudeau government lost the September 1984 election and a hard-won lands claim package was left unsigned. "I remember our concern during the campaign about what would happen if the Tories took government," says Pawley. "Unfortunately, our worst fears were realized. We couldn't get anywhere with the feds."

Pawley recalls Elijah being particularly insulted when the new federal minister for Indian affairs, Bill McKnight, failed to answer more than a dozen letters Harper sent on the issue. "This was one of the most difficult experiences that Elijah went through because he felt the agony and the pain of having been ignored by his counterpart."

The constitutional outcome would be no more successful. Elijah was a member of the Manitoba delegation attending the first ministers' conferences (FMCS) held to discuss the rights of native Canadians. It had taken intense lobbying to get Prime Minister Pierre Trudeau to agree to include the weaker constitutional amendment that would "recognize and affirm existing" aboriginal and treaty rights, and the wrangling left a bitter taste in the mouths of the country's aboriginal people.

"That experience taught us one important thing, Mr. Speaker," Elijah said in his maiden speech. "We know we can no longer sit back, we can no longer allow both levels of government to manhandle our lives and our future. We as Indian people must take steps to gain control of our destiny." His election, he said, had begun a process by which native people could fight for their rights in meetings with First Ministers "in the only arena that will have any proper effect."

Harper's participation in the ministerial meetings leading up to the conferences and in the conferences proper gave him a unique opportunity to carve out a pro-active role within the NDP and the country's native leadership. At that first FMC, held March 15 and 16, 1983, Elijah viewed himself as a student. "I was just learning everything at the time," he says. "I understood that the game was about power and control. That much I understood." His lasting impression from that first meeting was of Trudeau's demeanour. When native leaders wanted to pray before the session began, Trudeau quipped that if native people were going to beat their drums and pray before each session, then the others in the room would also have to pray to their god. "I found him to be insensitive and arrogant," says Elijah. "We look at the prayers as a way to focus, to bring us together. This is how we start our meetings."

By the last FMC, in 1987, Harper had matured, but he never felt like a key player in the constitutional game. "Often, I felt like a token Indian," he says. "I became more active, but I never felt that instrumental or effective."

Despite these feelings, Harper did work more closely with Manitoba native groups and their leaders during that four-year period to develop common strategies and goals. Together they made up a formidable native elite with a common history and shared views on everything from economic development to self-government.

Elijah's connections with this emerging elite led to subtle but significant changes in the way the Manitoba government conducted its business. Before 1981, when a native issue arose, a call would be made to one or two high-profile native leaders. After Elijah's election, the government's contacts grew. "It was a favourable, progressive movement," says Pawley, "that spoke to Elijah's kind of involvement. Elijah would not have been the one person out there or one of the few people grandstanding or claiming to speak for all the Indian people in the province. Elijah is very much a democrat. He wouldn't want to be the one person speaking for native people."

Elijah slowly emerged as a facilitator and key player in the long-term strategy. "Elijah, as an MLA, became an instrument, let's say, of Indian issues when we started to deal with constitutional matters," says Mercredi. In fact, Elijah was sufficiently important to the aboriginal cause that native leaders lobbied the premier directly to secure Harper a position as close to the action as possible.

Mercredi says he believes that Elijah's involvement on the cabinet's native subcommittee was at least in part due to the efforts of native leaders and long-time Harper friends Moses Okimaw, Phil Fontaine, Louise Chippawe and Murray Sinclair (now an associate chief judge of the Manitoba provincial court but then vice-president of the Manitoba Métis Federation (MMF) and Howard Pawley's constituent assistant.)

At the time, Mercredi was involved with the Manitoba Indian Brotherhood and the MMF. "I met with the chairman of the native caucus within the NDP," he recalls. "We insisted that Elijah be a part of the [native] subcommittee of cabinet. We said, 'Look, because of the constitutional issues you need someone who understands the issues within the inner cabinet, within the cabinet structure. And, while Elijah isn't a cabinet minister, it is important that he have access to the subcommittee and that he is a permanent member of it.' I remember arguing with Pawley, saying to him that you have to do things differently. While he may not be a cabinet minister, he should still sit on that committee."

Mercredi, in those days reputed to be an aggressive and often confrontational man, recalls that Pawley, as usual, sat and listened. "And then Elijah did become part of that committee and he got very involved in constitutional matters. And Elijah gained more confidence, in my view anyway, as his role and his responsibilities increased."

In this way, Mercredi says, Elijah became integral to the much broader native constitutional picture. "The machine that drove the constitutional agenda was the Manitoba chiefs," says Mercredi of the FMCs devoted to native issues. There were several reasons for this. Manitoba had a history of political activism that began soon after the 1951 changes to the Indian Act loosened the funding rules. By the early 1980s, native organizations were sophisticated, articulate players on both the provincial and the national scene. Moreover, the Pawley government supported aboriginal goals, offering native leaders a cherished seat at the negotiating table. (Native leaders would ask the same of Tory premier Gary Filmon years later but would be refused.)

Native leaders worked out an agreement with the Pawley cabinet that, whenever possible, the government would advance the native position during constitutional meetings. "And whenever they couldn't put forward our position, they would so indicate, publicly, that this government position was not supported by Indians," says Mercredi. "The other deal we made was that we would have the option of speaking in our own right if we wanted to."

At the FMCs, Harper sat at the table; behind him was a delegation of Manitoba chiefs. And should a point of contention arise, Pawley also offered to let the chiefs answer the questions. "If we wanted to intervene, we could, we could speak for ourselves directly," says Mercredi. Quebec allowed native women to speak, and Alberta had a few native spokespeople at one meeting as well. But, as a rule, only the politicians spoke.

Elijah, however, was never merely an emissary for native people. As his role in the native game plan grew, so did his status in the NDP caucus.

During those years, Pawley says, Elijah became the behind-the-scenes focus for formulating and then articulating Manitoba's position on native self-government. He travelled throughout the province to meet Indian and Metis groups to ensure that their views were incorporated into the government's position. "I think without Elijah having been elected and intimately involved in the decision-making, that it would have been very difficult to ensure that our position was consistent," says Pawley.

The native FMC process was launched in the dying days of the Trudeau administration. By the time of the final FMC in March 1987, the Mulroney Tories were entrenched in Ottawa. Between the first and last meetings, Elijah had learned some hard lessons. "We had a number of caucus members that just couldn't see this idea of aboriginal self-government," says Pawley. "Every time it came up, some of the old hackneyed concerns would come up. 'What do you mean by aboriginal self-government? We don't understand why you are supporting it, Mr. Premier. We don't understand it, Elijah. Native people aren't ready for it.' "

Pawley says the number of caucus members expressing such views was "substantial," and the experience was often a frustrating one for Harper. "We would go down to the conferences and then we would come back and either in cabinet or in caucus a member would question why we were so up front."

"I sensed it from day one," says Elijah, "a feeling that some people in caucus weren't pro-active. . . . I don't know if it was a result of not being interested or not wanting to deal with it."

Elijah spent quite a bit of time explaining to his own party what self-government meant to native people, trying to alleviate fears. "I remember talking about some things with Sam Uskiw, when he was natural resources minister and we were talking about treaty rights," says Elijah. (Uskiw was the long-time MLA for the central Manitoba riding of Lac Dubonnet.) "And he said, 'Well, if you have those rights, why don't you take them to court?' "

Harper had expected an NDP minister to be more supportive. "I knew that the courts were not really knowledgeable about aboriginal rights, not in the way they were years later," says Harper. Even the premier, who was supportive of entrenching self-government in the constitution, worried about public perception of such support. Nevertheless, Manitoba would be the only province at the FMCs consistently to support placing native self-rule in the constitution. "A lot of governments wanted a definition of self-government," says Elijah. "Manitoba wasn't pushing for that. Our position was that aboriginal people have been here since time immemorial, that aboriginal people have had their own governments and managed their own resources."

Harper took the self-government message throughout the province, to schools and public meetings. "The best way I saw was to explain things simply," says Harper. "What it is all about is to take control of your lives, manage your own affairs and determine your own future. We have never relinquished that right, even by signing the treaties. When we signed the treaties it was an exercise of our right to self-government. The First Nations signed treaties with the sovereign state of England as equals. England made promises to the First Nations, many of which have yet to be fulfilled. And the treaty-making process has never come to an end."

Self-government is, of course, more complicated; and, when necessary, he describes in more detail the kinds of relationships with governments that might result. "We should be able to make our own laws within our jurisdictions, like family allowance, policing—matters that are not criminal matters." In many ways, the process has already begun—Indian Affairs has been handing over the administration of various services, such as education and child welfare, to native people for more than a decade.

Elijah says that the specifics of self-government can be negotiated only after it is accepted that aboriginal people were on the land first and had been self-governing before the Europeans arrived.

Currently, land claims settlements with the federal government are concluded only after the signatories have agreed to give up their aboriginal rights. "When the federal government states that they want an extinguishment," says Elijah, "it is a recognition that the aboriginal people do have the right to land and resources."

This reality, says Elijah, must be recognized in the constitution in such a way that the diverse cultures of native people across Canada can be accommodated. "There are examples of forms of governments in place. Here in Manitoba we had clan systems, in British Columbia they have the potlatch. It isn't just a ceremony, it was a sophisticated form of government."

Some native leaders wish to move ahead as much as they can through changes to the Indian Act. Harper disagrees, as the government would not be forced to acknowledge the inherent right to be self-governing. The Indian Act, he says, is like a penitentiary with the Indian people as the inmates. Changing the act does not get the inmates out of jail. "When you change the Indian Act all you are doing is extending the chain a little longer, that's all.

"If First Nations people were totally independent, if they declared independence within Canada, then they would be the ones who would be providing money to the federal government instead of the federal government providing money to them, because they would have the land and resources and total control."

Harper also worries about those regions that are settling land claims before the essential question of self-government has been answered. Current land claims settlements leave the federal government in control even when they hand over territories. Native leaders are signing, Harper believes, because local conditions are so bad they need results sooner than any constitutional process can offer. "I know people are getting tired of these constitutional discussions," says Harper. "We have been negotiating for years and years on land claims and rights. It has been going on since I can remember."

Of course, building the institutions and providing the training needed to take control is a complicated process. Making self-government a reality will require a lot more educating of the general public. "I think it is a lack of understanding, of not knowing about aboriginal people," Elijah says of most of the resistance he has seen. "The perception is that we as Indian people get everything for free and there is some resentment because we should be doing our share," he says.

The essential question is one of power. Once you have the power, it is hard to give it up. Provincial governments do not want to give up control, particularly over resources. "What we are trying to achieve is to share," says Harper. "If we have self-government we would have jurisdiction over certain territory. Bands would control and own the resources. Management of those resources would often be shared responsibilities.

"Self-government is not a panacea to our problems, but it is a start. We are saying, 'Back off. We can control our own affairs.' If you are going to address problems—alcohol abuse, child abuse—it has to come from the community, from the people themselves. It can't come from anywhere else."

Throughout the native first ministers' conferences in the 1980s, Elijah's presence advanced the native cause. "In the ministerial meetings [held to prepare for FMCs] he was one of the official spokespersons for the province of Manitoba," says Mercredi. "Elijah, on occasion, would intervene as an Indian MLA, which is somewhat different than being an intervenor as an ordinary MLA, right? So he spoke from the heart, he spoke as an Indian who happens to be an MLA.

"It had a good impact because all the other aboriginal people could see that he was one of them, which was very important to us, because we didn't have very many friends in the constitutional process. Most of the [political players] were people who knew very little about Indians or Metis or Inuit, and rather than try and learn about us and genuinely understand us, they were more interested in putting us in a position of accounting for who we are and what we wanted."

Maintaining this balance of loyalties to his native constituency and his caucus was difficult for Harper, says Pawley, but he handled it well. "Elijah is a team player," says the former Manitoba premier. "There was no way he was going to say, 'Hey, I took this position but the NDP caucus would not support me.' He would not separate himself from the caucus or the party. At the same time, his collective commitment was to native people, first and foremost."

Acting as the bridge between people such as Attorney General Roland Penner, who had the lead on constitutional issues, and other cabinet ministers or caucus colleagues was probably the most valuable contribution that Harper would make in the early years as an MLA, says Pawley. "He played an essential role of making me more knowledgeable as premier, making Roland Penner more knowledgeable as attorney general, and making caucus more knowledgeable insofar as the issue of aboriginal self-government."

Of course, not everyone was satisfied. "The native people would sometimes misunderstand Elijah during that period," says Pawley. "He would have criticism heaped upon him for supposedly not standing up for them and making sure that the government did certain things. I think some of the most brutal criticisms of all came from the native community."

Most of the negative comments, whether backroom complaining or media criticism, focussed on Harper's lack of a public profile and the fact that, as Pawley's first term in office drew to a close, Elijah was still not a full-fledged cabinet minister.

It may have been unrealistic to expect that Elijah could have accomplished more. Nonetheless, scepticism about Harper's work and about the motivation of Premier Pawley, who talked about supporting native people but failed to appoint the province's only native MLA to cabinet, was growing.

Chapter Five

THE PLAN UNRAVELS

As the Pawley government's first term neared the four-year mark, grumbling about Harper's performance gained momentum. Comments about his quiet demeanour and low-key approach gradually turned into charges that he was not performing.

Much of the dissatisfaction was focussed on Pawley. The affable premier was accused by provincial native leaders of treating Elijah as a token Indian: why else had the province's only Indian MLA not yet been given a cabinet portfolio. Harper says he assumed that it would be just a matter of time, and in his own quiet way, he "pestered" the premier.

Pawley admits he was feeling the heat as the 1986 election approached. "Clearly, there was a need to move Harper up because the native community was unhappy he wasn't full-fledged," says Pawley. Opposition members of the House, in particular Liberal leader Sharon Carstairs and Tory Northern Affairs critic Jim Downey, joined the pack.

Privately, some detractors also complained that Harper was being overly influenced by Northern Affairs Minister Jay Cowan. "There was a problem of perception," says Pawley, "in that Elijah had a little office adjacent to Jay Cowan's, and those who wanted to be sarcastic would say that he was tagging along with Jay Cowan."

Cowan's uneven temper had gained him his share of enemies, some of whom charged that the Churchill MLA viewed himself as "king of the North" and that he had no intention of abdicating to Elijah or anyone else. Pawley rejects such sentiments. "Jay was as anxious as anybody to see Elijah move up." Besides, says Pawley, Cowan had expressed a desire to move on to other posts.

"I had a lot to learn about the aboriginal culture," says Cowan of the years he worked with Harper. "Elijah had a lot to learn about dealing with the more dominant culture in the legislature. And we both learned. I know he did. And I hope I did."

Pawley also felt that much of the criticism of Elijah was unjustified. "His contribution was much greater than a Louis Stevenson kind of contribution," says Pawley, referring to the former leader of the Manitoba Assembly of Chiefs and chief of the Peguis band. Stevenson, a long-time Harper critic, is known in Manitoba for his bombastic speaking style, heated and quick responses to breaking issues, and attention-getting manoeuvres.

"Elijah's contribution," says Pawley, "was where it counted. It was in decision making—and from an individual who was not hesitant to speak up." Pawley says that what most of Harper's critics missed was his behind-the-scenes work. In caucus, Harper provided the native perspective on every subject, be it housing or day care.

Ovide Mercredi says that Elijah's problem was two-fold—perception and reality. "It wasn't that he wasn't doing his work in the constituency. He was doing whatever was required of him as an MLA." But Elijah's ability to shine was limited by the fact that national Indian concerns predominated during the period. "These were the issues that were foremost in the minds of Indian leaders in Manitoba—treaty and aboriginal rights." Harper gained some profile on those issues through his constitutional work, but in the main, he was restricted to the provincial stage. On top of this, says Mercredi, "Elijah wasn't using the media very successfully."

Harper admits to feeling pressured by the backroom lobbying on his behalf and recalls hearing directly from Mercredi and others during this time. Elijah still speaks with a hint of discomfort about Mercredi and the others who made or passed on the criticisms. "A lot of people thought I should be more assertive and aggressive, but other people were putting pressure on the government."

Harper was not about to go public with what was happening behind the scenes, but some native leaders were pushing him to speak out against the government or resign. "There is tremendous pressure, in terms of some issues, to grandstand," says Elijah. "But what do you do after you resign? Where does it go from there?"

Steve Ashton, MLA for the northern riding of Thompson, says he was never pressured by his constituents as Elijah was. "People wanted Elijah," says Ashton. "It wasn't a question, often, of issues. Elijah was a lightning rod."

Harper recognized that his day-to-day work was all but invisible and that his loyalty to the Pawley team was a source of stress. One of the problems, he says, was that many of his critics did not understand the rules of the legislature, just as he had not when he was first elected. "So I had to explain—the process, the caucus, the government process—so that they would understand," says Elijah. "A lot of time people saw me sitting in the legislature, not saying anything, and they'd say, 'Why don't you get up and ask questions?' I'd explain that there are rules and procedures. They expected me to ask questions the opposition would ask."

He could understand the chiefs' disappointment. "I guess I figured that as politicians and as government you could change things. But then you find out about political will and that negotiations take time when you are working within the system. It can't happen overnight."

Critics such as Chief Louis Stevenson and Mercredi made Elaine Ediger angry. "I couldn't even face these people. I would get just livid. I think a lot of it was that they just didn't understand how the system works. And also, Elijah's not an aggressive fist-pounder-on-the-desks, table-thumper person. His style, I think, works far better.

"He is willing to sit across the table from you and he'll take forever to get his opening statement on the table. He'll sit and talk about how you are and how the weather is and what is happening in the world. He'll smile quietly, have ten cups of coffee and thirteen cigarettes, until the last five or ten minutes when he's quite comfortable, and then he'll say, 'This is my idea.' "

However effective, it was not a style that translated into television news or newspaper headlines.

Elijah was often depressed, not only about his job but also about his home life, recalls Ediger. Elijah's wife, Elizabeth, seemed unhappy in Winnipeg. "She did not like politics," says Howard Pawley. "She did not like Winnipeg." As well, alcohol abuse was taking a toll on the relationship. Elijah was known to drink periodically and would come to work late some days as a result, but Elizabeth's alcohol problems often seemed out of control. NDP insiders recall Elizabeth arriving at political functions in a foul mood and making a public display of it. Ediger says that, while Harper "wouldn't win any father-of-the-year awards," his sense of family ran deep and the problems in his marriage caused him great anguish.

During a few of those bleak periods in Elijah's first term, he would call Elaine at home. "I knew that he was reaching out and I thought that if anyone is reaching out, you should go. So I went when he called, and we would talk and talk about everything. It was very difficult to pull information out of him, but I would just keep talking and eventually there would be a response of some kind. It didn't happen that often. And it wasn't long term.

During one such conversation in 1985, Elaine asked, "Do you ever see yourself going into cabinet?"

"No," said Harper.

"Well, I do," she replied. "I really see a light at the end of the tunnel and I really do see you as a cabinet minister." That day—a day Harper says he does not recall—Ediger sensed that Elijah was doubting that he had been cut out for white politics. "Then he got on a plane and went off to these three community meetings and we never mentioned it again."

Around the same time, a handful of chiefs who were meeting in Winnipeg to discuss winter road construction in Island Lake called the president of the Rupertsland NDP, Ken Ellison. "Ken told me later that he had had a call from Rod Bushie [then chief of Hollow Water]. They put him on a speaker phone," recalls Elijah. "Rod says, 'I am sitting here with the chiefs.' The chiefs were named off. He even named off the chief of Red Sucker Lake. Rod was trying to say that everyone was talking about replacing me, and he asked about nominations and proceedings."

Elijah later was told that several people, including Ovide Mercredi, had met with the NDP executive of the election-planning committee just before Christmas in 1985 to seek help in ousting Harper. "Ken Ellison said that I was too grassroots oriented," says Elijah. The chiefs put forward the name of George McIver from Cross Lake to run against Harper for the NDP nomination.

Elijah suspected that the chiefs were not really aware of the leg work required to oust him. "I knew that the chiefs wouldn't go door to door to sell memberships. Some chiefs didn't want to be seen as supporting any one political party. Another problem was that if they did go around, they would be cornered with a lot of other issues." He was right. In the end, "it never went any further."

Mercredi denies he was ever a negative force in Harper's career. Rather, he says, he was helping behind the scenes. "There were friends out there for him all the time—Moses [Okimaw], myself, Phil Fontaine—who were always concerned about making sure that Elijah had an opportunity to succeed," says Mercredi. "Some of us were in a position where we could do that without asking his permission or letting him know that these things were happening in the background.

"Moses and a few of us met and decided that there was no sense in supporting the NDP if they were not going to demonstrate some willingness to have a native person as a cabinet minister."

Pawley dropped the writ on February 11, 1986. The NDP held a comfortable lead—thirty-four seats to the Conservatives' twenty-three—but it had not been an easy first term. In 1980, the year before the Pawley government came to power, the Supreme Court of Canada had ruled that a hundred-year-old law making English the official language of Manitoba violated the agreement that had brought Manitoba into Confederation in 1870. The province had thousands of pieces of legislation written in English only, and translation would be prohibitively expensive. As well, decisions had to be made about how to proceed on future legislation and government records. Conservative Premier Sterling Lyon had avoided the issue, leaving it for the NDP. "We wondered if we even existed, legally, as a legislature or not," says Elijah.

On May 19, 1983, the Pawley government signed an agreement in principle with the federal government to amend the constitution to mandate full bilingualism services in Manitoba by 1987. In return, Manitoba won a postponement of any court-imposed settlement.

"We started developing policies," says Elijah, "things like we would only translate truly essential laws and the more recent laws." As well, the NDP proposed that the provision of French-language services be determined by the percentage of French speakers in the community.

The proposed amendment unleashed a storm of protest throughout the province, fuelled by the Conservative opposition. The battle made national headlines and led, in 1984, to a resolution in Parliament supporting the extension of language rights. Shortly afterward, when Brian and Mila Mulroney visited Manitoba, an angry Tory MLA called Mila a whore. The slight sealed the enmity between Mulroney and provincial Conservative leader Gary Filmon forever, despite appearances of congeniality.

Even for a rookie MLA who had faced his share of racism, the anti-French vitriol was an eye opener. The Tories focussed their public attacks on the lack of public consultation; however, says Harper, behind the arguments lay a sea of bigotry.

"I, of course, thought the other official language should be native," says Elijah, only half in jest, "but I did not make my case."

After months of fighting, the Pawley government was forced to withdraw their bill, handing the matter back to the courts. Most important, however, the Pawley government introduced new legislative rules to apply to all future constitutional amendments, including mandatory public hearings on proposed changes to the constitution. It was these rules that would determine the fate of the Meech Lake Accord.

Harper began his reelection bid with Elaine Ediger as his campaign manager. Elaine had helped in other campaigns, but she was not prepared for the logistical nightmare of running the Rupertsland election. "We needed so much money," she says with a sigh of exasperation. "To get a plane off the ground cost $2000 and it was the only way to get into those reserves."

The early part of the campaign was spent trying to raise and save funds. "I organized a fund-raiser for him and lost fifteen pounds doing it," says Elaine. Dozens of people throughout the constituency were asked to pitch in. All the food—smoked fish, rice, bannock—was donated and prepared by the Native Women's Transition Centre. "It was phenomenal," Elaine says. "We cleared about $8000, for the campaign, which cost about $23,000."

The next task was to find a campaign office in Winnipeg. An acquaintance of Elijah's from Norway House, Norman Gunn, offered the NDP a "hole in the wall" on Higgins Avenue for only $300. "There was no heat," recalls Ediger. "I used to work with my fur coat on. We put office equipment on a table that had only three legs. I remember Elijah came along that night and hammered a stick in the ground for the other leg."

This time around, however, campaigning in Rupertsland itself was comparatively easy because of winter road access into the region.

On March 18, 1986, Harper handily won his second term, with 2302 votes to the Tories' 931 and the Liberals' 577. But the NDP, reduced to 30 seats, had a three-seat majority. The Tories were no happier. They had expected to capitalize on the French-language furor and were bitter

As minister of northern affairs in the mid-1980s, Elijah Harper travelled throughout northern Manitoba with his staff. He frequently dropped off friends and members of his family en route. (L-R: unknown, Elijah Harper, minister of northern affairs; Bruce Harper, Elijah's son; Elaine Ediger (later Cowan), co-ordinator of the provincial task force on hydro development; Lloyd Girman, deputy minister of northern affairs; Don Settee, Harper's executive assistant)

After he gave her several traditional native gifts, Elijah Harper received a thank-you kiss from Rigoberta Menchu, winner of the 1992 Nobel Peace Prize and human-rights activist in Guatemala. (11 November 1992)

Harper serves beaver meat at a traditional native feast in honour of Rigoberta Menchu (second from left). Menchu was a guest in the Aylmer, Quebec, home of Konrad Sioui (far left) of the Assembly of First Nations on 11 November 1992.

On 11 November 1992, Elijah told the story of Meech Lake to aboriginal visitors from Guatemala and Peru. Two weeks later he announced he was resigning as a member of the Manitoba legislature after serving for almost eleven years.

Elijah's former wife, Elizabeth Harper.

Harper signs autographs in Fort Frances, while on a speaking tour of northwestern Ontario in August 1990, a few months after the demise of the Meech Lake Accord.

Harper autographs a poster of himself for fans who have come to hear him speak in Fort Frances, Ontario, a few months after his stand against the Meech Lake accord. Harper received none of the money raised through such promotional efforts.

The key provincial and federal politicians in the North during the 1980s, all members of the New Democratic Party. L-R: Harry Harapiak (MLA—The Pas), Elijah Harper (MLA—Rupertsland), Jerrie Storie (MLA—Flin Flon), Rod Murphy (MP—Churchill), Steven Ashton (MLA—Thompson), Jay Cowan (MLA—Churchill). Ashton and Cowan later played pivotal roles in the Meech Lake saga.

Harper at a social gathering with Manitoba Premier Gary Filmon (far right).

Elijah's mother, Ethel Harper, in August 1992, a few months before her death from heart failure.

Elijah's father, Allan B. Harper,
in August 1992.

ELIJAH
HARPER
FOR
PRIME
MINISTER
HARPER
FOR
PRIME
MINISTER

Facing page: Native people from across the country gathered on the grounds of the Manitoba legislature on 22 June 1990, as Harper prepared to say his final no to the Meech Lake Accord.

This page: Elijah Harper, the day he was named minister without portfolio. (April 17, 1986)

Harper being interviewed on the Fort Alexander reserve in Manitoba after the funeral service for the father of Manitoba native politics, Dave Courchene, Sr. (12 August 1992)

Facing page: Elijah Harper speaks with Edward Schreyer, premier of Manitoba from 1969 to 1977, at the funeral of Dave Courchene, Sr. Harper held his first government job during the Shreyer administration.

Phil Fontaine, grand chief of the Assembly of Manitoba Chiefs, takes part in the funeral procession of his mentor, Dave Courchene, Sr. Courchene was former head of the Manitoba Indian Brotherhood, the precursor to the assembly. (12 August 1992)

Old and new collide daily in Red Sucker Lake, Elijah's home reserve.

The Northern Store, accessible only by boat, services the 300-plus residents of Red Sucker Lake reserve and a nearby Metis community. The Northern Stores have replaced the Hudson's Bay Company stores throughout the North.

Water sheds (to which water is pumped from the lake) serve as the reserve's main water supply. They are found throughout Red Sucker Lake. Only the school and nursing station have hot and cold running water and flush toilets.

Elijah Harper and Howard Pawley, premier of Manitoba from 1981 to 1986. Pawley made Harper the province's first native cabinet minister.

With Premier Howard Pawley looking on, Harper signs in as minister of northern affairs on 4 February 1987. Behind him stand other ministers, including newly elected MLA Gary Doer, who would replace Pawley as party leader in 1988.

Judge Murray Sinclair, associate chief justice of the Manitoba provincial court, would later co-chair the Public Inquiry into the Administration of Justice and Aboriginal People. Sinclair helped Harper in his first provincial election campaign.

George Hickes (left) and Elijah Harper. Hickes was poised to take the Rupertsland NDP nomination and bump Harper out of his job as a member of the Manitoba legislature, but the Meech Lake episode intervened.

Next page: The main road on the Red Sucker Lake reserve.

about their second-place finish with 26 seats. (Their anger was directed at Filmon and would reverberate within the ranks until he emerged as a statesman of sorts during Meech Lake.) Sharon Carstairs, leader of the Manitoba Liberal Party since 1984, took River Heights and became the first Liberal leader in thirteen years to sit in the Manitoba legislature.

On April 17, 1986, Harper was appointed minister without portfolio (translated in Cree as "minister who has no briefcase," says Harper, laughing). Harper could now attend cabinet meetings and be part of the discussions and policy making. He did not head a ministry, but Pawley says that much of the handling of native issues, including work on outstanding land claims, fell to Elijah. A Native Affairs Secretariat was created, through which Elijah aimed to co-ordinate all government department activities that affected the aboriginal people in Manitoba.

When a major cabinet shuffle was announced in February 1987, Harper was named minister of Northern Affairs. (Included in that cabinet was Gary Doer, former president of the Manitoba Employees Association and future party leader.) Although the Northern Affairs, posting seemed logical, some argued that it would further raise already overblown expectations. One of those who took this position was longtime NDP insider Lloyd Girman, who had served as secretary of the cabinet's native affairs subcommittee and become Harper's deputy minister soon after Harper was named minister without portfolio.

"First and foremost, Lloyd was seen to be a good negotiator," says Pawley about Girman's appointment as deputy minister, a point of particular importance as the province was in the midst of negotiations on land claims. Girman calls himself "an old hack" who joined the Pawley government during its first term to restructure the province's child welfare system. He had previously worked with the Manitoba Children's Aid Society and various Indian bands on related issues.

When Girman was approached by George Ford, clerk of the executive council, and asked to become Harper's deputy minister, he was told that the long-term plan was to make Harper minister of northern affairs, with Girman as his right-hand man. "I had no desire to be a deputy," says Girman. "I was cabinet secretary, which was a great fucking job. There is no line of responsibility. I was going around doing all the original constitutional stuff."

Eventually he gave in, but not before making a suggestion. "My argument was that they shouldn't make Elijah a minister of northern affairs," says Girman. "They should give him another portfolio. He had to deal with the party line, he had cabinet, and at the same time he had the Indian constituency to satisfy. I mean, Energy and Mines might have made more sense."

Despite his initial misgivings, Girman became the perfect foil for Harper. Where Elijah was co-operative, Girman was confrontational. Where Harper was gentle, Girman was abrasive. Yet they shared an absolute love of finding ways around stuffy bureaucrats and obstructive rules.

They set to work immediately, carving out a niche—first for the new minister without portfolio—apart from cabinet and from Harper's predecessor Jay Cowan, now minister of co-operative development. The first step was to get Harper some operating capital to launch projects. It was with this in mind that proposals for a Native Secretariat, a body that would work to centralize information on native program activities in government, and an Aboriginal Development Fund were launched.

"The issue wasn't money," says Girman of the plan and, particularly, the fund. "The issue was Elijah establishing himself." His dream was to see a real centralized, almost federalistic Indian government in Manitoba.

When Harper made the funding request to cabinet, all the backroom lobbying had been done, and Pawley was on side; but it was Elijah's job to sell it. "I want $2 million," Elijah announced quietly. Elijah sat for a couple of minutes as the buzz of protest grew. (Pawley was the kindest of men, but often the weekly cabinet gatherings degenerated into screaming or sulking matches in which the loser stomped out.) Harper listened, looking around the room, arms crossed over his stomach. "You know," came the quiet voice, finally, "I am getting pretty tired of being the token Indian."

"That was it," grins Girman. "Three minutes later he had the money."

Harper and Girman then focussed their attention on resolving the outstanding Northern Flood Agreement issue, working on constitutional issues affecting native Canadians, and helping unite the province's Indian leadership.

This last goal was in part to make Harper's life easier. "Every band in the province wanted to negotiate self-government," says Girman. "And every band in the province wanted their particular rights—hunting, fishing, gambling issues."

"It was something we needed to face and deal with," says Harper.

Harper announced he would negotiate only with a single body. The native community decided that their representatives would be the Assembly of Manitoba Chiefs. When the Manitoba Indian Brotherhood fell apart in the 1970s, Manitoba's chiefs divided into two groups along north-south lines. By the time Elijah and Girman had teamed up, there was a move to reunite, a trend Harper encouraged by providing funding for chiefs' conferences which brought the leaders together on a regular basis.

From that process emerged the Assembly of Manitoba Chiefs. A $320,000 grant was earmarked for the chiefs to review provincial statutes such as the Wildlife Act to determine what changes would be required to reflect treaty rights. Equal funding was given to the Manitoba Métis Federation for similar research.

Harper handed Girman the lead role in settling the outstanding Northern Flood Agreement deals. "All he said to me was, 'Settle it,' " remembers Girman.

The Northern Flood Agreement was a tripartite deal among Manitoba Hydro, the federal government and five northern bands who had suffered flooding damage from the Churchill River Diversion Project. Having so many parties involved made the issue more difficult to resolve, says Harper. One of Harper's biggest concerns was how much of any settlement would go to the consultants and lawyers that presented the chiefs' case. "One of the things we decided to do was to meet with the chiefs instead of the negotiators," says Harper.

In the end, a global settlement was presented—for signing by all five bands or none. The package provided money as compensation as well as guarantees of future help in the area of development. "You never knew the impact the flooding would have," says Harper about promises for the future. The most difficult parts of the negotiations were trying to put a financial value on loss of culture and assuring the chiefs that signing the deal did not mean that they could not seek additional compensation in the future if the flood-damage estimates had been too modest. "It was a lawyer's heaven," says Harper. In the end, however, the global approach did not work, and the bands continued negotiations into the 1990s.

Elijah also acted as translator between native leaders and the province's lead constitutional expert, Roland Penner. "It was really a hoot," says Girman. "Roland would have all these meetings with Indian leaders. Elijah and six Indians would sit while Roland pontificated for about a half hour. And then they would all get up and leave and go over to the St. Regis and have a real meeting. You sat with Roland and he would tell you everything you couldn't understand, and then you went and sat with Elijah and he would interpret it in a way that you could understand."

"Elijah wasn't a real mover and shaker in the cabinet, but he was truly underestimated in terms of the sort of depth he could have," says Michael Balagus, who worked in Pawley's communications department. "He didn't speak all the time, but when he did [cabinet] listened and it generally influenced the discussion."

Having a native cabinet minister also came in handy in meetings with federal officials, says Girman. Not long after Harper was named Northern Affairs Minister, the pair met in Winnipeg with then–Indian Affairs Minister Bill McKnight on treaty and land entitlements issues. The meeting between the tense, humourless McKnight and Harper was, Girman declares, "fucking great."

"They've got McKnight set up at the Westin [hotel] in a suite," recalls Girman. "His aides meet us downstairs and usher us up. We go in. This is a breakfast meeting and it is all very, ah, federal."

It was clear, says Girman, that McKnight had one way of handling Indians and one way of dealing with ministers of the Crown. "But he cannot deal with an Indian fucking minister," laughs Girman. "He was dog meat. Elijah turned him inside out and backwards. It was fun to watch."

None of McKnight's negotiating tactics worked: "You can't say 'I've been Indian Affairs minister for so long and I know more about Indians than you,' " says Girman. "And he couldn't say, 'I'm a federal minister and I have more power than you have as minister.' He was just slobbering. And Elijah knew exactly what he was doing." Despite Harper's deftness—he exacted a promise, then and later, from McKnight that a deal was imminent, and got his own cabinet to agree to a global package on land rights—McKnight never followed through and the issue remains unresolved.

A healthy lack of respect for political protocol also opened doors for Harper. One morning, in Ottawa with Girman and Manitoba Attorney General Roland Penner, Harper failed to show up at breakfast as scheduled. When he finally arrived, around 10:30 A.M., Penner was not in the best of humour. Asked where he had been, Harper replied, "Oh, I just had breakfast with Crombie." Harper had simply phoned the Indian Affairs minister and arranged a meeting. "He could get meetings all the time," says Girman. "None of the other guys could manoeuvre like that because they followed protocol too tightly. Elijah didn't give a shit. If he got rejected, he got rejected. But for Roland to walk up to Crombie's office and be rejected, that would be a major blow."

Elijah had another unconventional talent, which people found either attractive or disconcerting. "One of the most remarkable things about Elijah was that, without warning, he would get into a deeply philosophical mood. He was the one of the most eloquent people, weirdly eloquent," says Cliff Scotton, Pawley's former principal secretary.

In 1985, when NDP MLA Mary Beth Dolin died of cancer, Harper's speech to the Manitoba legislature revealed this surprising talent. Harper noted that Dolin had taught at the local school in Garden Hill and had paid him special attention after he was elected. He then ended his speech in his usual slow, calm voice: "Mary Beth Dolin's work and commitment to enhance the quality of life for many Manitobans, especially women, have made us walk tall and, with each step, taller. Mary Beth Dolin has left us. She has left her imprints, a direction that we should follow. We will all miss her dearly."

"He can be tremendously effective or a complete bomb," says Girman. "If there is an Indian in the audience, the man is un–fucking believable. An all-white audience and he gets uncomfortable and he tries to deliver a message he thinks the white audience wants to hear—and he fumbles."

While constitutional and lands claims issues took much of Harper's energies throughout this period, it was the day-to-day constituency duties—meeting with interest groups, attending caucus and cabinet meetings, answering the daily calls and requests for information and services—that took most of his time and energy. Harper was called on daily to prove he was accomplishing concrete things for aboriginal communities throughout the province, and it was in these matters he had to push the bureaucrats the hardest.

In the beginning, Girman says, Elijah would get frustrated when someone told him he wasn't allowed to do something for a reserve community because he had no jurisdiction; later, his ability to sidestep bureaucracy would take over. Girman recalls a meeting with Garden Hill leaders. Most of the meeting was in Ojibwa-Cree, but as they were leaving, Elijah turned to Girman and said, "We have to build them a dock."

"You can't build them a dock," replied Girman. "That is federal responsibility, federal jurisdiction."

"I've got to build them a dock."

"What we did," recalls Girman with a bad-boy laugh, "was build them a dock on Stevenson Island, which was in our territory. Then we floated it across the lake. We had to do shit like that all over the place. Weird shit."

Elaine Ediger says Harper would often play a key role in such problem solving. "Elijah would come up with one comment during the whole meeting, and that would be the answer."

"I know that even if something is a federal responsibility, there must be a way," says Elijah. "People really need help whether there are different jurisdictions or not. Something has to be done."

Girman says he eventually stopped telling Harper they couldn't do something and instead worked on ways to satisfy Harper's agenda. But it never got easier. Harper was responsible for forty-seven Metis communities, but only peripherally for the status Indians living on Manitoba's reserves. Yet, their needs—and demands—were never-ending.

Slowly, Harper's critics grew quiet. "Part of the ineffectiveness was attributed to the fact that he had no power base within cabinet, he wasn't a cabinet minister," says Mercredi. "And when he became a cabinet minister his image changed and the perception of Elijah changed as well, because now he could actually make decisions affecting the lives and affairs of the people within his constituency, because he was the minister of northern affairs. So he could help Indians in terms of hydro, he could help at least the Metis and the non-status Indians in terms of housing and in terms of expanding local government or dealing with local government."

At one point, word spread through the NDP caucus that Elizabeth had returned to Red Sucker Lake with the children. Rumour had it that she was demanding Elijah return too. "There was no way," says Pawley. "At that point he was already recognized as having done one of the best jobs as minister of northern affairs that had ever been experienced in the province and he was building his reputation."

Harper does not deny that tensions existed but says there were never any demands that he return to Red Sucker Lake. (His relationship with his wife is a very private matter; whenever the subject arises, Harper grows quiet and looks worried. He has no interest in stirring up old hurts and anger, he says.)

Being a cabinet minister also made Elijah a target of scrutiny and criticism in the House. Liberal leader Sharon Carstairs questioned Harper about his job appointments, specifically that of Lloyd Girman, and the dismissal of Girman's predecessor, John Morriseau, the former head of the Manitoba Métis Federation.

"Will the minister explain why a government dedicated to the principle of affirmative action and also committed to the concept of self-government would appoint as an advisor on native affairs, a non-native?" asked Carstairs on August 21, 1986. "Is the minister telling the House that no aboriginal citizen in the province could be found with the talents, education and empathy to fill this most important position?"

Elijah responded that Girman had been the most qualified applicant. "We have many people who are qualified, but unfortunately those people who were qualified didn't apply for the job," Harper said. Then he suggested that the role reversal of a white man serving as advisor to a native minister was rather refreshing.

In fact, Harper had searched through the aboriginal community and asked Phil Fontaine to apply for the job. In the years since he and Elijah had worked together in the early 1970s, Fontaine had continued to gain prominence as a powerful and respected native leader. At the end of his four-year term as chief of the Fort Alexander reserve, Fontaine had gone to work for Indian Affairs, where he eventually became regional director in Yukon. After three years in that position, he took a leave and returned to Winnipeg to finish a Bachelor of Arts degree at the University of Manitoba. His focus was political science.

Fontaine moved on to the Southeast Tribal Council, an umbrella body representing bands throughout southeastern Manitoba, and then to the Native Economic Development Program (NEDP). Then a new assignment with the Ottawa-based Assembly of First Nations beckoned. In 1986 he was appointed vice-chief of the Assembly of First Nations for Manitoba. He would spend three years in the post, the first two by appointment, the third after winning an election against fellow Manitoban Ovide Mercredi. It was in the early days of his AFN posting that Elijah approached him. But Fontaine needed a guarantee that he would get the job, says Harper, which was not possible. "He never put his name in."

In April 1987, a year after Elijah was appointed to cabinet, Tory native affairs critic Jim Downey charged Elijah with conflict of interest and demanded his resignation. A few weeks after Harper was appointed minister without portfolio, cabinet gave final approval to a $350,000 loan from the province's Communities Economic Development Fund to businessman Norman Gunn of Norway House, who had rented Harper the "hole in the wall" office during the 1986 election campaign. Six months after the loan was approved, Gunn declared bankruptcy.

Premier Pawley admitted that Harper was at the cabinet meeting as minister without portfolio when the loan decision was finalized, but pointed out that work on the application had been carried out before Harper's appointment. He rejected any notion that Harper had benefited by accepting the rental office from Gunn or that Harper had anything to gain by the loan. "It is the height of idiocy for the member for Arthur [Downey] to even suggest the removal of the member of Rupertsland under such circumstances," Pawley told the House.

"It was my first cabinet meeting," says Harper. "I didn't even know what was going on." The Gunn episode, however, gave Harper a taste of what he was in for as a cabinet minister and was one of his first tests in the adversarial system of white politics. "I took it seriously," he says. "I knew it could become really dirty. I guess I handled it okay, because we came out of it." But the jostling in the House did not suit his personality. "I'm not a good fighter," says Harper. "I just listen to people."

While his performance in the legislature was much improved, Harper was no star when peppered with questions. After the first day of debate in the House, Harper's staff would prepare him by raising probable questions and letting him go through the answers based on whatever information they had uncovered.

The Gunn affair and other queries about appointments and firings gave Harper a permanent dislike of Tory MLA and Indian affairs critic Jim Downey. "He comes off and shoots from the hip and the lip," says Harper, "and he never gives a straight answer. When I ask questions, I don't view it as me asking the questions. I see it as my constituents wanting to know something. But he takes it personally and he answers personally. I don't operate that way."

It had taken him years to earn the cabinet posting and, at least temporarily, to silence his critics. He should have been on top of the world. Instead, the daily attacks in the House and ongoing problems at home were weighing heavily on Elijah. One Wednesday morning in the fall of 1987, he disappeared. "He just didn't show up," says Elaine Ediger, who now went by her married name of Cowan. "I was getting these phone calls—'Where is your boss?' " Elaine could say only, "I just talked to him yesterday, as a matter of fact. I'll get right back to you."

"Cabinet meetings are every Wednesday morning," explains Girman. "Every Wednesday morning I panic. I panic for this reason. We have a big cabinet agenda. I don't want to go in and carry it through cabinet, it doesn't look good, right? Every Wednesday morning I'd say, '[Harper,] be here by 8:00 A.M. and I will give you the cabinet briefing and books and at 9:00 A.M. you'll be ready to go in.' Five to nine, he would show up and I'd be briefing him as we went down the hall."

On this particular Wednesday morning, Girman panicked as usual. "At five to nine, Harper was not there. Five after nine, not there." Girman headed into cabinet to do what he could with the agenda items. When he got out, there was still no Elijah. "I was getting ready to call the RCMP."

Instead, Harper's staff called the airlines to see if Harper had bought a ticket. "Hours later," says Elaine, "I got a call from him. He was in Red Sucker Lake. He had gone to the reserve to be on the trapline." It was moose-hunting season, Elijah's favourite time of year.

No matter where Elijah travelled, his deep love of the bush beckoned. When Harper speaks of a trip into the bush with a dog team or canoeing down the just-thawing rivers in the spring, there is love in his voice. Elijah had rarely missed moose-hunting season, and he needed this restorative time in the bush more than ever during the fall of 1987. In part, however, taking off was also simply Harper thwarting authority, even authority he had volunteered to work under.

Such a disappearing act might be tolerated from a backbencher, but not from a cabinet minister; and Elaine and Girman told Harper so.

Says Girman, "He walks in six days later and I say, 'Where the fuck were you?'

" 'I was on my trapline.'

" 'You're a minister of the Crown. You have responsibilities,' " an infuriated Girman threw back. " 'You don't just leave.'

" 'But that's what I do,' said Elijah. 'Every year of my life at this time of year, I go on the trapline.' "

The answer left Girman speechless. He suddenly realized, "This is how he keeps himself sane. This is what he does to maintain his Indianness."

Elijah sidesteps the fact that he was having a rough period in his personal life and that going to hunt moose was a convenient way to escape the pressure, just as he evades most inquiries about his personal troubles. Those close to him say that prodding does little. Those seeking information on his personal life must simply wait.

"There is a time when the moose season comes around—around September—when the moose gets active," says Harper when asked about the unexpected trip up north. "That's when I go moose hunting. I heard the call," he says, laughing. "I can't determine when the moose's time comes, so I go out there. I mean, I can't postpone it because of a cabinet meeting. This is our way of life. We put our life around it. That is how I was raised. When it is time for the geese to fly, you can't stop them."

He knew that not everyone could understand his love of the bush. Harper recalls talking to Attorney General Roland Penner as Penner was heading off on an exotic holiday during a legislative break. Penner asked where Harper was going. "I said, 'I'm going into the bush in a tent, have a bonfire and have some tea.' The way he reacted you knew he couldn't understand that I would do that and be able to enjoy it."

Harper's quizzical response to the panic of his staff when he disappeared was similar to his reaction to the panic over his finances. "He didn't see the importance," Elaine says. "He never knew how significant it was. But I was hysterical about his safety—it would just drive me crazy. There he was safe and sound, just doing his thinking, and he would come back just as if he was coming back from Bermuda—bright-eyed, smiling, a shine like you wouldn't believe, full of energy."

When Harper returned, Elaine insisted that there be a system to deal with future trips. It took a while, but eventually Elijah got better at letting Elaine know when he needed to head off for a break. "I would watch his mood, and then I would schedule a whole week off and he would really look forward to it.

"Howard Pawley was so understanding of him. Howard adored Elijah, he just adored him. And he was very understanding of him having to go back to the trapline, or whatever."

That understanding would be put to the test some weeks later when Harper got into a minor traffic accident. He had also been drinking. "I wasn't drinking every day or every night," says Harper. "I was drinking maybe once a week, or even once a month. If I knew I would be drinking, I always left the car in the parking lot." This night, however, Harper landed in serious trouble.

It was September 7, 1987, and Harper was drinking red wine with a friend, McLeod Fiddler, "talking about things" at the Marlborough Hotel in downtown Winnipeg. "Red wine is no good for me," says

Harper. "I don't know what's in there, but there is something about red wine." He left, got into his car and headed the few blocks to his Ellice Avenue home. While changing lanes he clipped the bumper of a tow truck that had come to a sudden stop. There didn't appear to be any damage to the truck, but Harper didn't stop. "I panicked," he says, letting out a nervous, tight sound. "And he followed me."

Harper knew the tow truck driver was behind him and knew the police would soon be at his door, but he went into his apartment and drank a couple of beers. He doesn't know what compelled him to drink more or why he just sat and waited. The police came and took him to the station, where he telephoned his lawyer and friend Vic Savino. When Harper finally got home, he called Elaine and Girman.

"He called very late, two or three in the morning," Elaine recalls. "He said, 'There is trouble. There's been a car accident and I've been drinking.' "

Girman played cards at his parents' house Tuesday nights and usually stayed overnight. At about 3:00 A.M. the phone rang. "I've got a problem. I have to quit cabinet," Elijah told Girman. After asking a few questions, Girman drove to Harper's apartment. Elaine Cowan was there. Yvon Dumont, a friend and leader in the Manitoba Metis community, would also stop in to offer support.

Girman says Harper was rambling by the time he got there. Elaine is more generous. "He was feeling, of course, as badly as anybody could possibly feel," she says. "But he wanted to do the honourable thing. He wanted to resign. I was still trying to find ways to fix it." It was suggested that Pawley's media liaison, Michael Balagus, be called to an early morning meeting. Later that morning, Harper also asked for Tory native affairs critic Jim Downey's phone number. "He said he wanted to tell Downey himself that he was resigning," says Elaine.

The next morning was a Wednesday, and Pawley had scheduled a cabinet meeting in his riding of Selkirk.

Girman called Pawley around 7:00 A.M. "Howard, we have a problem," said Girman, explaining the situation.

"Ooo," came the reply.

"Not what I wanted to hear," says Girman. "I thought, 'This is a crisis.' "

As in politics everywhere, when an embarrassing scandal has broken or is threatening, the spin doctors move into overdrive to do "damage control."

The primary question at that morning's meeting was what would cause the Pawley government, which had undergone several mini-scandals in the previous months, the least embarrassment. Although the accident had caused no damage, it would still be media and opposition fodder. Other members of the Manitoba legislature had been charged with drunk driving in the past—some more than once—but here was the province's first Indian MLA leaving the scene of an accident and, on his lawyer's advice, refusing to take a breathalyzer test. Various scenarios were considered, but no one doubted the need for Harper to resign.

"I told him nothing comes out 100 per cent in this—it's bad, it is a no-win situation—except you can come out of this appearing to have been very honest. You can tell the world first what happened and with great modesty," Pawley says. He found the episode particularly sad because Harper was gaining momentum as a cabinet minister. "I give him credit," says the former premier. "Some would have tried to dodge it or run away from it."

"All kinds of things went through my mind," says Harper when asked what he thought his options were. "But how else are you going to handle it? I mean, you have to handle it head-on. If you make a mistake or do something that stupid, admit it and deal with it."

A press conference was called later in the day. Harper gave a short statement, wearing the same grey-striped suit he had worn the day he was named cabinet minister. His eyes looked glassy, and his voice was quieter than usual. "As a result of my being charged earlier today with failing to take a breathalyzer and leaving the scene of an accident, I have asked the premier to relieve me of my ministerial responsibilities pending the outcome of these charges," said Harper, reading from his prepared text. "No one was injured in the accident. It is my intention to serve the people of Rupertsland as a member of the legislative assembly. The premier has accepted my resignation and it will take effect immediately."

He answered a few questions, including why he thought he should remain an MLA. "I have an obligation to the people who put me there as an elected member and they expect me to get up," he said. "I don't think people respect you if you lie down. I have to get up and serve my people."

He did not mention that resigning his seat would end the NDP's majority in the house. Only two weeks earlier, NDP MLA for St. Boniface, Larry Desjardin, had announced his impending departure.

"The staff just walked over and hugged him, the secretary, all the assistants. The phones didn't stop ringing," says Elaine. "It was like a funeral."

That afternoon Elijah and a staffer flew to Red Sucker Lake. "Basically he got off the plane, walked over and sat with his family, cried with his family, hugged them all, then flew back and there was a car waiting," says Elaine. Elijah was driven south to the Hazelton Residential Chemical Dependency Treatment Centre in Minnesota, which specialized in high-profile people with drug and alcohol problems.

Harper says his month-long stay in the U.S. treatment centre was one of the most positive experiences of his life. There he sat, with doctors, lawyers, athletes—people from all over the world who should have had everything but got into trouble because of alcohol or drugs. He says he spent a lot of time talking to the people in his unit. (Harper was even elected unit leader and put in charge of the opening prayer and of organizing various lectures.) "This one man, his name was John, and he was from Texas," recalls Elijah. "He told me one day, 'I'm a Republican, but if you ran I'd vote for you.' "

Although his problems with alcohol were minor compared to those of some fellow patients, Elijah was forced to face how serious the accident could have been. "What I realized after was that I needed it," he says of the treatment. "Everyone needs to do that, go through a process of what alcohol does to you. I mean, you can make mistakes, and that decision can change your life. I was very fortunate; it wasn't that serious. But that one instance where you become panicky could change your life. It is a philosophy: to totally abstain from alcohol is the only way you can be totally free."

Within hours of Harper's departure for Minnesota, the power struggle began. Flin Flon MLA Jerry Storie was named acting northern affairs minister, which was fine with Girman. What wasn't fine was that Storie had been assigned to take over Harper's office. "What you are about to do, perceptually, is close the door on Elijah's political career by moving someone else into his office," Girman told Pawley. The premier ruled that Harper's office should be left as it was. "I gave a clear signal that when he had paid his debt and the court had dealt with this, he would be brought back in," Pawley says.

Harper called his former staff twice, once about three weeks into the treatment and again just before he was scheduled to return home. By the second call, Harper was in good spirits and sounded positive. "He wanted his mail, he wanted the cabinet agenda—even though he wasn't a cabinet minister he still wanted to know what was happening," says Elaine Cowan.

When Elijah returned, he heard from all sides: some thought he should never have quit; others, like his old political rival Alan Ross, said Harper should resign his seat.

The cost of the detox program, says Elijah, was about $6000, which he paid. Some incidentals were paid for by the party. Harper pleaded guilty to the charges, was fined $450 and had his driver's licence suspended for a year. Elijah voluntarily extended the licence suspension to five years. (He had not reapplied for driving privileges by 1993.) "I was involved in this unfortunate incident and I have had to deal with it as honourably as I can," Harper said after his court appearance. "What I want to do is to continue on in my role as a member of the legislature representing my constituency."

On November 23, 1987, just over two months after Harper's accident, Pawley quietly returned him to his cabinet post, saying he had paid his dues. Liberal leader Sharon Carstairs suggested that Pawley leave Harper out of cabinet for the same one-year period as his licence suspension. Conservative Gary Filmon, whose MPs had had two drunk driving convictions, was more sympathetic. "He has been dealt with in a legal sense, and he has undertaken the alcohol rehabilitation program, and I believe he has indicated that his life is straightened out in that respect. So there is no other reason that he should be barred from serving in cabinet," said Filmon. Filmon also wrote a personal note to Harper expressing the same sentiments, a kindness Elijah has never forgotten.

This view corresponded to the opinion within the native community.

"The drunk driving charge wasn't something, really, that mattered to me," says Ovide Mercredi. "It affects mayors, it affects judges. I practice criminal law, so I see it all the time. To me it was not something that goes to the heart of a person's credibility.

"We see those problems ourselves in our communities. We don't get judgemental about that. Where Indians became judgemental about him was his appearance of ineffectiveness as an MLA in terms of dealing with the issues they wanted him to deal with, that they hoped he would deal with."

But unhappiness about Harper's return would continue through the new year, more fuel on the fire that would consume the Pawley government. Indeed, the election win had begun unravelling almost as soon as the votes were counted.

Chapter Six

MEECH LAKE DEATH WATCH

Things had changed since Harper's sudden departure and return to cabinet. With the Pawley government's majority shaved to the bare minimum, the mood in caucus was tense. Every vote in the House held potential disaster.

"We were in a very vulnerable situation," says Harper. "You had to be in the legislative building all the time. I remember being sick one day and having to come in. I was lying on the couch in case there was a vote. If you were on a trip, you had to worry all the time that you weren't weathered out." The legislative rules give MLAS twelve hours to return in the case of a crucial vote, hardly adequate for the peculiarities of northern travel. "Everyone was very uptight."

While many of Pawley's political difficulties were domestic, he also had to contend with strained extraprovincial relations. In October 1986, Ottawa had snubbed Manitoba by handing a multimillion-dollar contract to build CF-18 aircraft to a Montreal firm, although by every measurement the Manitoba bid was superior. Pawley and other provincial political and business representatives mounted a high-profile but ultimately unsuccessful campaign against the decision, which tapped into the ever-present sense of western alienation and permanently coloured relations between Mulroney and Pawley.

Tension over the CF-18 affair had barely subsided when the prime minister invited the premiers to 'a constitutional information-gathering session' at Meech Lake on April 30, 1987. To the surprise of the leaders, they emerged a day later having cobbled together a basis for amending the constitution in ways that might persuade Quebec to sign. The premiers' agreement included a promise to recognize Quebec as a distinct society and new power-sharing arrangements between the provinces and Ottawa.

The distinct society clause merely exacerbated French/English tensions in Manitoba. The power-sharing changes were of particular concern to Pawley, the country's only socialist premier; however, public opinion seemed to support the accord. The only concerns that initially bubbled through the general euphoria focussed on the rights of native people and of women, multicultural rights and the effect of the proposed new funding arrangements on new national social programs.

By the time the premiers gathered again, on June 3, 1987, at Langevin Block, the dissatisfaction over the distinct society clause and spending powers had grown. At least two premiers, Howard Pawley and Ontario Premier David Peterson, were convinced that changes were needed.

Pawley had also been pressured by Elijah and other native leaders to push for changes on their behalf, but others—even Pawley's own federal party leader—cautioned him to go easy. Ed Broadbent called at least three times. "He was terribly concerned that we were going to upset the boat on Meech and affect him negatively at a time when he was leading in the polls in the province of Quebec," says Pawley.

Pawley warned Broadbent that he was prepared to leave Langevin if he didn't get what he needed. "You can't do that," Broadbent pleaded. "We're just at the point of taking off nationally."

"It makes me annoyed when I look back at it," said Pawley two years later. "I'm not sure to what extent Ed played a proper role."

Proper or not, Broadbent would continue the pressure long after he had retired as NDP leader, acting as an emissary for the federal government by making surprise phone calls to various players.

The Langevin meeting, long and often rancorous, came close to collapse several times. In the end, however, Pawley's signature was on the newly created 1987 "Meech Lake" Accord. Pawley had won a clause stating that existing native and multicultural rights would not be adversely affected by the accord, but he had failed to gain any ground on spending powers.

Pawley says Mulroney assured the premiers that night that national public hearings would be held on the package, and it was on that understanding that Pawley signed the document. A few months later, only a few carefully selected groups were invited to make presentations in Ottawa. "That was the extent of his national hearings," says Pawley, anger in his voice. "We did not foresee that kind of manipulated display. I feel that Mulroney was Machiavellian throughout."

Pawley's signature carried one important proviso: changes might be sought on the basis of what Manitobans had to say in mandatory public hearings, during which every Manitoban has the right to speak. "Mulroney was warned as early as June of 1987 that there was a particular process in Manitoba, and warned that we had found to our detriment in the French-language debate that you don't proceed without a proper process," says Pawley. The warning would never be heeded.

The hearings kept being pushed farther down the priority list as the Manitoba government dealt with a major crisis in the government-run auto insurance industry. Moreover, NDP polls showed the Manitoba government's popularity plummeting as Liberal leader Sharon Carstairs's anti-Meech stance gained popularity.

Still, it was decided to hold the hearings in the fall of 1987, between legislative sessions, so that public input could be dealt with by the time the MLAS reconvened early in 1988.

Pawley is a nonconfrontational man who would not take on Ottawa out of vengeance, as he told the prime minister and the other premiers when he signed the accord. "I said, Manitoba is not going to subvert this [Meech] process by not signing it when everyone else has gone along, the nine provinces and the prime minister," says Pawley. "But we will go through our process, we will have our hearings. There will not be a rubber stamp. And we may very well be back to the table for further negotiations." (It was this comment that caused Bourassa to respond that not "a comma shall be changed, not a T uncrossed.")

The fall hearings would never be held.

According to Manitoba's legislative rules, the Pawley government needed unanimous consent from the opposition to introduce a resolution establishing public hearings. The resolution had been prepared several weeks in advance and Jay Cowan was to get consent. However, on July 16, 1987, the last day of the session, consent had not yet been obtained. "In fairness to Jay, it wasn't deliberate on his part," says Pawley. "Meech wasn't an important thing to him. Probably I should have said to him a few days earlier, 'Jay, did you get consent for that?' "

In a last-minute rush, Pawley approached the Tories, but the accord—in particular the distinct society clause—was causing strains within the Conservative camp. "The Tories were nervous," says Pawley. "They weren't prepared to do any favours to get on with the Meech process." They also did not intend to help the problem-plagued NDP government.

"If they had given consent," says Pawley, "we would have been into hearings in the fall of '87 and the process would have been moved along tremendously in Manitoba."

Pawley could sympathize with Filmon's predicament: members of Pawley's own caucus were also unhappy. As is normal practice after the leader has returned from battle, there had been extended applause and a standing ovation for Pawley when he returned to the House from Ottawa in June. But not everyone joined in. While people like Carstairs would be expected to sit on their hands, members of the government were not. "There were only two people that didn't applaud on our side," recalls Pawley. "Elijah and Gerald Lecuyer [the francophone MLA for Radisson]." Elijah was one of the first to approach the premier. "He was very clear and very up front: 'I don't like Meech,' he said. I indicated why, from our perspective, we had signed it, but I said it was not a rubber stamp. We were going to try and work to improve it."

Pawley and Ontario Premier David Peterson had fought hard at Langevin to safeguard aboriginal and multicultural rights guaranteed in the 1982 Charter of Rights and Freedoms, but native leaders were not satisfied. As usual, they had been excluded from the Meech and Langevin meetings and given no chance to voice their concerns that the new amending formula—unanimous consent of all provinces and the federal government, instead of the approval of seven provinces representing 50 per cent of the country's population—would make native self-government impossible. The formula would also make it difficult—probably impossible—for Yukon and the Northwest Territories—and their overwhelmingly native populations—to become provinces. In addition, native leaders were angered at the entrenching of the English/French duality without recognition of Canada's original inhabitants.

"If there isn't some improvement in Meech as it affects aboriginal people," Elijah told Pawley in private, "I will probably have to resign cabinet when the vote comes."

"Elijah doesn't grandstand," says Pawley. "He didn't threaten in caucus to try and influence caucus members, which goes to his credit. It was a personal discussion."

Harper stood before Pawley not merely as an MLA but as the representative of all native Manitobans. Indeed, the interests of his native constituents overrode his responsibilities to the New Democratic Party. Balancing these often conflicting loyalties had been a struggle from the day he entered the Manitoba legislature.

It was a strange position to be in, says Harper. Within aboriginal communities there is still very little understanding of white politics. "Ours is probably the first generation that even talks about politics with each other," says Harper. "Even now, we have problems with people not going out to vote, not relating to why you run for one party or another." While he was often in a position to introduce native concerns into the political mainstream, the lack of voting among aboriginal people meant that, in real terms, their political clout was minimal.

If Harper voted against the government on the Meech Lake Accord, it would be unfortunate but not a disaster: the rules would not allow one MLA to thwart the will of the House for more than a couple of days. However, Elijah was not alone. Particularly vocal among the behind-the-scenes dissenters in the NDP caucus were MLA Al Mackling from the west-end Winnipeg riding of St. James, Len Evans (Brandon), and two MLAS representing francophone ridings, Gerald Lecuyer (Radisson) and Larry Desjardin (St. Boniface). "Desjardin and Lecuyer believed the francophone minority outside of Quebec had been ignored," Pawley says. "And I remember Al Mackling complained like heck that I had signed it without caucus discussion."

Soon after Filmon's refusal to give consent, the opportunity to hold the hearings disappeared under the Pawley government's ongoing domestic problems. Upset by the federal government announcement that it would move ahead with a free trade deal with the United States, Pawley decided against fast-tracking the accord in Manitoba. Moreover, he says, it was becoming obvious that there was little hope that any changes Manitobans might suggest would be accepted. "There was intransigence," says Pawley.

In September 1987, not long after Elijah headed south for alcohol treatment, Larry Desjardin resigned his St. Boniface seat to take a private sector job. His departure left Pawley with twenty-nine seats and the opposition with twenty-seven; with the speaker in the chair, the NDP had a single-seat majority. Desjardin's resignation convinced the government to stay away from the Meech Lake debate—Lecuyer and Desjardin reflected francophone opposition to Meech, and the accord was sure to be an issue in the St. Boniface riding.

Another event contributed significantly to the eventual demise of the accord. On March 26 and 27, 1987, six months before Harper's drunk driving episode and just weeks before the Meech Lake Accord was hatched, the final first ministers' conference on native issues had been held in Ottawa. It was a bitter affair. In the four years that had passed since the inaugural FMC on native issues, aboriginal leaders had become dismayed by the provinces' increasing opposition to entrenching self-government in the constitution. As well, the Conservative Party was not renowned for its interest in native initiatives, and Mulroney's constitutional sights were focussed on Quebec.

Mulroney spoke comforting words, say native leaders, but then argued that aboriginal governments would never be able to "stand separate and apart" from provincial and federal governments. Not surprisingly, then, the March 1987 meeting ended with no agreement on the recognition of native self-rule.

Pawley believes the meeting failed in part because of problems within the native leadership: a lack of unity, confused goals and a failure to define what self-government meant before the meeting began. "There was no way we were going to write in self-government," says Pawley, "until we were able to resolve this, not just among white leaders, but among aboriginal leaders."

"I never saw the native leadership as a problem," Harper says. "There are always different issues to be resolved between the different native groups. I always blamed the governments. They never took us seriously."

During the final FMC meeting on native issues, British Columbia Premier Bill Vander Zalm argued against entrenching unconditional self-government. His province had 197 bands, about one third of the national total, and he feared the consequences if the province was forced to negotiate separate political pacts with each one. He was joined in his opposition by Saskatchewan Premier Grant Devine, Alberta Premier Don Getty and Newfoundland Premier Brian Peckford. (Ontario, Nova Scotia, New Brunswick and Prince Edward Island had tried for a statement in principle on native self-government, but Manitoba alone supported unconditional native self-rule.) While most provinces accepted the general idea of entrenching native self-government as a constitutional right, the debate became stuck on whether those rights should be defined first or agreed upon later through regional agreements reflecting different native traditions.

"Since our right to self-government is inherent, it cannot be created by the constitution," argued the Assembly of First Nations, calling for a review of all 483 treaties with a view to bringing them up to date. Native leaders also wanted the word "existing" removed from the 1982 constitutional amendment (Section 35.1), arguing that the word was being used by the courts to quash treaty hunting and fishing rights overridden by federal and provincial laws.

"There was a lot of emotion when the prime minister hit the gavel and said, 'This constitutional conference is coming to an end,' " recalls Elijah. Yvon Dumont, head of the Manitoba Métis Federation, cried at the end of the conference because nothing had been gained.

During the closing ceremonies, the president of the Métis National Council, Jim Sinclair, delivered an impassioned speech on behalf of all native people. He charged Ottawa with not having the guts to put sovereignty on the table, and specifically targeted Dutch-born British Columbia Premier Bill Vander Zalm. "It's a shame that you can come here and in a few years become the premier of one of the largest provinces in Canada, and you will not recognize the rights of our people."

When Sinclair finished speaking, the aboriginal delegates gave him a standing ovation. "It was the first time at any First Ministers' conference that there was some kind of demonstration," says Fontaine. "And then I think there was a sense that this thing had ended in failure but that it wasn't over, that we were going to continue with this struggle with a bigger and deeper sense of commitment."

The prime minister tried to defuse Sinclair's speech by acknowledging that the Metis leader's soul had been scarred by his experiences with the white system. "That was the most profound thing Mulroney said in six and a half years," says Phil Fontaine. "He finally recognized that the souls of aboriginal people have been scarred."

On April 30, 1987, barely a month after the failure of the final first ministers' conference on native issues, Mulroney and the premiers produced the Meech Lake Accord.

Throughout the follow-up Langevin meeting, native leaders could only mill about with reporters outside the building, gleaning what information they could. Phil Fontaine, now vice-chief of the Assembly of First Nations for Manitoba, and a handful of others spent the early morning hours watching events unfold on television until the premiers emerged with their agreement. "The deal had been cut," says Fontaine, "and we felt really abandoned, including by the people that we thought would go to the wall for us, the NDP government."

Some native groups were, if not happy, at least content with Meech. Non-status and Metis leaders were inclined to argue that without Meech the country would be locked in constitutional gridlock for decades and no progress would be made on any aboriginal issue. Yvon Dumont of the Manitoba Métis Federation was the most vocal proponent of this point of view. "If we defeat Meech Lake, I think we're fighting about the deck chairs on the Titanic because the ship of state is sinking."

This was not, however, Elijah's view. "A lot of people were insulted by the Meech Lake Accord," Harper told the Manitoba legislature just a few weeks later. The federal government was prepared to give the provinces decision-making power with respect to treaty and aboriginal rights, but "that could have been accomplished at the constitutional conference." The fact that such gestures were not advanced to native people, said Elijah, showed "a total lack of any kind of political will."

The timing of the breakthrough for Quebec was especially embittering for aboriginal people. Mulroney had told native leaders that he had wanted to end their final first ministers' conference with a deal, but Meech Lake showed that was a lie, says Fontaine. "If Mulroney had been committed, he would have made as strong an effort for us as he put out for Quebec. But there was nothing in it for him. There is nothing in it for any of them, except justice. And they didn't want that, of course."

Soon after the Langevin meeting, the national native leaders called another meeting in the Assembly of First Nations' Ottawa office. The Manitoba delegation arrived late—"We were formulating a position in Winnipeg," says Fontaine—but the AFN had not yet firmed up their position. After a discussion, Manitoba's was adopted. The message was two-fold: first, a missive to Quebec; second, bottom-line demands.

"We would never oppose Quebec," says Fontaine in explaining the strategy. "We would recognize you for who you are—you are distinct, you are fundamental, and it is important that you are afforded this recognition." However, the AFN's position was that aboriginal people are also distinct, the first people to occupy the land, and also fundamental to the country.

This principle and a demand that native representatives participate in all future first ministers' meetings would fall on deaf ears until it was too late. Native leaders kept hearing that this was the Quebec round and that they should be helping, not hindering, that effort. "You have to remember that Quebec is your ally," Indian Affairs officials told Fontaine and others. But native leaders were not fooled. "All you have to do is talk to aboriginal people in Quebec," Fontaine says. "It was just a line for the most gullible."

In Manitoba, Meech Lake was fodder for the opposition. Louis Stevenson, chief of the Peguis band and long-time Harper critic, demanded that Elijah resign for his 'unequivocal support' of Meech Lake. "That's the only way to prove native rights are a priority with him," Stevenson said.

But Harper disagreed. "I've made my concerns known to the premier, and our government's position is very clearly in support of aboriginal rights." He then said that the work he was doing behind the scenes would ultimately be more effective than quitting in a huff.

But such exchanges would become moot when, on March 9, 1988, NDP MLA Jim Walding voted with the opposition against the budget and the government fell. Walding had represented the Winnipeg riding of St. Vital for the NDP since 1971. Only hours earlier he had said he would vote with the government, but he had not been attending caucus meetings for months and had disengaged himself from his fellow NDP MLAS. He had even qualified his vote in favour of the government's throne speech just weeks earlier. "It is a speech from the Queen," Walding had told Harper. "You do not vote against the Queen."

"I couldn't believe it," says Elijah, who was sitting beside Walding when he voted against the government. At first, Harper was not clear on what the vote actually meant. "I knew we were in a tense and awkward situation, but I was not sure if we could last as a government or not."

The Tories were throwing paper in the air and hooting. Then there was a mad rush out of the chamber. "What's Pawley going to do?" the media kept shouting as they headed down the long hallway to the premier's office. "I don't fucking know," replied communications head

Michael Balagus as he slammed the door.

In the days that followed, the province's newspapers were filled with political speculation. Deep in the inside pages were a few paragraphs about a shooting. Hours after the government fell, a Winnipeg police officer, James Cross, had shot and killed an unarmed native man during a scuffle. The dead man was identified as John Joseph Harper, known as J. J.

Elijah heard the news the next day at caucus. Emotions were already high over the fall of the government. Then someone said that J. J. Harper had been killed. "I felt sick," says Harper. J. J. was the former head of the Island Lake Tribal Council. He had been a close friend of Elijah's and the two had often worked together when Harper was Red Sucker chief. "He was not the kind to pick a fight. My first thought was that something had been going on and he got in the way."

After some consideration, Pawley announced that he would step down, and the search began for his successor. Pawley's staff were devastated. They had been dumped from government by one of their own just when their own polls indicated that they were at 6 per cent and would be lucky to keep two or three seats across the province. Campaigners worked with a sense of impending doom.

Elaine Cowan again took charge of Elijah's campaign. For the first time, Harper's nomination went uncontested. Rupertsland was one of the few NDP ridings the party expected to hold, but given the mood of the electorate, nothing was sure. "I knew that we were not going to be the government," says Elijah.

Moreover, Harper's attention was soon diverted from the campaign by events following J. J. Harper's shooting. Within thirty-six hours of the incident, an internal police investigation exonerated Constable Cross. Native Manitobans were outraged. Only months earlier, three white Manitobans had been brought to trial for the murder of Helen Betty Osborne, a Cree teenager from The Pas, who had been killed sixteen years earlier. Much of the testimony in the trial centred on racism. In the end, only one of the men had been convicted, and many questions were left unanswered. Now J. J. Harper had been shot while walking along a deserted Winnipeg street, and the man who pulled the trigger had been cleared of wrongdoing in a matter of hours.

Elijah and his deputy minister, Lloyd Girman, attended J. J.'s funeral in Island Lake. "It was un–fucking believable," recalls Girman. "I have been on every reserve in this province and half the reserves in this country, and I was shit scared. There was me, two other white guys, Elijah, and a thousand other Indians all sitting in this wake for three days. Emotions were running so high."

Elijah pressured Attorney General Vic Schroeder for a full-fledged inquiry into the treatment of natives within the Manitoba justice system. "I felt strongly that we needed to look at the treatment of aboriginal people and policing," says Harper, tears coming into his eyes as he talks about J. J. and the inquiry. "I did not want the announcement to be seen as an election ploy—I know some people will say that—but I looked into my own heart and I felt something had to be done."

"I have never seen Harper push that hard," says Girman. "He was pushing with emotion. He wanted this inquiry." With the polls pointing to a serious NDP defeat, Harper wanted an announcement before the election: the NDP might be reluctant to launch what could be a messy inquiry, but the Tories would be sure to refuse.

Schroeder eventually suggested that an inquest be held under the Fatal Inquiries Act. "But it wasn't enough," says Elijah. "The act was very limited. It could only probe into the actual cause of death. It couldn't talk about the officers—if they had the right kind of training—or many other things."

For weeks Girman fed insider information to his friend Gordon Sinclair, Jr., a columnist at the *Winnipeg Free Press*. "God love the man, he went hard at it," Girman says. "I would call him every day and tell him what was going on. And he was writing stories and the pressure was starting to mount."

Indeed, NDP candidates, including the attorney general, found voters asking why there wouldn't be an inquiry. "He [Schroeder] came back in Monday morning, called Elijah over and said, 'I've changed my mind. I think we should look at this a little further,' " recalls Girman.

But the bureaucrats had been getting pressure from police to keep any investigation small. Even Harper and Girman were getting anonymous phone calls telling them to back off. "You picked up the phone and someone on the line said, 'If you guys keep pushing, you'll be in trouble,' and shit like that," says Girman. "Elijah and I were panicking. I was driving with my seat belt done up and going the speed limit."

The government made its decision, and Harper was to deliver the statement on the steps of the legislature before the hundreds of protesters gathered there. But when Harper picked up the statement on his way out the door, it said that there would be a beefed-up inquest.

"I was mad," says Harper. "I went to Howard [Pawley]'s office. We had decided we were going to have an inquiry, and I wanted to make that statement.' "

"Harper walked out to the crowd," says Girman, "stood in front of them and announced an inquiry."

During the last cabinet meeting, two days before the election, the inquiry was one of several orders in council delivered to the attorney general for approval.

"He wouldn't sign the aboriginal justice inquiry," recalls Girman.

Throughout the day, Harper and Gilman waited, assuming that premier-to-be Filmon was being asked to clear the order. "We sat there until six o'clock that night," says Girman. Then, finally, the order came back signed.

Manitoba's Aboriginal Justice Inquiry would be cochaired by Associate Chief Provincial Court Judge Murray Sinclair, an Ojibwa, and Justice Alvin Hamilton of the Manitoba Court of Queen's Bench. It would cost the provincial government just under $3 million and be the most far-reaching inquiry into the treatment of natives in Canada's justice system.

On April 26, 1988, Conservative leader Gary Filmon became premier of Manitoba, yet he again had failed to make the gains many had expected. The Tories won just twenty-five seats; the Liberals took twenty. The NDP had twelve seats and held the balance of power.

If Mulroney had hoped that Filmon could guarantee passage of Meech in Manitoba, Filmon's minority government and Carstairs's newfound power quickly dashed such thoughts. At a press conference two days after the election, Carstairs stood with her rookie team and made a statement that would come back to haunt her. "The Meech Lake Accord, in terms of Manitoba, will not be a viable issue," she said. "Any government will have grave difficulty getting such a resolution passed in the Manitoba legislature, which means, in essence, that Meech Lake is dead."

Filmon soon announced that Meech Lake would not be a priority until his economic agenda had been established: the two were, however, inextricably connected. Federal transfer payments to Manitoba had been notoriously slow ever since Pawley's announcement that he was putting the Meech Lake Accord on the back burner to protest Ottawa's free trade plans. While in opposition, the Tories had promised they could renew a federal-provincial agreement for economic development, but it would not turn out that way.

It soon became apparent that federal bureaucrats had been instructed to put the heat on Manitoba in any way they could. "Nothing was ever substantiated in terms of a formal directive, but there seemed to be a pretty clear feeling at the federal level that they shouldn't proceed at any great speed with anything to do with Manitoba," says one former Filmon staffer. "And, certainly, very little got done." Finally, after months of denying rumours of the federal Tory tactics, Filmon announced the long-awaited public hearings on the accord.

On December 14, 1989, less than a month after Prime Minister Brian Mulroney won his second majority government, Filmon stood in the Manitoba legislature to introduce the Meech Lake resolution. Two days later, on December 16, Quebec Premier Robert Bourassa announced that he would use the constitutional notwithstanding clause to bypass a Supreme Court ruling against Quebec's French-only sign law. Manitoba had been assured in private conversations that "they were going to come out with a reasonable solution to this that wouldn't cause us too much grief," says a Filmon staffer. "Filmon talked to Bourassa on the Sunday, and Bourassa said, 'I did what I had to do. You do what you have to do.' It was very cordial."

When Filmon called Mulroney's office, he was told that the prime minister was heading into caucus and didn't have time to talk.

On December 19, Filmon stood in the Manitoba legislature and withdrew the accord, stopping a process that would have killed the deal and buying time to assess the fallout from Bourassa's announcement. His action was misconstrued by, among others, the federal government. "They did not understand that if we did not pull it on the Monday or Tuesday, it was going to public hearings and we couldn't stop it," says Greg Lyle, Filmon's former principal secretary.

In an attempt to dissipate some of the tension, Filmon opted to hold public hearings on the kinds of constitutional amendments Manitobans would like to see. This did not satisfy the legislative requirement to hold hearings on the actual accord resolutions, but it was hoped that the exercise would focus growing tensions and highlight the major stumbling blocks.

The hearings were held throughout the province in April and May of 1989. More than three hundred people made presentations, including several native groups. Manitoba Attorney General Jim McCrae was forced to sign a document committing the province to the principle of native self-government after a showdown in Garden Hill. (The document had already been signed by NDP leader Gary Doer and Liberal representative Jim Carr.) Hundreds of area residents refused to let McCrae leave the hall until he got permission from Filmon to sign the one-page declaration, which stated, "The Creator has given us the right to govern ourselves."

In April 1989, Louis Stevenson, the high-profile leader of the Assembly of Manitoba Chiefs, told the constitutional task force that the signing of the accord had been a betrayal of native people. "We must bury the myth that the French and the English are the two founding nations of Canada," Stevenson said. "The Indian people must be accorded the recognition that they are the original owners of this country and are in fact the first founding nation." It was not a message Ottawa wanted to hear from a mere "interest group" jockeying for position on the constitutional bandwagon.

The recommendations that emerged from the Manitoba process included replacing the distinct society clause with a "Canada Clause" recognizing the distinct nature of Canada, including the contribution of aboriginal peoples and Canadians of different racial and ethnic backgrounds. The document recognized Quebec as distinct but specifically stated that the Charter of Rights should not be overridden by this recognition. Accord supporters saw the document as a direct affront to the heart of the accord; Manitobans viewed it as a reasonable compromise.

Reasonable or not, Mulroney seemed in no hurry to move the process along. "My sense was that they [federal government officials] were saying, 'If we can't get this the easy way, we will do it the hard way,' " says Lyle. " 'We will get them close to the deadline, get them scared about the breaking up of Canada, and then put the pressure on them.' "

Recognizing the squeeze play, however, did little to assuage Manitoba's growing fears that their mandatory public hearings would box them in at the end. No one, says Lyle, not even Filmon, wanted to give up hope that a miracle—perhaps a perfect package that Manitobans could accept unchanged—would present itself before the June 23, 1990, accord deadline. Yet Filmon vowed over and over that he would respect Manitoba's procedures, that the hearings would be full and open, and that he would be bound by the results.

"When we said that the hearings mattered, they [the federal government] said, 'Yeah, hearings matter, and this is how you get around them,' " says Lyle.

It was impossible to believe that the animosity between Filmon and Mulroney was for show. A handful of Manitoba reporters watched Filmon unleash his venom on Mulroney in December 1989, just as the Meech Lake debate was heating up one last time. The reporters had asked to sing a few Christmas tunes to entertain Premier Filmon and were granted a rare private audience. After returning the reporters' favour with a respectable rendition of Julio Iglesias's "Of All the Girls I've Loved Before," Filmon was presented with a Christmas gift by his staff: a Brian Mulroney doll. "Where's the noose?" asked Filmon, looking inside the box. The premier cracked joke after joke about the doll. The face of the doll was an uncanny replica of the prime minister—"true to life," a staffer quipped. Filmon immediately peeked into the doll's pants and said, "You're right. No balls."

While Mulroney's secret game plan and Meech Lake's growing troubles took up much of the public's attention between 1988 and 1989, Harper and the eleven other NDP MLAs got used to life on the back benches. After years of establishing a power base from which he could accomplish concrete things, Harper was now native affairs critic. He applied pressure to get native groups funding to prepare submissions to the Aboriginal Justice Inquiry and pushed for compensation for northern trappers whose equipment had been destroyed in forest fires, but he could not implement these measures himself.

Moving to the back benches also meant a cut in pay. As a result, Elijah became overextended on his credit cards, largely because of travel expenses that went beyond his constituency allowance.

Harper's reaction to being called to account for his bills, says Cliff Scotton, was always a mixture of bewilderment and surprise. "He would say, 'That much? What are the bills for?' " Despite payment schedules and restrictions, however, Harper's ability or inclination to deal with his finances never improved. "I saw it as a big heart," says Girman. Others saw it as either a cultural difference or a criminal impulse.

Harper is the consummate politician on the subject. He offers no extra information about his accounting troubles and appears genuinely perplexed by his creditors' preoccupation with payment. "I have a different perception of money," he says. "People look at it as if it is God, you know? But native people don't see it as such. I was never taught that. You share what you had."

In "the south," as Winnipeg is called by northern natives, "you have to have money now," says Harper. "It is so central to everything. And anything you do on the outside of that becomes almost criminal. It is a different value. People want to have money, they want control, they want power." Even today in Red Sucker Lake, he says, you can go a long way without cash.

The perception in the native community, says Elijah, is that he is rich. He works in the city, has a high-profile government job and access to government largesse. "People are in dire straights sometimes," he says. "There are lots of people I tell I don't have money and they get mad at me. It is hard to say no sometimes." Often, he would give out personal loans—thousands of dollars, he says—that he did not expect to see again.

"He literally just shares his pay cheque with all his friends and all his family," says Doer, who was forced to deal with Harper's money problems when he took over as leader of the party. "At one point, they cut off his phone. [In fact, Harper has not had a home phone for years.] I would find out after talking to Elijah that he had just paid for some of his uncle's funeral back in Red Sucker Lake and had to fly in some relatives. That was more important to him than the thirty-day cut-off of his telephone."

In 1992, two debts would make the news: Air Canada sued him for an outstanding account of more than $13,000, and a reporter claimed that Elizabeth had been forced to sell furniture and seek welfare because Harper defaulted on support payments. Harper responded that both problems were supposed to have been cleared up; and, indeed, he had resumed his support payments.

Harper says that, despite the critics who accuse him of being irresponsible, his conscience is clear. "The important thing is caring about each other and how we feel about each other."

Harper came to recognize the need for damage control in white politics, but his heart was not in it. Harper never really understood why the media—or anyone else—would be interested in trying to uncover things in order to hurt someone's reputation. Howard Pawley and others appeared able to accept Harper's foibles; but after the government's defeat, Elijah's support network was gone. Girman says Harper spent hours in Girman's office talking about his problems and trying to sort out the financial mess, which included a separation agreement with Elizabeth.

"It wasn't that he was angry," says Girman. "It was that he was just hurting."

There were a few bright spots in Elijah's new life as an opposition MLA. During a trip to Manitoba in 1989, Quebec Premier Robert Bourassa met not only with Premier Filmon and the official opposition leader, Sharon Carstairs, but also with NDP leader Gary Doer. One of the main native concerns with the Meech Lake Accord was how the Northwest Territories might attain provincial status if unanimous provincial consent were required. Doer raised the issue with Bourassa, who replied by asking why the issue couldn't be dealt with after the accord was passed. "He never disagreed with any substance," says Doer. "He would disagree with process—when you could change it—so you never got into a big fight."

Bourassa's comments behind closed doors lent credibility to the native leaders' worry. "Bourassa said, 'Why should we give up our resources?' " says Elijah, reporting what he was told by Doer after the meeting. "That kind of thinking reinforces the impression that it is control that Quebec wants. He doesn't want to let go."

The decision to become a province should be made by the residents of the territories in consultation with the federal government, says Elijah. Unanimous consent is as irrational as giving all the provinces a veto on whether Quebec should separate. "Would Bourassa allow that? Wouldn't you think that that would be of more interest to Canadians than the question of allowing the Territories to become more Canadian and part of unity?"

In July 1989, Harper was invited by the Red Sucker Lake band to appear at an Assembly of First Nations conference in Quebec City. When Indian Affairs Minister Pierre Cadieux took questions, Harper stood at the microphone last. "I am a member of the Red Sucker Lake First Nation and I am representing them at this AFN conference. I am also a member of the Manitoba legislature," Harper told the minister. "Are you prepared to include in the Meech Lake Accord protection for aboriginal treaty rights and recognition of native self-government?"

Cadieux hedged and gave a non-answer, says Harper. "I told him I would not support the accord as is when it came to the legislature. They didn't take me seriously then."

On November 30, 1989, Harper spoke to hundreds of NDP delegates gathered in Winnipeg to elect a new federal party leader. He told the delegates and soon-to-be leader Audrey McLaughlin a story in the traditions of his forefathers.

"The story is about a man, an aboriginal man, whom I will call Cha-Cha-Canoe, which means blackbird in my language," Elijah began.

"One day, Cha-Cha-Canoe encounters two strange people coming on to the land. He welcomes and invites these people to his house. He shares his home and many other things with these two people. One is named Jack and the other Jacques. Jack and Jacques become very comfortable in the house. As days go by, Cha-Cha-Canoe begins to notice some discontent developing between his guests.

"Jack wants to control the whole house and Jacques wants a part, a distinct part of the house with a prominent identity and notices in a language he can read and write. Jack thinks all signs and notices throughout the house should be in his and Jacques's language, together.

"Cha-Cha-Canoe is totally bewildered and confused as to the behaviour of his welcomed guests. After weeks go by, Cha-Cha-Canoe is amazed and astonished to find Jack and Jacques are not prepared to share the house or many other things. Cha-Cha-Canoe suddenly finds himself shut out of the house. He looks in through the window and sees Jack and Jacques talking at the table. He hears Jack and Jacques arguing as to who built and designed the foundation and the structure of the house.

"Many years go by. Cha-Cha-Canoe tries to make contact with Jack and Jacques without any success. Cha-Cha-Canoe is able to survive and finds after a decade that Jack and Jacques seem to be controlling everything. Cha-Cha-Canoe finds that Jack seems to have the upper hand in running the affairs of the house.

"Cha-Cha-Canoe notices the house to be crowded. He is surprised to find nine brothers of Jack have moved in, and Jacques appears to be very upset and uncomfortable with the living arrangements that are developing.

"Finally, one day, Cha-Cha-Canoe is invited to his house for a talk. He is advised he can bring three of his aboriginal brothers with him.

Jack also invites his two cousins as observers. Cha-Cha-Canoe finds Jack and Jacques are still arguing about the house and Jacques still wants a unique place. Cha-Cha-Canoe and his three brothers are welcomed at the house and fed a fine meal.

"Then, Cha-Cha-Canoe and his brothers find out Jack and his nine brothers want to know what rights Cha-Cha-Canoe and his brothers should have to the house.

"Cha-Cha-Canoe and his brothers find out that Jack and his nine brothers, along with Jacques by association, have prepared a statement about the founding and the building of the house. There is no recognition of Cha-Cha-Canoe and his brothers. One by one, they make strong, passionate and forceful speeches for recognition, but to no avail. After four days of sitting around the table, there is no progress. There is great disappointment and disillusionment as there is reluctance by Jack and others to accommodate the wishes of Cha-Cha-Canoe and his brothers. The brothers go home at least with full stomachs.

"After a day or so Jack calls his nine brothers along with Jacques to a special dinner. Jacques's requests and needs are to be discussed. Jack twists his brothers' arms to accommodate and try and bring Jacques into the family.

"Cha-Cha-Canoe and his brothers are disturbed and angry at Jack, as Jack did not really use his influence, when the opportunity was there, on behalf of the aboriginal brothers. There is still no mention or recognition for Cha-Cha-Canoe and his brothers.

"After all this, Cha-Cha-Canoe says: 'They have wished that we would have been long gone and disappeared. At least we know now that they know we still exist. Through our beliefs, our traditions and culture, by welcoming and sharing, we have been and will continue to be a proud and great people and nation. Our constitution is far greater and superior.' "

"This," Elijah told the delegates, "is where the story ends for now. I believe it is up to the New Democrats to continue that story and this challenge. I believe we have that obligation to build a better Canada. Aboriginal people want to be part of this country and want to be recognized as being the First Nations and for the great contribution made by the first citizens of this land in the development of this country."

When Harper told this story, he knew that the tide against Meech was building. Ed Broadbent, a consistent Meech Lake supporter, was being replaced as leader. Audrey McLaughlin had voted against the deal in the House of Commons primarily because of its failure to deal with aboriginal concerns.

He could not know that Newfoundland would rescind the accord in April 1990, in response to Quebec's refusal to accept changes, or that a month later a federal government committee would recommend a companion resolution that would, among other things, recognize aboriginal people in the body of the constitution.

Nor could he know that he would not have to rely on any of these signs, however hopeful, because he would do the job himself.

Chapter Seven

THE DEAL IS DONE

Tensions surrounding the Meech Lake Accord increased as 1990 dawned and the prime minister continued to play his waiting game. A series of events helped to increase the sense of foreboding: a meeting of First Ministers in Ottawa in November 1989 ended in stalemate; Manitoba and New Brunswick released reports recommending changes to the accord; and testier players had been introduced into the negotiating mix.

Finally, on March 21, 1990, the constitutional train left the station again when New Brunswick Premier Frank McKenna released what he called a "companion resolution" to come into effect when the accord was proclaimed. The suggestion triggered a ridiculous dance between those who sought changes to the accord and those who vowed that not one letter could be altered. Since a separate document would deal with contentious issues, McKenna and others argued, Quebec could claim the accord had passed as originally agreed. But if Quebec was amenable to such a smoke screen, it wasn't willing to admitting that publicly.

Of the five items in McKenna's resolution, two were of particular interest to native leaders: the creation of new provinces should not require unanimous approval, and native issues should be placed on the agenda for the next round of constitutional talks. (Other items included the federal government's obligation not only to preserve linguistic duality but to promote it; a statement that the accord could not override women's rights; and the provision that public hearings would be held on future constitutional amendments.) The second proposal was considered by angered native leaders to be a token gesture. Nothing in McKenna's resolution responded to questions about why native people could not represent their own interests at future First Ministers' conferences, or why their fundamental place in Canada's history was not noted.

McKenna's move, which eliminated New Brunswick as a threat to the accord, isolated Manitoba, but not for long. On April 6, Newfoundland rescinded approval of the accord, making Clyde Wells federal government enemy number one.

A day after McKenna's televised announcement, Prime Minister Mulroney established an all-party panel of members of parliament, dubbed the Charest committee after chairman Jean Charest, to travel across the country to hear opinions on McKenna's resolution, and, by default, the accord.

In the period between the 1987 Langevin meeting and the Charest committee hearings in April 1990, the strategy of the Assembly of First Nations and the Manitoba Assembly of Chiefs was legal rather than political. Native leaders believed the amending formula proposed in Meech—some items requiring unanimous approval, others following the existing 7/50 rule—ran counter to guidelines laid out in the constitution and was therefore unconstitutional. (As well, native leaders believed that by focussing on this legal "mistake" they might avoid being labelled anti-Quebec.) The goal was to get one of the governments that had not yet passed the accord to challenge the amending formula in court. "We knew we could not do it ourselves because we couldn't make a reference to the court of appeal or the Supreme Court with the same speed the governments could," says Fontaine. "We were running out of time."

Native strategists and legal advisors met with Deborah Coyne, Clyde Wells's constitutional advisor in Newfoundland, Filmon's constitutional legal advisor James Eldridge, and various officials in New Brunswick. Paul Joffe, the Assembly of Manitoba Chief's legal advisor, left the New Brunswick meetings surprised by the officials. "They were totally freaked out by the spectre of [Quebec] separation," says Joffe. "They were prepared to agree to anything."

Joffe found Filmon, his advisors and Manitoba opposition leaders to be more open, even if they did not necessarily agree with the native strategy. Joffe was also impressed by Fontaine's access to and comfort level with Manitoba officials, especially when compared to the experience of Quebec's native leaders with provincial bureaucrats. One day Fontaine, who had been elected head of the Assembly of Manitoba Chiefs in August 1989, suggested that he and Joffe drop by James Eldridge's office to get some information. "Fontaine walked in and Eldridge said he was busy," recalls Joffe. "Phil put his face to Eldridge's, and said, 'I don't give a fuck what you're doing, I want a meeting.' Eldridge said okay."

However, native leaders found it impossible to interest anyone in their approach. "In Manitoba, they feared being accused of reviving the old French-language debate," says Fontaine. "Newfoundland wasn't interested in anything legal—they wanted to go the political route. And New Brunswick was already in bed with the feds."

By the time the Charest hearings made it to Manitoba in 1990, the legal approach had been dropped in favour of a political and educational attack. The Assembly of First Nations published *Drumbeat: Anger and Renewal in Indian Country*, a book outlining concerns that in no way opposed Quebec's legitimate demands for recognition. If there was an error in this strategy, says Fontaine, it was in not spending time educating and wooing the media. As the deadline approached, native leaders found it almost impossible to interest the media in the points they had been raising for three years.

The Assembly of Manitoba Chiefs made their case before the Charest committee on April 24, 1990, just sixty days before the Meech Lake deadline. Fontaine and several Manitoba chiefs read different parts of the document: "Our profound opposition to the Meech Lake Accord has nothing at all to do with a rejection of or lack of sensitivity towards Quebec," they noted off the top.

Then their objections were outlined: the accord failed to recognize the distinct contribution of aboriginal people to the country; naming Supreme Court judges from lists provided by provinces only discriminated against the native majority of the two territories; every province would have veto power over the creation of new provinces; native representatives were not automatically included in future First Ministers' conferences or in future negotiations on Senate reform and fisheries; no process for self-government was set in place; and, finally, the opt-out clause for national cost-shared programs failed to offer special safeguards for native programs. The accord would have to be changed.

"We were quite satisfied with our presentation," says Fontaine, "although we thought Dorothy Dobbie was an ass. I remember when we were making one of our points, she whispered to someone, 'Well, who is going to pay for this?' And this was the woman who was supposed to be parliamentary secretary for the minister of Indian affairs."

Not long after the Charest caravan left Manitoba, Lowell Murray and Norman Spector began cross-country bridge building.

Fontaine attended one of the Manitoba meetings with Metis leader Yvon Dumont, members of the Société Franco-Manitobaine and representatives from women's groups. After each group expressed their reservations about Meech, Murray spoke in reassuring tones. "He tried to leave us with the impression that there was going to be something for aboriginal people," says Fontaine, "that it would be okay, don't worry. That we will deal with these things. We will do something for you."

Fontaine was struck by the fact that the media tended to believe federal representatives rather than others who had been at the meetings. "Spector was saying there was a good possibility that a local agreement could be reached," says Fontaine. But as Fontaine saw it, there had been only vague promises: nothing had been offered that would lead one to conclude that an agreement might be possible. "It was part of a very fascinating process that we were all getting sucked into," says Fontaine of the federal government spin.

The Charest committee report recommended that a companion resolution with reforms come into effect after Meech Lake was passed. Of the twenty-three recommendations, two directly dealt with aboriginal concerns: the admission of new provinces should not require unanimity but be determined by the federal government and the would-be provinces, and aboriginal issues should be placed on the agenda for future constitutional talks.

A joint response was prepared by the Assembly of First Nations, the Four Nations of Hobbema in Alberta, the Assembly of Manitoba Chiefs and the Grand Council of the Crees.

"Although the report identifies issues of vital concern to aboriginal peoples, its conclusions and recommendations fail to put forward the concrete solutions consistently urged by aboriginal witnesses before the committee," read the statement. "Aboriginal peoples are distinct societies in Canada. Nothing is more conspicuous. This is an undeniable fact, and every Canadian member of the special committee is aware of this. Why then does the special committee lack the courage to state this elementary fact? Why then do we continue with the myth of only two founding peoples and only two languages? Why put a fundamental lie in Canada's constitution? This is the time and this is the place to correct this error. There will not be a better time and we, the First Nations, are not willing to wait."

But no one was listening.

Days after the Charest report was released, Lucien Bouchard quit the Tory party, saying the companion resolution was unacceptable because its recommendations weakened Meech. The accord's June 23 deadline was just weeks away and the premiers, suspecting they were being toyed with, threatened to take over if Mulroney didn't act. Finally, Mulroney called the premiers to a dinner meeting in Hull on June 3, 1992.

There would be seventeen people in the Manitoba delegation—the three party leaders and political staff, legal advisors and representatives of groups opposed to the accord. Phil Fontaine was invited to be an observer with the Manitoba delegation, but Fontaine wanted native leaders to represent themselves and told Filmon so.

"It wasn't a good meeting," says Fontaine. "Filmon was in a particular mood—not feisty, but he took a hard position." Filmon rejected Fontaine's request for a seat as one of the province's delegates.

"I speak for all Manitobans and I will represent them," Filmon told Fontaine.

"I don't want to belabour this point," began Fontaine.

"You *are* belabouring the point," interjected Filmon. The premier agreed that the position of the native people was unique, but he would not change his mind.

Fontaine canvassed several Manitoba chiefs about not going to Ottawa. Some worried that the Assembly of Manitoba Chiefs might appear petty or that something important would be missed; others, however, told Fontaine to do what he thought best. "We had taken the position that we wanted to be full and equal participants at the table and to accept less would be compromising our position," says Fontaine of his protest.

The Assembly of Manitoba Chiefs did send emissaries—Lloyd Stevenson; a lawyer from the Peguis band; AMC constitutional advisor Al Torbitt, and Paul Joffe—to keep an eye on things. In Ottawa they linked up with the lead native players, Assembly of First Nations representatives Georges Erasmus, Ovide Mercredi and Konrad Sioui.

On Sunday, June 3, the premiers and the prime minister met for dinner at the Canadian Museum of Civilization in Hull. On Monday morning, meetings began at the Ottawa Convention Centre.

"Our people kept on trying to lobby Newfoundland. They met with Quebec, Manitoba and New Brunswick," says Fontaine. "We discovered that there was very little information getting out, that we had as much information as these people and others who were supposed to be part of the team of bureaucrats who were supposed to be kept informed. I ended up having as much information there as Doer and Carstairs. And I was in a better position than they were," concludes Fontaine, "because I didn't compromise our position."

In Ottawa, native people were treated "as the lowest of the low," by participants and the media, says Les Campbell, then chief of staff for NDP leader Audrey McLaughlin. Campbell describes native leaders giving interviews in the parking lot while delegates and observers were questioned—more often and at greater length—in the comfort of the convention centre.

Throughout the week, sympathetic politicians attempted to update the Manitoba natives. After a briefing by Paul Tellier, Audrey McLaughlin spoke with the native delegation. "It was demeaning to everyone," says Campbell. "As soon as she [Audrey] launched into her secondhand account, she knew it was demeaning."

About midweek, Doer, Carstairs, McLaughlin and Liberal MP Ethel Blondin met with Erasmus, Mercredi, Lloyd Stevenson and Joffe to pass on what they had heard. "They, of course, were very concerned that their rights were not being considered," says Carstairs. "And all we were really doing was being an information bank for them, saying that this is on the table, to the best of our knowledge, which isn't any better than yours, really."

Mercredi says that asking Campbell for a delegate pass did not leave him especially frustrated because it was the kind of treatment native leaders had long come to expect. Fontaine agrees. "At that time we weren't really concerned at all about how we were treated. We were interested in getting the thing understood and we were there to secure some concessions. We had made a commitment and taken a position and we were going to see it through."

As the week wore on, Fontaine realized that only one thing was absolutely certain: eventually the accord would have to go back to Manitoba.

An interesting dynamic was also developing within the Manitoba delegation. Before leaving for Ottawa, the three party leaders and their staff had whittled the Manitoba task-force recommendations to three: a change to the amending formula for Senate reform and the creation of new provinces; protection for the Charter of Rights and Freedoms; and adoption of the Canada clause, which stated that the fundamental characteristics of Canada included aboriginal people and a multicultural mosaic. The mood in Manitoba would not let them manoeuvre much beyond these basics, but they were optimistic. "You had this sense that maybe there was a state of the play which was moving toward a consensus," says Greg Lyle, then strategist for Filmon. "They had tried to do the right thing with the Charest report. You had the dinner on Sunday night and people were really trying to save the country—and that was sort of exciting, that is how politics is supposed to work." The euphoria would not last long.

Both NDP and Tory insiders say they thought that Sharon Carstairs might break from the others. The Tories and the NDP, who had ruled Manitoba for decades, were united in a disaffection for the newly emerged Liberals. Since the 1988 election, the two parties had periodically worked together on house strategies to destabilize the Liberals. "In terms of personal relationships, we had none with Carstairs," says Lyle.

Jean Chrétien, who was running for the leadership of the federal Liberal party, had been giving mixed messages about the accord—first criticizing it, then saying little, and finally seeking a compromise involving add-ons for outstanding issues before the June 23 deadline (also the date of the Liberal leadership vote). Manitoba delegates worried that Chrétien's strategists, who were intimately involved in the backroom negotiations, would bring Carstairs on side. But the fears evaporated on that first Monday when Sharon Carstairs's federal contacts gave Manitoba an edge in the talks.

"I arrived in Ottawa at two o'clock on the Monday afternoon and was called into a meeting with Eddie Goldenberg, Eric Maldoff and a lawyer from Toronto, John Rae, and was given a document which was supposed to be the basis of discussion Monday morning," says Carstairs. Goldenberg told Carstairs he had received the document from Mulroney's principal secretary, Stanley Hartt. She was told that she was being given the information because Chrétien wanted her to have everything Filmon had. But Carstairs soon discovered something was amiss.

"I went from that meeting to a meeting with Filmon and realized I had a document Filmon didn't have," explains Carstairs. She showed it to him.

Grey Lyle says the premiers had been told the document wasn't ready. "The premier went back in and said, Sharon's got it. At this point we knew—this was a fix, the whole thing was a fix. That first night it was a big deal that the dinner had established a good tone. And then we knew that they were lying first thing in the day," says Lyle. "You started off the week with hopes dashed by a concrete demonstration of a real lie. Maybe that's how it works in Ottawa, but it doesn't work that way in the provinces."

Stanley Hartt made a furious call to Maldoff and Goldenberg, who were sharing a suite at the Château Laurier, soon after Filmon headed back into the meeting to discuss the accord. Maldoff in turn called Carstairs. "Hartt screamed at them that I had broken the deal," she says.

"Eric," Carstairs told Maldoff when the message was relayed back to her, "I'm not playing this game. If you guys want to deliver things to me from Stanley Hartt, and try to set me up to be a wedge with Filmon, forget it."

Carstairs had been aware of the connections between Mulroney's and Chrétien's staffs for some time. "I first heard of Stanley Hartt's involvement in January 1990," says Carstairs, "of his realizing that this thing was out of control and something had to be done. So there was this alliance on the one side between Stanley Hartt, Eric Maldoff and Eddie Goldenberg, and on the other side, the prime minister, Lowell Murray and Norman Spector," she says. (Hartt, of course, maintained his primary allegiance to the prime minister, as the others did to Chrétien.)

Carstairs says a number of assumptions—none of them positive—motivated the feds to approach her through the Liberal connection. "We were bit players, and we were not very bright," she says, sarcastically. "We were from the hinterlands, and besides, I was a woman." Primarily, she says, the leak was an attempt to divide the Manitoba delegation. "Mulroney . . . felt that if Chrétien gave me documentation then I would play along with this game."

But the strategy backfired. Carstairs's decision to share the document united the seventeen people on the Manitoba team. "We established a relationship of trust," says Lyle. "This group was being attacked by these other people; they were trying to screw us and we fought back."

The three leaders carried the new "team" message in front of the cameras: "We were sitting together every day and countering the federal strategy," says Lyle.

During the next break, federal envoys told the media that the premiers were hung up on Senate reform. This was a lie, according to Filmon's briefing of his staff. "There was a broad discussion on a number of things—the Charter, the distinct society clause, that sort of thing," says a member of the Manitoba delegation. "We saw these guys saying it was all about Senate and we said, we're being set up." Several members of the Manitoba delegation blitzed the media. "We said, these guys aren't telling the truth—just straight up, no screwing around. This is what happened. This is what they are *saying* happened."

The only two Manitobans consistently inside the meeting room were Filmon and Jim McCrae, minister of constitutional affairs. Periodically, the province's legal experts were asked in to interpret the ramifications of various proposals.

As the days passed with no deal in sight, those outside the main meeting noticed a distance developing between themselves and their premiers. It also became apparent that Wells and Filmon were the focus of attention. "I think they [federal strategists] felt that if Manitoba was left by itself, given our history, we would not be the one to say 'No' to Canada. And I think by and large they were right," says Lyle.

This "not-me" was a major Mulroney tactic, and it forged the bond between Wells and Filmon: neither wanted to leave the other alone at the mercy of federal forces.

This is when the cracks began to appear—not between the members of the delegations and their premiers, or even between Wells and Filmon, but in everyone's ability to retain their resolve against an avalanche of fear mongering. "The pressure, ultimately, was that you—as an individual—are killing Canada," says Lyle. "That was the type of tactic they used on most everybody in the delegation—primarily the leaders, but everyone else too."

On Thursday afternoon, Gil Rémillard, Quebec's minister of intergovernmental affairs, told Carstairs that the group was prepared to give Manitoba a letter signed by prominent lawyers indicating that the Charter of Rights would not be adversely affected by Meech Lake's distinct society clause. "That is not good enough," Carstairs told Rémillard.

Doer and Carstairs were called into a meeting Thursday evening. "We were presented with a whole battery of constitutional lawyers. We were never presented with a deal," says Carstairs. "We were asked a series of questions—what would be acceptable and what would not be acceptable, what would work and what wouldn't work."

That night, the CBC reported that Carstairs and Doer had rejected a tentative deal reached by the premiers. The same message was repeated in the federal media briefing.

The next morning Carstairs met with Wells and Chrétien's advisors Goldenberg, Rae and Maldoff. It was a tense meeting. Wells was showing the strain of the night before. "Clyde told me he had an offer," says Carstairs. "He was terribly distraught . . . very cold like Clyde gets when his rational being has taken over."

"We are going to get the premiers to sign this side document to say that the charter is not affected," Wells told Carstairs.

"That is not what you are going to get." Carstairs told him about the Rémillard meeting: the document was simply a letter signed by lawyers.

"You're wrong, Sharon."

"I have had this meeting with Gil Rémillard, and you are not going to get this," insisted Carstairs.

"Yes, I am going to get this," said Wells.

Carstairs says that, up to that point, she had insisted that any promise about the charter had to be absolutely enshrined in the constitution along with the accord. "But he was so convinced he was going to get this premiers' document that I said, 'Okay. It is not as good as what I want, but it is a heck of a lot better than this lawyers' letter that Rémillard is talking about. So go for it.' "

Wells told Carstairs that the Friday meeting would last a half hour. He was wrong. In the meeting, Wells discovered that Carstairs had been right: the promised document was merely a letter signed by jurists. It was one of the few remaining unresolved issues, since discussion of the Canada clause with its recognition of native people as a fundamental characteristic of the country, was to be put off until an unspecified future round of negotiations.

The premiers took a break to wait for the legal text. "Wells came to us, presented it to us as a lawyer—not as a premier, and certainly not as my friend: this is what is agreed, this is acceptable to everyone," says Carstairs.

"Clyde, is it acceptable to you?" asked Carstairs.

"Yes, it is acceptable to me," he responded.

But when Wells saw the legal text a few hours later, a clause that would allow the first ministers to review the impact of the distinct society clause had disappeared. Wells was outraged. The meeting broke up with both Filmon and Wells refusing to sign. From that moment, Wells took himself out of the process, deciding to take the document to Newfoundland where others could make the final decision.

Although Sharon Carstairs was growing increasingly discouraged, leaving became less feasible. "The only thing that stopped me from packing my bags and going home was the understanding that we had to do the best we could," says Carstairs. In conversations with the crowd waiting outside the building, she found so many people "who weren't judging Manitoba, who weren't judging Quebec, but who were just saying, 'God, you guys have got to do something.' That's what kept me there, the fact that they were so non-judgemental."

All week long, native strategists had continued their push, hoping to make a breakthrough. Their only official meeting took place on Wednesday morning with Norman Spector, secretary to the federal cabinet for federal-provincial relations. "He said he wanted to listen to us, to incorporate some of our points," says Sioui. The problems were outlined, but the meeting ended with no assurances.

AFN Chief Georges Erasmus and Konrad Sioui pressured Quebec, Ontario and Newfoundland for face-to-face meetings. Ovide Mercredi and Ethel Blondin gathered information and pressured Filmon, Wells and, when possible, Bourassa's people. Finally, Erasmus and Sioui were granted a meeting late Wednesday night with Quebec's minister for intergovernmental affairs, Gil Rémillard. For months, Erasmus and Sioui had tried to convince Quebec that native people shared much with Quebec and that they could help each other.

"We knew that, without Quebec, we would get nothing," says Erasmus.

In the meeting with Rémillard, Erasmus asked about the unanimity clause for creating new provinces, particularly in the Northwest Territories and Yukon.

"The majority of the inhabitants of these territories are indigenous," Erasmus said. "Why do you fear that we would have our own provinces? Is it because we are indigenous? Is it because you want to expand and grab a piece of the Northwest Territories, or what? Is it because you are afraid that the Inuit and the Crees in northern Quebec will eventually break from nouveau Quebec and that you would then lose it? Or is it that you want to access Labrador? What is it? This is our land. If they want to have the status of a province, it is none of your business."

"This is not negotiable," Rémillard told his visitors. He added that Quebec believed native interests were protected by the 1982 constitutional provision regarding existing rights.

"He simply said it was in the highest interest of Quebec to keep the veto on the creation of new provinces, and that this was not negotiable and that he would never agree to the fact of losing the veto," recalls Sioui.

The next day Erasmus and Sioui waited for Rémillard to arrive. "We ran at him, to ask him for a further explanation," recalls Sioui.

"It is not negotiable," came the curt reply. "You have to swallow it, because this is it."

"I saw flames in Georges's eyes," says Sioui. "I have never seen Georges so angry and I have worked with him for a long time. We were the leaders—we felt that we had importance in it all—and we were kept at the back door."

The AFN duo also met with Newfoundland Premier Clyde Wells and Ontario Premier David Peterson that week, again late at night and after much cajoling. "Peterson was very inflexible," says Erasmus. "He took the same position as Rémillard." Erasmus and Sioui sensed that Wells was listening, but they knew he didn't have room to move.

As the week progressed, visits by white politicians slowed: by Friday, even Carstairs was no longer answering her cell phone. A growing sense of defeat was settling in.

It was in this atmosphere that Manitoba's leaders, like Clyde Wells, agreed to take home the document and its companion resolution "for appropriate legislative or public consideration and to use every possible effort to achieve decision prior to June 23, 1990."

The companion resolution promised Senate reform within five years; the Territories to be included on the list for Supreme Court of Canada appointments; and aboriginal conferences to be held every three years. Everything else, including the question of new provinces, was put off for future discussion.

"We had the basics of what we were looking for," says Greg Lyle, explaining Manitoba's acceptance of the document. "We had the process for aboriginal meetings. We didn't have the Canada clause, but we felt that there was a momentum, that it would be extremely hard for them to resist without pissing off the rest of the public. We had a deal that was liveable."

Erasmus says that the native delegation never even considered accepting an offer of observer seats in the convention centre to view the signing. He, Sioui and others retired to the AFN office to watch the congratulations, self-aggrandizement and self-satisfaction of the premiers and prime minister on television.

And then it was over. The Manitoba leaders grabbed a few hours' sleep before boarding the Manitoba government plane to head home. Dawn had not yet broken.

Paul Joffe, anxious to distance himself from the Ottawa experience, drove to Montreal before dawn, worried about the call he would soon make to Assembly of Manitoba Chiefs leader Phil Fontaine.

Up in Red Sucker Lake, Elijah Harper pondered what would happen next. The Rupertsland nomination meeting was set for June 23, 1990, but Elijah was all but convinced it would be put off again since so much attention would be focussed on the accord's June 23 deadline. Still, party organizers were growing impatient. If the nomination meeting went ahead as planned, Harper believed he would be at least twenty votes short of a victory. George Hickes, a rival candidate, had signed up more than four hundred people.

Elijah says he was worried but still optimistic that his past work and his contacts would pull him through. He had yet to make the rounds of the Island Lake reserves, where the bulk of his support had traditionally been. If the nomination date was extended, Elijah felt he could still beat Hickes.

Elijah caught only glimpses of Saturday evening's events on television during a visit with his parents. "I knew I'd get the details when I got back anyway."

The specifics reached him sooner than he expected. The next day, the Red Sucker Lake chief knocked on Saul Harper's door to say that there was a call for Elijah at the band office. The caller was Phil Fontaine.

"Elijah, let's talk about what happens now," said Fontaine. "You are probably going to play a key role in this." Fontaine talked about strategy with regard to the public hearing process and the legislative rules. He did not say that he wanted to kill the accord.

"I am only one person," Harper warned Fontaine. "I will need someone there to second the motion. I can't do it alone." He added that the

Assembly of Manitoba Chiefs would have to take care of public demonstrations and the political legwork.

He also suggested that the assembly might want to consult the former deputy clerk of the Manitoba legislature, Gordon MacIntosh. "He's had a lot of experience," Harper said. "He won't need much research. He has the rules in his head and knows the constitution. If the chiefs want him, I'll call him."

Harper had originally hoped to spend another week in the North, but he said he would return to Winnipeg the next day to meet with Fontaine.

On the plane from Ottawa, the Manitoba leaders had talked of the hurdles they might face in achieving the ratification of the accord they needed to be able to go ahead with public hearings. Filmon would not admit to having any dissenters among his MLAS, although Gilles Roch had already crossed the floor to join the Liberals and Gerrie Hammond had publicly raised questions about women's rights.

"I admitted I had some problems," says Carstairs. One of those was francophone MLA Gilles Roch. "I don't know how it will go," she told Filmon. "I won't attempt to control him."

Doer said he might have a problem with Len Evans, who was concerned about the spending power provisions and the effect on national social services, and with Maureen Hemphill, who was vocal on a number of issues, including multicultural, aboriginal and women's rights.

"He didn't mention Elijah because he kept thinking—and I think all of us kept thinking—that we had gotten more for the aboriginal people than we had before," says Carstairs.

The breaking of party ranks is rare, usually a sign that the leader has lost the confidence of his or her troops. If conscience or constituents demand such an unusual action, a member usually makes the point in a way that does not damage the party or the leader. Moreover, party discipline tightens according to the importance of the issue. With the unity of the country at stake, protocol was expected to override individual protest.

Phil Fontaine and the other native leaders did not care about such niceties. While they preferred to work within the constitutional framework, they were in no mood to be forgiving. Elijah sat in the middle, both a status Indian and a member of the Manitoba legislature. Native to his core, he also had an insider's understanding of the white system.

As always, he sought guidance from personal advisors, native and white. One of the calls went to Lloyd Girman. "It was about 1:00 A.M. Monday morning when he phoned," says Girman. "I was half asleep."

"I'm wrestling with a problem," said Harper to his former deputy minister.

"That's nice," said Girman, trying to clear the fog from his brain.

"I'm getting a lot of pressure from the chiefs to vote against the Meech Lake Accord."

Early the day before, Girman had received a call from Gary Doer's legislative assistant, Lesley Turnbull, who was looking for Phil Fontaine's home phone number. In the course of the conversation, Girman recalls, "Turnbull said, 'We've made a deal. Georges Erasmus is going to kick and yell and scream but allow it to go through. In Manitoba there's not going to be much opposition. The House will vote on its conscience and Elijah can vote against it, but it's not going to make any difference.' "

Girman was wary and told Turnbull she had better call Fontaine, because "it may not cut it in Manitoba."

"I don't think it will be a problem, but that is why we need Phil's home number," replied Turnbull. "We're going to phone and clear it."

"Gary felt that Erasmus would go for a deal," Turnbull says when asked about the call. Doer's feelings were based on conversations he had had with Erasmus the previous week. "It was one of the reasons Gary would go for a deal—if Erasmus okayed it."

"I don't know how they could get the impression we were happy," says Erasmus. "We were getting more and more upset all the time.

"We met with Manitoba, Ontario and Quebec and made it very, very clear what our concerns were. Why were we bothering them if we were going to be happy? We made it clear that we couldn't live with what was there. There was no way we were changing our position after the past three years."

When Harper called early Monday morning, Girman felt that Harper's course was clear. In Girman's opinion, Harper's time with the NDP had all but run out. "You have one constituency left that you have to deal with," Girman told Elijah. "The only consideration is that you are an Indian, and the Indian community is speaking to you and that is where you have to take your guidance and direction from."

Harper, says Girman, was living in the netherworld between white and native politics, buried in personal stress. One side was asking him to break the most basic rule of the other—party loyalty. "He was feeling this massive sense of responsibility."

While Harper spoke to Girman and others, Doer, Carstairs and Filmon prepared the text for televised speeches scheduled for the following day; but they soon discovered that their sense of accomplishment was shared only by those who had been inside the convention centre. The general public exuded a hostility that native leaders would later be able to harness for their own purpose.

"There were a number of groups that understood the principles and didn't like the principles—that was fair, that was understood," says Lyle about the final package. "But the vast majority of the public who were upset about it were upset about process."

If fury was driving those seeking to kill the accord, process became their vehicle. By the time the premiers returned to their home provinces, the groups who had been fighting the accord on different fronts for three years were united in their disgust over the way the game had been played. Process had become as important as content. Elijah's role would be to force everyone to ask how corrupt that process could become before someone stopped it.

Phil Fontaine's lack of knowledge of legislative rules may have been his greatest asset. Others might have been cowed by the legislative obstacles before them, but Fontaine was oblivious to the enormity of the native undertaking. Fontaine arrived at the Charter House Hotel restaurant for their Monday morning meeting before Harper did, and he sat in a corner booth, nervously awaiting his only real weapon.

Despite the fears and anxiety Harper had been experiencing, says Fontaine, he looked "very quiet and unassuming," as always. Laughing, Fontaine adds, "And he had a good breakfast."

There are several versions of this breakfast meeting, and as many answers to the key question: how solidly on side was Harper? "I have it on very good authority in the aboriginal community that Elijah was not going to say no," says Sharon Carstairs. "He was saying, I will lose all my credibility within my party, I'll lose my seat. At first, he agreed to say no for one day and then move on to day two."

Fontaine is wary about revealing what Harper's feelings were that morning, since he fears that outsiders will misread any hesitation on Harper's part as opportunism. Fontaine believes that Harper's concerns about his future, and the pressure all native leaders would likely face, were legitimate.

"He is a hero, you know," says Fontaine. "We talked, and he was concerned about his career. George Hickes was overtaking him. 'Don't worry about that, Elijah,' " I said. " 'We will take care of that because you are key in the process.' "

Harper warned Fontaine that the native leader might be expecting too much from him. "I can stall it, but that's about all I can do. I can make a symbolic gesture."

That was a start. "What we have to do," thought Fontaine as the meeting ended, "is come up with a position that we can develop a strategy around. We know that Elijah is a key figure here. How he plays that out is not clear yet. But we are willing to put Elijah up against the creativity in the legislature."

They talked a little longer, but Fontaine was already thinking ahead. "My main concern was getting a commitment from Elijah to meet with the chiefs."

Hours later, as Harper headed to the legislature for a caucus meeting, Fontaine went to Fort Garry Place, a hotel and apartment complex where the chiefs were gathering. (All sixty-one Manitoba chiefs and hundreds of other delegates were coming to town at the expense of the federal government for a health conference.) Fontaine told the chiefs that Harper had some concerns about his future if he should stand against Meech.

The chiefs created a nine-point plan that included acquiring legal counsel, getting as many people as possible involved in the public hearing process, and generating a letter-writing campaign. Ovide Mercredi and Donna Greshner, a constitutional lawyer from Saskatchewan, wrote up the plan. It was presented and adopted.

When Harper walked into the NDP caucus meeting that morning, he found that he was not alone in his concerns about the accord. Brandon East MLA Len Evans had consistently opposed the accord because of his fears about the spending power provisions. A canvass of the room led Doer to conclude he would carry eight of his twelve members. The assumption was, however, that three of the four opponents would note their protest after the document made it past the public hearing hurdle.

Elijah told caucus that he and the chiefs were exploring their options. Doer had already spoken with Phil Fontaine and Ovide Mercredi, who were united in their anger. "They were upset about two things," says Doer, "what was in it, and the way they were treated."

"I know this puts you in an awkward position," Elijah told Doer. "If you feel awkward, I am prepared to sit as an independent."

Doer insisted that this was not necessary, but he and other caucus members warned Harper to be cautious, that he might find it impossible to turn back once he took the first step. "I knew that he would speak out against it," says Doer. "I knew he would vote against it." The question was when.

Like Pawley before him, Doer considered the potential ramifications. Filmon would need unamimous assent in the House to allow debate on the accord to begin immediately. If Harper refused to vote in favour of setting aside the rules, the public hearing process could not begin. Alone, Harper could hold the process up by refusing the necessary unanimous consent for only forty-eight hours. Still, any delay might be troublesome.

The party House leaders had met to work on the plans for province-wide hearings. "The idea was that we would go right into hearings," says Lyle. "We had, possibly, two weeks. Even if you had a lot of people talking, you could have three panels around the province and you could get it done. You could still give the appearance of holding hearings. You could still actually hear a lot of people. But it was tight—everything had to work when we got to that stage."

Harper made a few rushed phone calls from caucus, including one to Gordon MacIntosh. Harper told MacIntosh that the chiefs had problems with the accord and might seek his services.

Harper headed back to the St. Regis Hotel, his mind spinning. In the meeting hall were more than a hundred chiefs and band councillors; more were arriving all the time, both past supporters of Elijah and those who had not been impressed with his performance. Harper told the gathering what he had already told Fontaine: things were rough for him in the NDP and this would only make matters worse. He wanted assurances that he would have the chiefs' support. He warned them that they must be prepared to bear the kind of pressure that had been directed at Filmon and Wells. "Let me warn you, there will be threats," said Harper. The fallout, in funding cuts and other "punishments," could be devastating.

The chiefs listened and reassured Harper that they would stick by him.

Finally, in a sweat and with heart pounding, Harper told the chiefs his decision. "I will say no."

Chapter Eight

ANGER UNLEASHED

From the moment Elijah Harper nervously promised to say no to the Meech Lake Accord, he began a journey back into the native fold. His transformation from Manitoba's first Indian MLA to Canadian aboriginal hero began with Fontaine's wish to calm Harper's fears and show him that the chiefs and the native people of Manitoba would support him to the end.

The legislative session was scheduled to begin at 1:30 P.M. the next afternoon, Tuesday, June 12. That morning, Fontaine asked the three hundred or so chiefs and participants at the health conference to walk with a drum group from Fort Garry Place to the Manitoba legislature, a fifteen-minute hike through downtown Winnipeg, in time for the session.

The delegates were already fired up. That morning, a cocky Mulroney was quoted in the *Globe and Mail* as saying that he had "rolled the dice" on the timing of the week-long first ministers' conference, creating a crisis atmosphere in order to help focus participants' minds. "Every chief had that *Globe and Mail* article," said Doer, who also found Mulroney's gleeful admission hard to stomach. "Mulroney was bragging. It was a stupid thing to do, especially when we still had hearings in Manitoba."

Almost two hundred native people took the walk to the Manitoba legislature that afternoon. While specific plans had not been made to do so, the marchers assumed they would enter the building and watch the proceedings from the observers' gallery; but nervous legislative guards, seeing the native procession approaching, panicked and locked the doors.

"I don't know why they did that," said Fontaine, still incredulous long after the event. "It was a real blunder." Indeed, it unleashed the fury that fuelled the native cause for the next two weeks. Fontaine and others shouted at the guards to let them in and tried to force their way through a partly open door.

Inside the chamber, there was an air of anticipation. Doer, Jay Cowan and current NDP house leader Steven Ashton knew what would happen, but few others did. Ashton had met several times with Tory Deputy House Leader Jim McCrae—who also served as justice minister and attorney general—and Liberal House Leader Reg Alcock to work out the logistics of passing the accord. Ashton, an accord supporter, knew that Harper was likely to refuse leave but did not inform the other house leaders. He was convinced the accord would pass before the deadline, so there was no reason for him to break caucus secrecy.

Harper's heart was racing as he waited for his cue. Since telling the chiefs of his decision, he had been able to think of nothing but what he would do during the next day or two. "I knew when the time came, that first no would be really hard," says Harper. "I didn't know what kind of reaction there would be. I didn't know what was going to happen." He had told the chiefs and Doer that he would make his decisions a day at a time, and he had not insisted that the accord must die.

None of the reporters in the press gallery above Speaker Denis Rocan's chair had, as yet, paid particular attention to Harper; none were aware of the drama taking place outside the building. Only a few cameramen captured Fontaine's angry face as he and several dozen supporters tried to push their way into the building.

The session began with a brief prayer; then Denis Rocan, a Tory francophone first elected in 1986, called on Deputy House Leader Jim McCrae.

"Mr. Speaker, I wonder if there would be leave to move directly to orders of the day?" said McCrae.

"Is there leave of the House to move directly to orders of the day?" asked Rocan.

There was a muffled response, and nods. The House agreed and Filmon stood.

"Mr. Speaker, I wonder if there would be leave for me to move a resolution respecting the Constitution Amendment Act 1987?" asked Filmon.

There was a chorus of MLAS mumbling "leave" to indicate their agreement to bypass the rules that would delay debate on the accord for the customary forty-eight hours. Then, in the back row, Harper shook his head.

"No," he said in a barely audible voice.

For a few seconds everyone scanned the benches, unsure that they had heard correctly.

"No leave?" asked Rocan, looking around the room and then at Harper. "Leave is not granted?"

Harper shook his head again.

"Leave is not granted," ruled Rocan.

McCrae, pausing only briefly, stood and asked that the House be adjourned until the following day at 10:00 A.M. Leave was called for again, and the day's proceedings ended.

The scene had taken less than two minutes; the forty-eight-hour clock had been started. In two days, Harper would no longer be able to stop the motion from being introduced into the legislature. Debate would begin on the Meech Lake Accord, public hearings would proceed and, when they were complete, a vote on the accord would take place.

Harper looked dazed as he left the legislature with a dozen local reporters in tow. Native supporters, having finally gained access to the building, crowded around him as he was guided by Fontaine and others to the vast marble staircase adorned with its two life-sized bisons just inside the building's main doors. Elijah stood high on the stairway in front of a single microphone. His voice was so quiet that people had to push closer to hear. "I believe the decision that I made is the right decision," he said. There were cheers and applause. The drum group began a beat that would echo through the halls of the Manitoba legislature for the next two weeks.

At the bottom of the stairway, Elaine Cowan watched, overwhelmed. Harper had called her a few days earlier to talk, as usual seeking counsel, help and support. "He felt that he was going to be public enemy number one," she says. "He felt that he might have to do this, that this was what he was supposed to do, but that it was going to kill Canada. That's what he thought."

"When I saw him walking down that staircase, I thought, this is it. I knew there had to be a reason. From the time he was first elected, I knew there was something else, a reason for it, and this was it. It was incredible, a dream."

Harper expanded on the reasons for his decision, haltingly at first, and then with more clarity and strength as the days passed. "Look at the relationship with Canada in terms of when the Europeans came here. We shared our land and resources with strangers, the people who came to our homeland," he said. "That is the biggest contribution any society can make and yet we are not even recognized as having contributed that—and that is so frustrating. The Canadian constitution doesn't even mention this, not even as a founding nation of this country. There are only the French and the English.

"We are a caring people. What makes you a great nation, a great person, is what you are able to give. And certainly aboriginal people have demonstrated that. Aboriginal people are the most accommodating people in this country and I believe it's about time that you allowed the aboriginal voice to be heard."

"He has every right to do that," said a flustered Filmon to reporters. "I think, though, that he is under the misapprehension that in some way he can block the process, when all he can do is delay it."

"Every day that we come closer to the twenty-third of June without either passage or defeat in the Manitoba legislature makes it that much more difficult for all concerned," offered Carstairs. She repeated her resolve to do what she could to see the accord through and appeared upset by the turn of events. Others in her caucus, however, admitted to different feelings, says Elijah. He was told by Liberal member Avis Gray that "a lot of MLAS in caucus are clapping silently when you say no."

Said Doer that day, "If the first ministers had agreed with Manitoba's first position that aboriginal people are a fundamental characteristic of Canada, this wouldn't be happening."

Behind the scenes, there was a sense of impending chaos. The Tory and Liberal house leaders had been in almost constant communication with their NDP counterpart since the leaders' return from Ottawa, yet they had known nothing of Harper's protest, and they were angry.

"I felt personally betrayed," says Reg Alcock, the Liberal house leader. "This came as a complete surprise."

Alcock says the three house leaders had agreed to get the debate on the floor as quickly as possible, which meant Tuesday. "We wanted to maximize the time for debate and public hearings," says Alcock. "The agreement I negotiated with [the other house leaders] was that it was important that we speak as one voice to get debate into the House. Once debate began, all bets were off."

Still, the assumption was that, depending on how Ottawa responded, Harper might allow the debate to begin the next day. Indeed, Harper was insisting he would decide day by day. "I deliberately didn't say, 'We are going to kill Meech,' " says Harper. "In case something came up, I had to be open." Even if Harper did not retreat, however, debate would begin on Thursday, although it would be a few more days until public hearings could start.

"Gary Doer told us, Filmon and myself, that Elijah was just going to go along with it for one day," says Carstairs. "And the next day he said, 'I don't know.' "

Elijah and his supporters left the legislature that Tuesday afternoon for Fort Garry Place. Inspired by the day's events and fuelled by his anger over the locked doors and "rolled dice," Fontaine called on every Manitoba aboriginal person and all other supporters to sign up for the hearings. Like a modern-day drumbeat, the call went out—by phone, fax, word of mouth—through a complex native network. "We told people what our strategy was. It was to get people out to the hearings," says Fontaine. "We told them to get their friends, their enemies, sisters and brothers. It was important to get people out."

The rules stated that everyone who wished to be heard had to be given an opportunity to appear. The immediate strategy of the native plan was to stack the meetings with as many people as possible; the rules stated that everyone would be allowed to speak for as long as they wished. "We were going to get our elders to come and speak. And they can talk for hours, speak for a whole day," Elijah says, laughing at the thought. "And it would have to be translated."

But it would take more than speeches to kill the accord. Expertise would be needed to work out a more detailed plan.

Earlier that day, Harper had asked fellow MLA Jay Cowan to call Gordon MacIntosh to explain that the chiefs had agreed to retain McIntosh and that they would be in touch. Since his days as legislative assistant to the former Northern Affairs minister, Harper had remained close to Cowan, who was an expert on the rules of the House and a top legislative strategist.

Cowan was a Meech Lake supporter—"I thought it important that Meech Lake succeed to keep Quebec in the process," he says—but he sympathized with the native arguments and believed they had every right to push their cause. He decided to assist Elijah and the chiefs. His goal, says Cowan, was to help them gain enough leverage to force concessions from Ottawa before Meech became a reality. A protest by Elijah would be an irritant, but not lethal to Meech, he reasoned.

Gordon MacIntosh, deputy clerk of the Manitoba legislature the year Harper was elected, was the second pro-Meech white advisor drawn into the native strategy that week. "I had some fairly strong views about Meech Lake," says MacIntosh. "I was very concerned that if it didn't pass it would threaten the unity of the country."

MacIntosh was an expert on legislative procedure. A year before he resigned as deputy clerk in 1985, he had accepted a contract with the Manitoba government to rewrite all the rules of the House in light of current practice. Cowan explained that Harper wanted advice on whether one person could kill the accord in the legislature.

"Theoretically, it is possible," said MacIntosh, although he got the impression that Cowan did not agree (and MacIntosh himself thought the chances were remote). "The rules are rather loose. They are really intended for a group of people who have a common objective. Sooner or later, votes can be put together under the rules to get things done."

MacIntosh did not hear from the Assembly of Manitoba Chiefs or Harper for the rest of the day, and he began to wonder if he was really part of their plan. But that night, on the way to a family dinner in the revolving restaurant of the Fort Garry, MacIntosh bumped into Harper on the steps of the hotel. Harper was heading out from his apartment in the complex.

"Come meet Phil," Harper said, leading the way to the lounge. "By the way, what do you think of Meech?"

MacIntosh paused, wondering how honest to be. "I think it should go through to keep the country together," he said. Harper seemed unfazed.

MacIntosh was introduced to Fontaine and others who were sitting at the table. Fontaine explained that they were looking for help on House rules. In reply, MacIntosh gave his opinion of Meech Lake.

"We don't want you for your personal views," Fontaine said. "We want your professional advice."

"Okay, but we will have to meet first thing in the morning," replied MacIntosh. "There is no time to waste." They agreed to meet at MacIntosh's downtown office at 8:00 A.M. "It was a tremendous conflict for me," MacIntosh says. "On the one hand I was concerned about what would happen if Meech Lake didn't pass, and on the other I was trying to help people who were oppressed and discriminated against."

His decision was, he says, influenced by his belief that the accord would not die as a result of the native protest. "I understood that there was a risk to it," he says, but he increasingly saw his involvement as an opportunity to give native leaders some leverage.

The handful of people at the 8:00 A.M. meeting would become the core strategists at every meeting—Elijah, Phil Fontaine, Ovide Mercredi who had flown in to help, Al Torbitt, Lloyd Stevenson and Jay Cowan.

The meeting set out the day's assignments: Elijah would say no again that afternoon to keep things on hold; MacIntosh would begin research on the rules immediately and would check the order paper introducing the accord for any potential problems. The group agreed to meet again at 4:00 P.M., with Cowan coming a little earlier so that the two rules experts could exchange information. MacIntosh and Cowan began drawing up charts of what the daily proceedings might look like.

MacIntosh had not glanced at a rule book since his 1984 contract. "I recalled the routine procedures; it was the finer points I had to become familiar with again." Once he started, however, he found that the details came back quickly.

While MacIntosh pored over his rule books, the Assembly of Manitoba Chiefs called Winnipeg lawyer Jack London to ask him to advise the chiefs at the afternoon meeting. London had some experience with aboriginal rights cases, but he had never been professionally involved with the assembly. He had met Fontaine years earlier when the then-chief of Fort Alexander had asked for help to prepare an appearance before a legislative committee studying amendments to the municipal property assessment act.

London had been vocal in his opposition to the Meech Lake Accord, believing it "would balkanize Canada in terms of the delivery of social services." He had appeared as an accord critic in the media and had written articles against it. But by the time London showed up at the Fort Garry that Wednesday, he had been converted. "I've changed my mind," London told a reporter on June 12, the day Elijah said his first no. "Or, at least I've fought the battle as best it could be fought."

The pressure-filled week in Ottawa had changed his mind, he says. He watched the crisis mentality take hold among the participants and even became, he says, a victim himself. The CBC had flown London to

Ottawa at the start of the week to do colour commentary. Obviously, no breakthroughs came on the Sunday—or for days afterward—but London was in town at CBC expense, and so he was invited to appear on "The Journal" that evening with Meech supporter Peter Russell of the University of Toronto.

"I said that I thought Meech was not going to be successful—that they weren't going to be successful at the first ministers' conference unless everybody, and that included Quebec, made concessions," London recalls.

When the interview ended, host Barbara Frum and a producer said that they were going to redo the piece for Central Canada.

"Why?" asked London.

"Because you expressed your opinion," Frum said.

"She said that the purpose of my participation was to give an observation based on some kind of objective set of standards," says London. "So we did it again in Ontario. I was asked different questions and I don't think that part about concessions appears in the second go-round."

Later, London says it struck him that both he and Russell had said the same thing from opposite viewpoints. "I began to wonder why it was that mine was opinion and his was fact." That incident and others the same week had led him to conclude that the fight was over.

"I don't see what I can offer," London told Fontaine's office.

"They'd like you to come down anyway," came the reply.

"It was a busy day, and I said to myself, 'Am I going to do this?' And as I was saying that to myself I went outside, I walked down Broadway and Main and went into this huge room, which was stifling hot, cameras everywhere, four or five hundred people in the room."

The basement meeting room in the Fort Garry is a monument to excess. Every wall, window well and light fixture is painted or adorned with cherubs and full-figured women. London thought, "What an absurd place for a group of aboriginal people to be holding a meeting on the future of Canada."

Up front that afternoon sat Gary Doer, Sharon Carstairs and Jim McCrae. They had agreed to appear before the native health conference delegates to explain why they were supporting the latest package.

"I am not here to sell the deal," said Doer, the most forthright of the three. "I am here to apologize to you for failing to get the objectives set out in the [Manitoba] task force report." Nonetheless, Doer said, without the package, constitutional reform and native aspirations could be delayed for decades. McCrae and Carstairs echoed the sentiment. The room was hostile.

An hour later, with the meeting looking like it might carry on indefinitely, McCrae got up to leave, saying he had another commitment.

"You should have walked out of the first ministers' conference," shouted one delegate.

"You have a commitment to Manitoba: now stay there!" demanded another, as a woman grabbed McCrae's arm and ushered him back to his seat. Others moved to block the exit. Forced to stay for another ninety minutes, McCrae was livid. "The tactic used this afternoon reminds me of how I felt in Ottawa," he said.

There was one other piece of important business at the meeting: a special ceremony to present Elijah with an eagle feather, a symbol of strength.

Harper was wearing a red rose in the lapel of his special occasion suit; his hair was braided rather than in its usual loose ponytail. Hours earlier he had sat in the House, fingering a two-inch-high stack of pink message slips, and said his second no to the accord, this time to thunderous applause and whoops of approval from supporters sitting in the public gallery.

The feather ceremony is usually private, but organizers allowed the television and newspaper cameras to document this event.

"We want to present one of our most prized symbols to Elijah Harper for the courage that he has displayed in standing up to oppose something that was wrong, and having the courage to risk things that he holds valuable in order to do this," said elder Paul Huntinghawk. "We want to present him with an eagle feather and we want to do this in a sacred way. We want to do this on behalf of the concern that we have in our hearts for each other, for our children and for their future. We want him to know that he does not stand alone, that we are behind him."

Elijah stood up, looking damp under the lights and somewhat humbled by the presentation.

"Elijah, it took a lot of courage to do what you did and we know that you had the backing of the chiefs," continued the elder. "But we want you to know that you also have the backing of the people, the people who are watching from the sidelines. It took courage to do what you did. Now you have to go ahead, and you have to go further.

"You have to do a lot of other things, because we're all going to keep watching you now, for inspiration. We watch our leaders and we want you to know that what you do, we approve of. I would like to present you with this eagle feather and we pray for you. If you take care of him, he will take care of you. That feather, that bird is coming anywhere if you talk to him, and you can hear him when he is coming. The owner is our leader. You be strong, you be strong from now on, and his words are going to be strong."

Harper looked sombre as he took the eagle feather in his left hand. The elder called for the honour song and a procession to circle the room. The drums echoed loudly. Elijah led with awkward steps. Two recent graduates from medical school were asked to accept the honour of following immediately behind him. Phil Fontaine fell in next, with the chiefs. Phil, in a sports jacket and golf shirt, smiled broadly as he walked. Ovide Mercredi, in his usual dark suit, hugged a woman who was in tears. Elijah walked around the room shaking hands. The camera lights caused him to sweat profusely. He was smiling.

With the circle complete, Harper spoke to the crowd. "As the first treaty Indian MLA in this country, I hope that I have not failed you, that I have stood up for the rights of aboriginal people. And I hope that you will continue to support me in that stand for ourselves and our children. So, with these few words, thank you very much for this sentiment."

There was a standing ovation and long applause. From that day on, Harper and the feather would be inseparable, and the image of the two together seared into the Canadian psyche.

Jack London was watching the proceedings when Fontaine and Mercredi made their way over to him. "There is a meeting later this afternoon with the counsel we have hired for Elijah Harper—Gordon MacIntosh. Please go to that meeting."

London went. In the room were Elijah, Jay Cowan, Lloyd Stevenson and Al Torbitt. Not long into this first strategy session, London understood the goal. When he returned to his office after the session, he opened a new file: "The Blockage of Meech." "It was clear to me from that very moment."

That Wednesday afternoon strategy session was especially important. The Meech debate would begin the next day, and Elijah had to be ready with points of order and matters of privilege to slow the process. MacIntosh had worked out a minute-by-minute analysis of each proceeding and what could be done with it to stall debate. Others, such as Lloyd

Stevenson, prepared questions for the legislative question period.

Jay Cowan had an important piece of news: the order paper giving notice that the Meech Lake Accord was to be debated in two days' time had not been filed correctly. According to the rules, the forty-eight-hour countdown could not begin until the document was filed with the clerk and distributed to the members in the legislature before the House adjourned. When Harper said his first no on the Tuesday, the order paper had been blank. The error was noted and a new order paper listing the resolutions was brought into the House before adjournment; however, it was not distributed before the members left for the day. It could be argued, therefore, that notice had not been given on Tuesday and that debate on the accord could not legitimately begin on Thursday.

Cowan had picked up on the error and queried NDP house leader Steven Ashton. Ashton, another northern MLA, was also offering Elijah advice on the rules when he could.

"I went back to [Tory House Leader Jim] McCrae and said, 'There is a potential problem here,' " says Ashton. "He said, 'Don't tell anybody.' But it wasn't a question of not telling anybody. People already knew."

The native strategy meeting was a short one. London would represent the interests of the Assembly of Manitoba Chiefs, particularly in any discussion with federal officials; MacIntosh would do the same for Elijah. Having watched federal government attempts to divide other allies, the chiefs had decided that there would be no direct contact between Harper or Fontaine and federal officials. The approach would also emphasize to Ottawa that the ideas and strategies being developed in Manitoba represented the collective decision-making of the gathered chiefs.

During the next two weeks, federal officials would try time and again to co-opt individuals who might be able to influence Fontaine or Harper, just as the feds had tried to divide the Manitoba delegation in Ottawa. Fontaine recalls getting a call from someone he had not heard from in years. He could only laugh—both at the tactic and at the stupidity of the federal government.

MacIntosh left the Wednesday meeting for the legislative library to research the order paper technicality.

"Early on we weren't sure if this was really a strong point or not," says MacIntosh, "but the more I got writing it, the more I saw that, in administrative law, if you don't have notice on something that may affect your rights, it can be critical to the decision that is eventually made.

"I kept thinking through the other points, making changes, making sure that the logic was correct and that the flow in the argument was right." The federal government had instigated a state of crisis in order to get things done, and it was for precisely such situations that the rules had been written, MacIntosh would argue. Therefore, they must be strictly adhered to.

He drafted Thursday's action plan in time for an 11:00 A.M. meeting at the legislature. "My blood was running pretty fast," he says. "We had to make decisions. We had to go through the draft. I wanted to make sure Elijah was comfortable with the draft and had input from whoever wanted to give it, but particularly Jay and Jack."

"This could be the bomb," MacIntosh told the chiefs, and for the rest of the day, the point of order would be referred to by the players as "the bomb."

"What do you think the speaker's ruling will be?" asked one chief.

"I have to warn you," replied MacIntosh, "the speaker does not always rule just on the merits of a particular point of order. He may consider other issues, sort of the will of the House. And, of course, there are political considerations."

Just after noon MacIntosh and London raced back to MacIntosh's office to incorporate suggested changes to the document MacIntosh had written. MacIntosh desperately wanted to get the revised document back to Elijah well before he had to go into the House at 1:30 P.M.

Harper waited at the legislature building. From then on, he would have to focus on every nuance in the House. One memo warned him to watch for anyone trying to catch the speaker's eye, because they might be about to introduce something that would derail the native plan. He knew that Cowan and Ashton would offer him guidance where they could, but it might not be enough. He sat in the caucus room, lit yet another Export "A" and waited.

At this point, says Girman, all the attention and energy of the Canadian people—native and non-native—the federal government and the NDP caucus were concentrated on Elijah. "There was an enormous weight of responsibility," says Girman. In various conversations, Harper wondered aloud if he was doing the right thing.

London and MacIntosh set off for the legislature: they had ten minutes before Harper had to go in. When a truck pulled in front of them and stopped, they became practically apoplectic. London finally pulled the car up to the legislature doors and MacIntosh ran into the building as the bells were ringing.

In the caucus room, MacIntosh handed Harper the seven-page point of order, a five-page matter of privilege and a few other motions in case they were needed. Harper was reading the documents as he headed down the hall and into the chamber.

MacIntosh, Fontaine, Mercredi, London and a few others watched the proceedings on television in the NDP caucus room. The gallery was filled to overflowing. Embarrassed by the locked-door episode, the government had publicly apologized and had set up a room with a closed-circuit television for the hundreds of observers who couldn't fit into the gallery.

The preliminaries out of the way, Harper took up five minutes to comment about the locked doors and to recommend that the policies of gallery attendants be referred to a committee for study. The motion was seconded by Ashton. Jim McCrae and Reg Alcock also spoke on the subject.

The speaker then welcomed various guests in the gallery.

Elijah stood again. "Mr. Speaker, I seek your advice. I have a point of order regarding today's order paper. I would like to know when I should raise it, now or after the question period."

"We will deal with that matter after oral questions," said Rocan.

Harper then began a series of exchanges about the accord with Premier Gary Filmon. "Can the premier tell the House and the people of his province why he returned home without any changes to the Meech Lake Accord?" began Harper. He would ask all the questions during the next hour. They were directed mostly to Filmon, with a couple to the minister of northern affairs, Jim Downey, and to McCrae as justice minister and attorney general.

Finally, question period ended and Denis Rocan called on Harper to present his point of order.

"My point of order relates to the resolution of the first minister [Filmon] and government house leader [McCrae] appearing on today's order paper," began Harper. "These motions, Mr. Speaker, appear to be out of order because no notice was given.

"On Tuesday, June 12, Order Paper and Notice Paper No. 145 was distributed. It contained no notice of motion. I have a copy available for you here. To my knowledge, this order paper was the only one distributed to MLAS on Tuesday before adjournment of the House."

He then went through the arguments as agreed.

"This is not a time for illegalities, for breaking rules," Harper said. "It is a time for order. It is a time for due process. . . . I ask that the motions of the first minister and the government house leader be struck from the order paper."

Inside the caucus room there are thumbs up and a collective sigh of relief. "I had tried to write the way he speaks," says MacIntosh. "He spoke so well—it sounded so good."

Steven Ashton stood to respond. This was significant for two reasons. It signalled that Elijah was not alone; the NDP caucus was behind him—at least on this point. It also separated Ashton from the other House leaders, who became so angry they later refused to speak to him.

Ashton spoke of the history of native people in Canada as a trust that had been betrayed over and over again. "I believe that you, Mr. Speaker, have to deal with the point of order raised by the member for Rupertsland in that context," said Ashton. "If our constitutional changes are to have any legitimacy, it has to be through the proper process."

McCrae stood last, arguing that Harper should have raised the issue on the Tuesday. "We are here today to debate a matter and to do the business of Manitoba and to do the business of the nation," concluded McCrae. "Mr. Speaker, I suggest we get on with it."

Rocan asked for fifteen minutes to study the "very, very complex point of order."

Everyone stood, hovering as if not sure what to do. Harper turned to Cowan and they talked; Ashton joined them. Reg Alcock sat shaking his head. Filmon turned to McCrae and seemed to be asking, "What is going on?" The two men entered into an intense conversation. McCrae responded.

"I am pretty sure," says Greg Lyle, "that the advice McCrae had [for Filmon] was not just that it had been fixed in terms of the house leaders, but that it was fixed in terms of what would stand up against a challenge. No one wanted to go to all this effort and then blow it on a technicality."

The announcement of such a short recess distressed those sitting in the NDP caucus. MacIntosh had predicted a lengthy recess and doubted that Rocan would reconvene the House that day if the point was going to get an honest examination. "Either the speaker seriously misjudged the nature of the point of order and the seriousness of it," thought MacIntosh, "or he had his mind made up."

MacIntosh turned to London. "I'd say it is sixty-forty against it going in our favour."

Harper had returned to the caucus room. London remembers he was very nervous, pacing. "We talked a bit, chatted, to try and relax him," London recalls. "At one point I called him over to the window looking over the legislative grounds." The pair looked out at the Louis Riel monument in the distance.

"You know, Elijah, if we're successful in this, and if we stick it through, it is quite possible that one day there is going to be a monument to you next to the one of Louis Riel," London said.

For the first time that day, Harper smiled. "Does that mean I'm going to have to be hanged?"

Fifteen minutes passed. Then half an hour.

"A lot of things were running through my mind," says Elijah. "What if we had to vote? What were we going to do? What was I going to do? I figured at that time that we had a pretty good case." Even if the ruling went Harper's way, however, it did not mean his work was over. "If he ruled in my favour, the government would challenge the speaker." That in turn would demand a countermove, and on and on until the deadline was reached.

Finally, almost an hour after the speaker had recessed the House, the bells rang. "I would like to apologize for taking so long," began Rocan after everyone was seated. "It is similar to the first minister who went for a dinner and came back a week later. I went for fifty minutes." There was sparse, nervous laughter. Then everyone held their breath.

"I have reviewed the points raised by the honourable member for Rupertsland and have concluded that they are valid."

The word "valid" hung in the legislature. In the NDP caucus room everyone waited for the "but." It did not come. Rocan's ruling would force the government to file the motion anew. Once filed, Rocan said, the resolutions could not be discussed for four days. The additional two days had been added to guarantee time for translation into French. He was doing this, he said, to ensure "that every step in the process is totally above question, to guard against any possibility of a subsequent court challenge to the validity of the actions taken in the House."

The ruling meant that instead of the debate beginning on the Monday, the latest date native strategists had hoped for, no debate could start until the following Wednesday—three days before the Meech Lake deadline.

"I didn't catch on right away," says Harper. He was barely able to make his way back to the caucus room through the crowd of supporters and media. "But I knew we had another two days."

"From that moment on," says London, "Elijah became a truly central character in the piece. It was only once the ruling of the speaker was made that he had any real significant decision to make. Real decision-making comes when you know you have the power."

Applause followed Harper as he headed to the caucus room. The drums were beating and euphoria permeated the hallways. Inside the NDP caucus room, the native leaders and their strategists sat quietly. "We're not talking party here," says MacIntosh. "We're talking solemnity."

Fontaine and Jay Cowan stood together near an open window on the second floor. Jay described how the chiefs could use this moment as leverage. "Jay was still talking about a meeting with the prime minister," says Fontaine. "He told me that we had scored with Meech, that this was a moral victory."

Fontaine, however, saw much more. "We had done it. I couldn't see for the life of me how they were going to do all this. The number of people on the speaking list was growing every day and we had already figured out how we were going to handle the public hearing process.

"I knew that it was over," he says, tears welling at the memory. "I had an overwhelming sense of, of . . . that it was over, that we had done it, that we had this tremendous power. You don't get many moments like that, not in one lifetime."

"I did not fully understand what they had hoped to accomplish," says Cowan. "I think, from their perspective, they had wasted a hundred years, and another hundred years was not going to make a lot of difference."

An emergency chiefs' and strategists' meeting was called by Fontaine a few hours later.

"This meeting of the chiefs is one I will never forget," says MacIntosh. "It was the first time I had been at a meeting with all the chiefs. There were speeches I wish were recorded. The emotion and the logic melded together to make great observations on what was unfolding."

Phil Fontaine chaired the meeting, calling on all the chiefs to speak. Elijah spoke of his role, his background, how he had been raised to have concern for his people and with the knowledge that everyone had to do what they could. Mercredi talked of how Elijah had slept on the floor of a hotel room the night before and how they had burned sweet grass and smudged the smoke at sunrise with an eagle feather.

"Everyone knew that the moment was significant, how they were going to use that moment," says MacIntosh. "It was solemn—not sad by any stretch of the imagination. I think some of us were overwhelmed by the success—not the power, but the obligations that could be exercised."

The speeches focussed on how the moment fit into the continuum of native history.

"We understand that, in the short run, this will cost us," said one chief. "They will penalize us. We will not be able to get what we are entitled to. But it doesn't matter. We must be able to stand with pride in the eyes of our grandchildren, and it is for them that we must take our stand."

"This meeting changed me," says MacIntosh. "This meeting brought home to me what my role was. It wasn't just a concept; it showed me through their stories how the history of aboriginal people has to change. I had a greater perception of how they had been overlooked. It was so clearly wrong that they wouldn't be recognized in a constitutional amendment before anyone else."

London found the meeting an equally profound experience. He had thought of himself as an important player, but the chiefs' meeting "was about a recognition of just how limited we really were in our ability to perceive the continuum of time and the importance of the struggle of these people. We are from the privileged class; we can't know that intuitively."

London learned a new way of doing things from Fontaine. "Phil is the epitome of a man who listened to his environment, very carefully processed the information and the innuendo, and then made a decision."

At the meeting, says London, "I watched the consensus model of decision-making operate for the first time and recognized that my preconceived notion—that the world should operate in a certain manner—was ridiculous. I was watching a decision-making methodology from which we have a lot to learn."

Similar chiefs' and strategists' meetings would be held daily until the deadline had passed. Each meeting began with a Cree or Ojibwa prayer and an opening comment from Fontaine. London would then brief the chiefs and answer any questions. Then each chief was called upon to speak. There was no time limit on their comments and no interruptions allowed. If necessary, there would be a second or third round of comments. Elders and band councillors were also allowed to speak. People would often leave the room to consult with elders and others back home.

"And then, at the end of a period of time, we would know what it was that we were supposed to do," says London. "No one ever put their hand up in the air. There were always different numbers of people around. There was no concept of quorum because, as I learned throughout the weeks, there was a network of information delivery back and forth into the regions and then back to the centre. It didn't matter if a person was sitting in the room or not, they were part of the process.

"I was never part of the directing force, Gordon MacIntosh was never part of the directing force, Jay Cowan was never part of the directing force. The only directing minds in the entire episode were those of the chiefs and of Harper—the chiefs because they were the intellectual resource, thoughtful, strategic minds, and Harper who put up the nerve and the guts for the fulfilment of those objectives. Neither could have done it without the other. They were really a partnership."

But all was not harmonious. While the Manitoba chiefs sat discussing what to do next, questions were being raised about the whereabouts and role of Assembly of First Nation's Chief Georges Erasmus.

Although everyone had insisted that absolutely nothing could be done after Harper said his first no, Erasmus and other national native leaders had met in Ottawa on that same day, June 14, 1990, with Justice Minister Kim Campbell, Indian Affairs Minister Tom Siddon and Senator Lowell Murray to make one last plea.

"We had gone through this before, in the early '80s," says Erasmus, referring to the about-face on indigenous rights during the patriation of the constitution. "We thought there were still some clauses that could be added [to the Meech Lake Accord] that we could live with while waiting for the next round." These included a distinct society clause for aboriginal people; an amendment on the northern boundaries; reversion to the original amending formula for the creation of new provinces; and the right to have native leaders sit at all constitutional negotiating tables as equals.

Erasmus left the meeting disappointed. "The debate seems to be between English and French Canadians," he told reporters after the encounter. "We aren't even the meat in the sandwich."

Despite the rejection, the Assembly of First Nations continued to strategize. Erasmus says it was an AFN decision that Mercredi head to Manitoba while Erasmus made his way to Newfoundland. The feeling was that Elijah's protest would amount to little more than a gesture. Erasmus believed the only opportunity to influence events would be in Newfoundland, where the prime minister and several premiers were taking Premier Clyde Wells up on his promise to let them make their pro-Meech case before the House. As Erasmus drove to the east coast to lobby (and then to holiday in the area after the accord deadline had passed), he kept in touch with the AFN by car phone in case there were any major developments. But the car phone did not work well in the Maritimes, says Erasmus, and without knowing that events were heating up in Manitoba, he drove on. He would eventually make it to Manitoba, but only after the major decisions had been made, reducing him to little more than a figurehead in the dying days of the accord. Elijah soon discovered, however, that even Erasmus's limited role was seen by some as too much.

Chapter Nine

ON THE RAPIDS

Finally, after three years of begging for attention, native leaders suddenly found Ottawa keenly interested in the possibility that they might have something to say.

"Once it happened, there were feds everywhere," says Greg Lyle. "They had constitutional experts in town should there be another ruling. There was certainly a full court press. But it was sort of like closing the barn door after the horses."

By Friday, June 15, the day after the ruling, the mood in the Manitoba legislature had shifted dramatically. Filmon appeared almost giddy. He answered reporters' questions with due seriousness but it appeared as if a great weight had been lifted from his shoulders. His comments had less to do with Harper and the NDP than with the faulty process that had led to this precipice.

The feds also had Newfoundland to worry about. Clyde Wells had returned home feeling abused after his week in Ottawa. A year later, he said that signing his name to the final document, as qualified as the signature was, was "my biggest regret about that whole seven-day dinner."

When debate in Manitoba was stopped, Wells says, "the red light went on. It was not going to be easy, if it was achievable at all." Still, Wells said he did not have a sense then that Meech Lake would die in Manitoba. He kept in touch with events through daily phone calls to Filmon and less frequent talks with Sharon Carstairs. In exchange,

Wells passed on information about events at his end.

Federal officials increased the pressure on Filmon, Carstairs and Doer, but their tactics had little impact. The mood had changed. The party leaders seemed to know that it was out of their hands and that the chance of the accord passing was now slight.

Still, no one would admit that the accord was truly dead. "No one ever sat down and said, 'It is over,' " says Lyle. "But all the individuals in the system pretty quickly started saying that it was gone." Nonetheless, the native leadership remained on guard against a surprise attack from the Filmon Tories or Ottawa. The first offensive, reasoned the native strategists, would be a challenge to the speaker's extra forty-eight-hour delay for French translation, since the resolution document had already been translated. But the appeal did not come.

"We were just going to do what was being asked," says Carstairs. "And part of that was based on our anger over the roll-the-dice scenario, in which Mulroney got too cute by half."

When asked by Jack London if the Liberal caucus would honour all the House rules, Carstairs replied, "There will be no violation of the rules, Jack. If you guys can play this thing up, straight, and get your rulings and do your thing, then don't worry about the Liberal party."

"Even if we all passed the accord, if we broke the rules then the whole thing could be thrown out in court," says Greg Lyle, explaining why the Tories did not mount a counterstrike. "It wasn't just a matter of getting political agreement. You had to be doing things in a way that was demonstrably right, because there was no question that there were still many people opposed to this thing, and they would continue to fight it."

At least three Meech opponents in the NDP caucus were anxious to publicize their opposition, but Doer felt that it made better political sense to leave it to the aboriginal people: they were the only group that had the true moral imperative to fight the document. "If the accord is to falter, it should do so on the justice question about aboriginal issues and not on other items like Len Evans's position on spending power," argued Doer. After much heated debate, Doer's view prevailed.

On the day of the ruling, Carstairs placed a call to Bourassa. "It was late Thursday when I realized that the no was probably going to extend all the way through," says Carstairs. "I phoned Robert and I said, 'If there is any way you can convince the prime minister to do something . . . you have to do something.' "

"This conversation never happened," Bourassa coolly demurred.

The next day, rumours started floating that Lowell Murray would be travelling to Winnipeg to talk to aboriginal people. "At that point, I thought maybe we were still going to get something," says Carstairs.

Friday was a turning point for Harper, the day he stepped out of his fear and walked into the arms of his native supporters, never to look back again. The moment came at the Winnipeg Convention Centre, where the Assembly of Manitoba Chiefs and supporters had gathered after the day's legislative proceedings. Hundreds of native people were arriving daily from across the country.

Harper walked in to a standing ovation. When the cheers died down, Fontaine called Harper up to the microphone and explained that some women had asked to make a presentation to show Elijah their appreciation of his efforts. Dozens of women lined the perimeter of the room. One by one, in a slow procession, they walked up to Harper, gave him a hug or kiss and handed him a rose. Some exchanged a few words with him. As Harper's hands grew full, he passed on a bundle of flowers so that he could accept more.

When the line was finished, Harper stood at the microphone for several minutes, tears in his eyes, the camera lights highlighting the angry scar under his chin.

"It's been . . . ," he began, a sob catching in his throat. He coughed, then continued in an agonizingly tight voice, "a very difficult week for me." There was another long pause as he squeezed his eyes shut again. Others in the room began to cry. "Because what I am doing I feel . . . I feel it is not just for aboriginal people [but] also for other people in Canada."

A sentence finally complete, there was brief applause. The tears were still in Elijah's voice as he continued.

"I love this country, too. That's why I've said we shared this land with other people. But the strength that I got was from all of you, and also from all the elders, the prayers that have been placed to our Creator. And I believe he has answered and heard our prayer.

"Last night I phoned home, and I spoke to my dad." Harper stopped again, checked another sob, and then carried on. "And he assured me to continue the fight. And the elders at home have been building fires in the evenings and praying for us—not only for me but for the leaders, so that they may make the right decision. And I believe we have made that decision, the right decision, but we still have to go through a few more days. And I can assure you there is support to kill the Meech Lake Accord."

It was the first time that Harper had stated that he was working to ensure the accord did not pass. The political hedging was gone. He had one purpose—to be the instrument of the native fight—no matter where that took him. Elijah Harper had returned to his world and he was welcome.

The applause was thunderous.

"All I am going to say is thank you very much for your help, and I've tried my best to do the right thing with the advice of people—Phil, Ovide, the chiefs and our legal counsel—and every little thing they have done this week has helped us be strong and united. I still call upon my elders to continue praying to ask for knowledge, to ask for understanding, to ask for wisdom; but also to keep us strong, to have that courage, and also to endure, because all those things are what will make us strong.

"It is strength that helps unite. Although we are poor people we are strong, and I can tell you we have won a moral victory in Canada." He paused to let the clapping stop. "The struggle is not over. We still need to be united and be strong."

He then invited everyone to a demonstration on the grounds of the Manitoba legislature on Thursday, June 21, three days before the accord deadline. The day had been declared Aboriginal Solidarity Day, and thousands of native people from across the country would be part of the event.

A native woman stood at a microphone to respond. "I recognize you as being, in my mind, the only hope for aboriginal people in Canada right now to have that voice, that single voice, and I give you from the bottom of my heart, and I know I carry it from my people, my heartfelt thank you," she said, tears in her eyes. "I feel very humble."

"His position all along was symbolic," says Phil Fontaine, who was there watching the scene. "Elijah got pulled along with this tremendous show of support by the aboriginal community. They were looking to him. They were already seeing him as this important figure."

Months later, aboriginal people would talk about where they were when Elijah stood up for them, how they watched every moment on television, how they cried when they saw him crying. The sense of the empowerment of aboriginal people across Canada was there in the room with Harper that day. Their strength was his strength, he says.

Harper will speak of the roses ceremony for a long time afterward. The crying, Harper will feel compelled to insist, was not because he felt weak, but because he was overcome by the strength and power coming from the outpouring of affection.

"The feeling I got was overwhelming," says Harper. "It was from the people there. And I felt this sense of responsibility, a sense of 'do something' placed on you as the only one," he says. The tears are there again as he speaks. "But once I went through that, I was ready to take on the world, there was so much power."

Ovide Mercredi also spoke that day. "What you saw there is part of what is happening in our society," he said, "the healing of the soul of our nation, and that cannot be stopped. And we will not allow anyone to stand in the way of the full expression of the aboriginal spirit."

Federal officials, oblivious to the transformation in the aboriginal community and its supporters, descended on Winnipeg, well-worn pressure tactics at the ready. The message to the provincial party leaders was simple: set aside the rules and anything else standing in the way of the Meech Lake Accord.

"But it simply wasn't a question for us," says Greg Lyle. "The process question made it an even bigger issue. We had fought for the rules in the first place. We had told Ottawa what the rules were. We'd gone and done speeches, press conferences—everything we could to let them know—but they had made their own decision. They had done the "roll-the-dice" thing."

Threats were also coming in from Quebec: Bourassa vowed Quebec would reject any future constitutional negotiations dealing with aboriginal issues if the native lobby killed the accord.

The Filmon government did what was required in the House, according to the rules. A second notice of motion had been filed the day of the speaker's ruling so that debate could begin the following Wednesday, June 20. Whether by design or omission, however, the government failed to cut off the list for public hearings. By the end of the first week more than 600 people were scheduled to speak. By the time debate began the following week, there would be almost 3500.

So many phone calls, telegrams and fax messages were pouring into Harper's office from across the country that staff from other MLAS' offices were called in to handle them. The response was mostly supportive, but a few people disagreed with Harper. "Do not think that the rest of English-speaking Canada will thank you for defeating the Meech

Accord," wrote Hamilton-West Conservative MPP Richard Allen. "Initial polls tell us that your province is now the only one where a majority are opposed to the new constitutional package. The rest of us want to get off the French-English preoccupation. . . . *We* want to see this country whole again."

Typically, Harper's days began with dashes between NDP caucus meetings and strategy sessions with the chiefs and other advisors. Harper would then acquaint himself with the statements he was to make and any problems that might arise in the House. As the threat to the accord became more obvious, television, radio and newspaper interviews were added. The media, which grew to include dozens of national and international journalists, stalked his every move, as did his supporters. He was forced to change hotels repeatedly by police who worried for his safety after death threats were called in.

On the weekend, eleven armed aboriginal guards appeared. Elijah's family had received an anonymous telephone call from someone who threatened to kill the entire family. A guard assigned by police followed Elijah everywhere. Carstairs, Doer and Filmon were also offered police protection. Carstairs accepted after receiving a threatening letter. Gordon MacIntosh asked a friend in the police department if he could have someone pass by his house regularly. MacIntosh's wife was expecting a baby any day.

One of the few calls Harper accepted personally during that first week came from Howard Pawley.

"Of all the members of the House, there was no one, in my view, who knew less about the rules of the House—or who cared less about them," says Pawley, laughing. "I imagine Elijah had never opened that little blue book, the rules book, in all the years he was sitting there. And then, to see him getting up on technical procedures and questions. . . ."

The incongruity of it all delighted Pawley, but his telephone message was a serious one. "Elijah, you know I disagree with what you are doing, because with all its defects, I think that we might be better to go ahead and take the commitment for further rounds on aboriginal items. At the same time, if I were you, Elijah, I would continue to do what you're doing. If you back down at this point—and I am speaking to you now as a friend—I think you will lose credibility."

Elijah listened and then responded in his usual quiet way. "I don't like this notoriety. I am looking forward to getting back to the trapline and looking up at the stars at night."

Says Pawley, "He didn't enjoy it, but he recognized that he had a responsibility that he couldn't avoid. He had matured, there was no question. He had moved from the local stage to the provincial stage to the national stage and he got everybody's attention. Everyone else was taking credit for what Elijah was doing, and he quietly waved the feather and said no. You could hardly hear him say no and he clearly wasn't enjoying the limelight."

It was because of who Elijah was, says Pawley, that Canadians were drawn to his cause and allowed him to stand as an expression of their own frustrations with the accord.

"They felt they were seeing one honest politician. They saw integrity and honesty. They didn't know about aboriginal issues. All kinds of people in Manitoba who had never shared Elijah's aspirations for aboriginal self-government were cheering him on."

Federal government officials, however, saw things differently, and they were trying to meet with Fontaine, Harper or anyone else who could influence the course of events. The native advisors had decided that only Jack London would accept calls from federal government officials. London would be the Assembly of Manitoba Chiefs' senior bureaucrat, the person to deal one-on-one with Mulroney's bureaucrats. Fontaine, as the assembly's leader, would deal with his equals, the prime minister and the premiers.

"I was to be the ears and eyes of the chiefs in discussions with the federal government," says London. But despite all he had witnessed and admired about the aboriginal ways of doing things, London still found it hard to let go of the notion that he could play a key role as negotiator. "There was still this little last vestige of me that was playing lawyer in the classic sense—with a certain amount of control over the file."

London returned to his office to find a message from Stanley Hartt's office. He returned the call. The conversation with Hartt would be the last time London overstepped his role.

"Hi, Jack."

London was struck by the familiarity of the greeting.

"I don't think we have ever met," replied London. Hartt suggested that they had, but London was not convinced. Even if they had, their acquaintance was not of the first-name sort.

"Jack, I wonder what can be done to alleviate this situation."

"It seems to me," replied London, outlining some thoughts, "that there is a window of forty-eight hours within which the federal government has to respond massively, in a way that I cannot define for you, but in a way so surprising that it would lead to a change in the position of the chiefs. By Monday, it is gone."

Hartt asked for a hint. London had been given no instructions from Fontaine or any other native strategist from which to extract an answer. There had been rumours that native leaders might be swayed by a treaty of some kind. While London did not say so directly, he could not help but hint that the prime minister should come to Winnipeg to make an offer.

"The prime minister would not make the trip and expose himself unless there is absolute certainly of the result," said Hartt, adding the now-familiar federal line. "This is the Quebec round. It is their turn. The companion resolution contains a number of points designed to advance the interests of other people, including aboriginal people.

"We would like to find a way to cause them [native leaders] to focus on the historic moment and their notoriety, and how they can turn the moment to their advantage without destroying the country."

London responded only that the people who had hired him understood the moment. "They understand the leverage that they have. And you have to understand that, too," he told Hartt.

Hartt suggested that there could be meetings and that the government was prepared to send the highest level delegation, mentioning Senator Lowell Murray and Justice Minister Kim Campbell. He also said that there might be room for talking about concessions "if [the native leaders] would start with them in negotiations." Hartt also told London that he had met the day before with Georges Erasmus and other national native leaders in Ottawa.

"You should understand that the people who are in control are in Manitoba and that you are not dealing with the national level," replied London. "You will have to focus your attention and efforts here in Manitoba and not with the national leadership."

The conversation ended with Hartt saying he would speak to the prime minister. London indicated that he would confer with the chiefs. London had the distinct impression that the federal government had no idea what to do.

The next day, Fontaine told London that he had heard about the call with Hartt and about London's suggestion of the prime minister's involvement and the possibility of compromise.

"Those were not your instructions," Fontaine said, politely but firmly. "You are simply a recorder in the process. You are to discuss, take information and then bring it back for processing. You have no independent authority to make a decision."

"It was at that point," says London, "that, finally, fully and completely, I recognized that it was the chiefs making a decision as a group, and that no one else would be involved in that decision-making process."

Over the weekend, London worked with MacIntosh and Jay Cowan to prepare for any surprises in the Manitoba legislature, which was scheduled to resume sitting the following week, and to decide on strategy to deal with the high-level federal delegation that was expected on the Monday.

On Saturday night, the team gathered at the Assembly of Manitoba Chiefs office. "They handed a note around indicating no one should say anything, but that we should just go to the Southeast Tribal Council Offices on Ellice Avenue, because there was concern that the place was bugged," says Gordon MacIntosh. When everyone was gathered at the new location about half an hour later, MacIntosh presented ideas on strategy for the legislature, and Cowan talked about procedures.

The biggest fear was that the Filmon government would find a way to suspend the rules of the legislature. "We were really into it by then, the greyest and most obscure rules," says MacIntosh.

On Sunday, June 17, London and Fontaine agreed to accept a call from the prime minister in order to finalize the agenda for the Monday meeting.

"When the prime minister comes a callin', you don't turn him away at the door," says Fontaine. "But our position was already established. We weren't into any horse-trading. Still, we understood that if the prime minister called and there was an indication that they were prepared to deal, this would bring pressure on the group. It is not every day that the prime minister calls."

When the phone rang, London answered. Fontaine picked up an extension.

"Hello, Jack," said Mulroney.

London cringed. "I have Chief Fontaine with me," he replied.

"Good morning, Chief Fontaine," said the prime minister.

Mulroney said he understood that Indians had legitimate needs and demands, and that there was a problem with trust. Without Meech, however, there would be no structure to deal with those issues.

"I am sending the delegation and they have the authority to speak on my behalf and to make decisions on my behalf," said Mulroney. "They are bringing with them a package that I am certain you will find more than acceptable. I hope that these negotiations will prove fruitful."

"Prime Minister, as we have said repeatedly," said Fontaine, "we will be happy to hear the representatives that you send and to listen to them very carefully, but we are not prepared to enter into negotiations."

"Well, there can't be progress if people aren't willing to discuss and talk," said Mulroney.

"My understanding, Mr. Prime Minister," interjected London, "is that my clients are prepared certainly to hear fully what has to be said; but they are not prepared to indicate that they will discuss or negotiate. They are prepared to listen."

Mulroney talked a bit more and finally said, "It will be in order if you listen, even if there is no dialogue."

Fontaine and London thanked the prime minister for his call. Then London added a parting shot. "I understand that you are going to the airport to greet Nelson Mandela this afternoon. Would you give him our love?"

"I'd be happy to convey your good wishes to Mr. Mandela," came the reply.

Less than a minute later, the phone rang again. It was Stanley Hartt.

"I hope you didn't misunderstand what the prime minister said when he talked about the delegation coming," Hartt said to London. "Of course his expectation is that there will be discussion."

"That is not so," replied London, pulling out the notes he had made during the call. "Let me read the quote of what the prime minister said." London read the comment. "If you take the position that we agreed to a negotiation," London told Mulroney's chief of staff, "or that we are agreeing to a negotiation, I am releasing the transcript, just like the *Globe and Mail* did." (London was referring to the fact that the newspaper had printed the entire roll-the-dice interview with Mulroney after the prime minister claimed he had been misquoted.)

"I understand your point," replied Hartt, and hung up.

Fontaine says that although Mulroney must have been aware of the power the native leaders were wielding, "I think there was still an underestimation of this whole thing."

Fontaine called an emergency meeting of the chiefs that afternoon to decide what position to take with the federal delegation and how to react to any offer. "We hadn't decided if we wanted to talk to them," says Fontaine. "As far as we were concerned, no deals. We wanted to kill Meech—it was racist."

MacIntosh had planned to stay home that day to do more research on the legislative rules, until Elijah called, asking him to come to the chiefs' meeting. Margaret MacIntosh had started her contractions that morning, and MacIntosh asked her what she wanted him to do. She said that this was history in the making and she wanted to go with him—perhaps there would be a room she could stay in while the meeting went on.

There was no convenient room, so Margaret sat at the back of the meeting doing breathing exercises and accepting water and words of encouragement from hotel staff and some female chiefs while discussions took place and calls went back and forth with Ottawa officials. "I remember the smoke," says Gordon MacIntosh. "Export 'A's are very popular. The room started filling up."

Harry Swain, deputy minister of Indian Affairs, called MacIntosh during the meeting and said that Mulroney wanted to talk to Elijah. "Elijah had taken the position that he would listen to the chiefs and thought it was best to maintain communications as they already were," said MacIntosh. The message was passed on—Harper would not speak to Mulroney.

Elijah was particularly stressed at the chiefs' meeting: he had hardly slept all week and he knew there was at least another week of manoeuvring before it would be over. There had been a warning that he would be assassinated in the legislative building that day at 2:00 P.M., so he had changed his schedule. Throughout the week, (any) car that would be transporting Elijah was checked over before he got in, and the driver watched the rear-view mirror nervously to see if they were being followed. "I was always on edge," says Harper, although he worked hard to put the threats out of his mind.

"People outside the fraternity of the legislature might not understand the weight that was placed on Elijah, or the significance of standing apart from not only the majority in the legislature but, in particular, your colleagues," says MacIntosh. "To stand up in the House as a lone voice is a difficult thing to do. There are few who have ever done it. All the planning and all the advice are not nearly as significant as standing up."

Elijah sat next to MacIntosh throughout the meeting, drinking a large McDonald's milkshake. Shortly after 2:00 P.M., MacIntosh told Harper that the dreaded hour had passed. Elijah simply grunted.

MacIntosh was finding it hard to concentrate because Margaret was now in full labour. She borrowed the only cell phone in the room to call the doctor, and he ordered her to the hospital immediately. MacIntosh left the building to get the car and walked into a wall of television camera lights and reporters. "It was like mosquitoes."

"Gord, what's going on?" shouted one.

"You look mad, sir," cried out another.

"I'm going to get my car to take my wife to the hospital. We're having a baby," said MacIntosh. The camera lights were immediately turned off. When MacIntosh reemerged from the building with his obviously pregnant wife, the reporters seemed surprised that he had been telling the truth. As the couple made their way to the car, a lone camera light turned back on. "Hey," exclaimed the cameraman, "that's a good story."

An hour later, the MacIntoshs' second child was born. They named him Gordon Elijah Mueller MacIntosh.

Throughout the afternoon, London jockeyed with Hartt over the telephone. The lawyer had two main points—the chiefs were prepared to listen only, and the government delegation had to be made up of representatives from Mulroney's office, not bureaucrats, particularly not Roger Tasse or Indian Affairs Deputy Minister Harry Swain. "They were technicians—Tasse on Meech and Swain on relations with Indian people," says London. "If we were simply there to listen, then the people delivering the message should be political people."

Hartt argued that "I can't send Lowell Murray in there just to hand over a message," but eventually gave in.

The chiefs' meeting lasted six hours. As London relayed messages from Ottawa, the chiefs discussed every option: some felt no meeting should be held; others felt that the government should at least be heard. Oscar Lathlin, the chief from The Pas, talked by phone with elders and others on his reserve for more than two hours. "When we make a decision, we have to make sure we have the support at home," he later told a reporter. An elder encouraged Lathlin to keep fighting. "He said a prayer for me over the telephone. That's what keeps me going."

Three hours into the meeting, consensus not to negotiate with the federal delegation had clearly emerged, but other details were still unresolved. The chiefs spoke frequently of their distrust of Mulroney and his government and of what little hope they held out for the next day's meeting.

Fontaine, Harper, Mercredi and London held a press conference in the assembly offices an hour after the meeting broke up. Fontaine began by asking the cameras to be turned off for a minute. He was upset about an article in that day's *Winnipeg Sun*. Legislative reporter Donald Bennam had named Fontaine as the brains behind the entire native operation.

"I want to say one thing not for public consumption," said Fontaine. "Donald Bennam's article today that suggested that I am the mastermind behind this—I'm not. Anything that we have done, we have done collectively. I just want you to understand that. There is no mastermind here. There is all of us."

Fontaine then delivered a brief statement from the chiefs.

"Prime Minister Brian Mulroney and Chief Phil Fontaine of the Manitoba chiefs have agreed that a meeting will be held on Monday, June 18, 1990, at 8:00 A.M. in Winnipeg, Manitoba, at the law office of Jack R. London, Q.C., between representatives of the prime minister and representatives of the assembly for the purpose of having the Assembly of Manitoba Chiefs listen to the representations and proposals of the prime minister on the current impasse on the Meech Lake Accord and the companion resolution. I call on all Manitoba chiefs to come to Winnipeg as soon as possible and report to the office of the Assembly of Manitoba Chiefs."

The reporters asked about the telephone conversation with Mulroney and who would be in the Ottawa delegation. No one answered.

The next morning, Mulroney's top political aides—Stanley Hartt, Lowell Murray, Norman Spector and Paul Tellier—flew into Gimli (supposedly to avoid media hordes) and then drove to Winnipeg.

"I know all of these characters," says Howard Pawley, "and I can't think of any individuals sent from Ottawa who would have less rapport with aboriginal people."

Copies of Ottawa's proposal were delivered to Jack London's office at 7:00 A.M. so that the chiefs and their advisors would have time to read it and prepare any response. There were seven pages and a covering letter from Mulroney. "Success in these efforts is an important component of Canada's future unity," wrote Mulroney. "I, too, wish that together we could have made more progress. But let us not overlook what has been accomplished in the past and how close we have come to making even more substantial progress."

The document contained several promises: aboriginal people would be involved in establishing the agendas for future first ministers' conferences on aboriginal issues; the date of the first meeting would be accelerated; the Canadian government would commit to recognizing aboriginal people as a fundamental characteristic of Canada; native leaders would be invited to attend future FMCs when issues directly affecting them were discussed; and a royal commission on native affairs would be established.

It took about fifteen minutes to read. "Is this what he meant by a new package?" asked Fontaine. "There is nothing new here." There were nods of agreement all round.

Twenty-six chiefs, band councillors and other native leaders, including Chief Louis Stevenson (in full headdress and buckskin jacket), were in the boardroom minutes later when the federal delegation arrived. London was to act as chair, and Fontaine was to say thank you to signal an end to the gathering.

Notably absent was Georges Erasmus, although the head of the Assembly of First Nations was expected in Winnipeg later that day.

Elijah had been so busy with strategy and caucus meetings and media interviews that he had been oblivious to internal Assembly of First Nations tensions. One night when Harper and Ovide Mercredi were preparing for an interview the following morning on "Canada A.M.", word came that Erasmus would be making his way to Manitoba shortly. "Ovide was upset with the credit newspapers had given Georges," recalls Elijah. "He said that the newspapers were making it sound like Georges was part of the process, but he hadn't been."

Harper says that the question of how Erasmus was treated during that period was raised more than a year later, when Mercredi was elected the new head of the Assembly of First Nations. "People thought that Georges had not been given the prominence that he should have been as national leader," says Elijah.

Erasmus says that he would have been in Manitoba sooner, except that he had been impossible to reach in the Maritimes. When he arrived in Newfoundland on Sunday, June 17, an airline ticket to Manitoba was waiting for him.

Insiders, however, say that while political etiquette required that Erasmus be invited to Manitoba, no urgent invitation had been issued to him. Both Mercredi and Fontaine had had their disagreements with Erasmus in the past—many of them over the Meech Lake Accord. Reporters had been asking throughout the week where Erasmus was and whether the Assembly of First Nations was using Manitoba to further its cause.

"The AFN includes all the chiefs of Canada, so we are using the people here," said Erasmus upon his arrival in Winnipeg on Monday, June 18. "It doesn't make much sense to keep such close daily control over it, so they're in charge. But we have a joint general strategy. The strategy is to either improve the deal or to find ways to frustrate it so we can get beyond the twenty-third and start all over again," he said. Mercredi would later make it clear that he was upset because Erasmus had not clearly stated that the work was being orchestrated solely out of Manitoba.

On the way into the meeting with the chiefs, Lowell Murray was caught by reporters. "I am here as agreed to speak to the letter that he [Mulroney] has sent to the chiefs and they have agreed to hear me on this matter," he said. He sounded uncomfortable, unsure of himself. "The objective of course, is to, ah, to, ah, break the, ah"—he struggled, then recovered—"the procedural impasse in the Manitoba legislature so that MLAS here will have the same opportunity as MLAS in the rest of the country, namely to vote on the Meech Lake Accord and the companion resolution."

The meeting lasted forty-five minutes and went exactly according to the native plan.

"Murray launched into a half-hour talk—a monologue—on the history of French-English relations," says London. "There was limited reference to aboriginal issues."

"It was almost contemptuous to aboriginal people," says MacIntosh of the talk and the government offer.

When Murray was finished, London asked Spector and Hartt if they had anything to add. They said no.

"I want to thank you for coming," Fontaine said. "The meeting is adjourned."

London escorted the federal delegation out.

"Should we stay?" asked Murray. "Should we go back to our hotel or should we go back to Ottawa?"

"I think you should do whatever you think you should," replied London before returning to the boardroom.

Lowell Murray was furious. Never before had he been dismissed in that way.

There was a brief meeting of the chiefs that afternoon at the Southeast Tribal offices. It was agreed that there was nothing else about the federal offer to consider.

"I knew that the die was cast, that there wasn't going to be an accommodation of any kind," says London.

On the way to the Manitoba legislature Elijah saw Yvon Dumont, head of the Manitoba Métis Federation and a spokesman for the Métis National Council, walking near the legislature. When Harper got to his office, there was a letter, signed by Dumont, urging him to give up the fight.

"He must have gone over to my office to drop off his letter," says Elijah. Dumont would warn a week later that Elijah and his supporters had "set us back fifty years."

Later that day, in reference to Dumont's letter, Mulroney stood in Parliament and referred to the fact that there were native leaders representing eighty thousand aboriginal people in Canada who supported the accord.

Dumont was an old friend of Elijah's, and his role in the Meech Lake saga still perplexes Harper. "There is a feeling of brotherhood or kinship," Harper says of relations between Indians and the Metis. "They are distinct nations—totally different—but we support each other."

Reading Dumont's letter, Elijah recalled Dumont's tears at the end of the last native first ministers' conference, and wondered why the Metis leader was so supportive of the Mulroney plan when the Manitoba Metis community was divided on the issue.

Elijah's nomination meeting was still scheduled for June 23, and early in the week Lloyd Girman got a call from a Manitoba NDP staffer about it.

"Elijah isn't going to be there," said Girman. "I think you have a couple of options. Go ahead with the nomination—and the following day the press will report that Elijah Harper, who just saved Canada, loses his nomination—or put it off for three months, postpone it due to circumstances." The party decided to postpone the event for several months. George Hickes would eventually run in the newly created Winnipeg riding of Point Douglas, and Harper would be left alone in Rupertsland.

As the Ottawa delegation made its way back to Ottawa that Monday, Harper stood in the legislature to say his fifth no, delaying debate once again. The pressure was getting to him: his eyes seemed permanently watery, there was almost always sweat on his brow, and he blinked very slowly in front of the camera lights. He was smoking more, and he even had one drink in the evening to help him sleep.

Later that day, Harper was again given a standing ovation by more than two hundred supporters at the Winnipeg Convention Centre. Again, he found it impossible to control his feelings. "I don't know if I can speak at this time, because I feel very emotional," he began, tears rolling down his cheeks. Again he spoke of his father in Red Sucker and how he had spoken to him the previous night for strength and guidance.

"Mulroney had the power to call a royal commission at any time," Elijah told reporters when asked about the government's offer. "We have had studies of aboriginal people for many years. We have a special parliamentary committee on self-government. There are a number of recommendations that are sitting on the government's desk. There is nothing in the Meech Lake Accord that will benefit aboriginal people."

He was asked what he thought he had gained by his protest. "I think what we have accomplished up to this point is that we have made the general public aware of aboriginal issues," he said. "And that what we are fighting for is a democratic process for all people—not only in Manitoba, but for the entire constitutional process."

"By this point, they [the native leaders] knew they had the support of the people across the country," says Sharon Carstairs. "If they had not had the public support, they may have been prepared to accept the recommendations that Lowell Murray put forward—the royal commission and all the other things."

Canadians were simply dispirited, she says. "They were furious with the roll-the-dice prime minister. They felt that they had been terribly betrayed."

With the failure of Mulroney's delegation, the pressure increased on the three Manitoba party leaders. Debate was to begin in two days' time, on Wednesday. Publicly, Ottawa was demanding that Manitoba suspend the rules. Lowell Murray declared that these rules, referred to by some federal officials as the most democratic in the country, should be changed: "I would find it incredible that one MLA can tie up the legislature in knots indefinitely."

"They knew the rules," says Carstairs. "They just thought they'd finally get us to capitulate, that we would be willing to break the rules. They never understood us. They never thought we were important enough to understand. They never understood Clyde Wells, and they never thought he was important enough to try and understand, to try and find a way to work with this man, to make it acceptable to him."

"They were doing the 'You said you would make every effort possible,' " says Greg Lyle. " 'You're not making every effort possible.' . . . They knew they had fucked up. They were really getting desperate."

Rumours began to fly that the federal government was working on a scheme to move the deadline, despite repeated claims that this was impossible.

The three party leaders knew that the three thousand names on the speakers' list for public hearings would make it impossible to complete the hearings before the Saturday deadline. They worked on their statements for the debate, knowing that these would be the only official record of their thoughts on events in Manitoba once the Meech Lake Accord died.

On Wednesday, debate finally began on the accord in the Manitoba legislature, but only after Elijah refused a request to dispense with the forty-minute question period. He carried the entire session alone. With the eyes of the country on him, Harper visited the spectrum of native issues: the constitutional impasse, aboriginal self-government, Supreme Court rulings affecting native rights, native education, treaty rights and health care, aboriginal child-care centres, and hunting and fishing regulations.

When question period was over, Filmon was finally able to introduce the accord. For almost an hour, Filmon outlined the history of the accord in Manitoba, then stated, "I believe this package is worthy of our support."

Carstairs responded to the calls from Ottawa to invoke closure by quoting from Mulroney: " 'You will not be able to get me to ever cut off debate on a constitutional resolution. They can go on for as long as they want—for years,' " she read. She then called on Canadians to set aside their disgust with such an untrustworthy prime minister and "say yes to Canada."

When Doer, too, said he would support the proposal, the three had fulfilled their promise to Mulroney: they had stood in support of the accord.

Only a few NDP members had promised to speak on the accord and, without additional speakers, it was questionable whether debate could carry on through the Friday sitting. Then Liberal MLA Gulzar Cheema stood, followed by long-time accord opponent NDP Len Evans and others. An attempt to have the House sit beyond 6:00 P.M. failed.

The next day, Aboriginal Solidarity Day, thousands of aboriginal people from across the country marched on the Manitoba legislature. There was dancing and singing and, until the public-address system failed, the demonstrators listened to the goings on in the legislature.

On the way into the House on Thursday, Elijah told reporters that he had every intention of carrying his protest through to the next afternoon. "The support I got here today gives me the strength," he said. "I feel somewhat confident, but tomorrow we will see what happens."

One of his regrets, Elijah says later, was that he was so busy he didn't have time to enjoy all the people who came to support him. "I kept being put in a room and told to take it easy. And I just wanted to feel, to be with the people. Some of the people told me it was the first time they had walked proud down the streets."

Inside the House, Elijah again took up question period and was then called upon to speak to the accord. His speech had been drawn up in consultation with the native strategists. "Our relationship with Canada," said Harper, the eagle feather in his hand, "is a national disgrace.

"What we are fighting for is democracy, democracy for ourselves and democracy for all Canadians. And we will use the democratic principles in this country to obtain our rightful place in Canada." He then raised many of the issues he had been speaking about in the legislature for more than a decade.

"We are prepared to hurt a little," he told the House that day in closing. "We are prepared to wait ten years; we are prepared to wait fifteen years. We are prepared to wait for twenty-five years because we believe in what we are fighting for. We are not interested in short-term solutions. What we are fighting for is for our people, for our children—for the future of our children, our culture, our heritage and what we believe in. Most of all, we are fighting for our rightful place in Canadian society and for democracy for aboriginal people and, indeed, all Canadians. Thank you."

Around three o'clock, Filmon informed Carstairs and Doer that the prime minister wanted to talk to the three of them at five that afternoon.

"I just looked at him and said I didn't particularly feel like talking to the prime minister," says Carstairs.

"Well, neither do I," replied Filmon, but he didn't think there was much choice.

"So we all gathered at his office," recalls Carstairs, "and it came to five, and then five-thirty." The phone rang. "It was Lowell Murray," says Carstairs.

"You people have to invoke closure," demanded Murray. For the first time the request had come directly from the prime minister's office.

" 'There is no bloody way at all,' " Carstairs says she replied. " 'The whole process is ruined. You've abused it, and I will have no part in any further abuse of the system. Nothing.' [Murray] huffed and puffed and said that if that was our attitude, Newfoundland was going to pass it and we'd be the odd man out."

The three Manitoba leaders were barely able to contain their disgust. They had been in close contact with Wells. For days, he had not been sure how the vote would go, but the previous night, he had finally taken a count. He had told Manitoba that the accord could not pass in Newfoundland.

Wells was told by federal government officials sometime Thursday afternoon that Manitoba was about to pass the accord. Both Carstairs and Harper assured him that only a miracle would get it through Manitoba. "I told Wells that I would not allow unanimous consent to sit beyond 12:30 P.M. on Friday," says Elijah.

On Friday morning debate in the Manitoba legislature continued until 12:30 P.M. The legislature must adjourn at that time unless there is unanimous consent to extend the sitting. Speaker Denis Rocan asked if there was leave to extend debate. Elijah Harper, holding the now-famous eagle feather, shook his head. "No, Mr. Speaker."

The House was adjourned. The accord could not be passed in Manitoba before the deadline. There were wild cheers outside, but they could not be heard inside the chamber.

Elijah walked into the caucus room and hugged MacIntosh. "We couldn't have done it without you," Harper said.

"No, no," replied MacIntosh, feeling quite emotional. "It was you and the chiefs who did it."

While the House was sitting, Lowell Murray had gone on television to say that the federal government was investigating the possibility of asking the courts to keep the clock ticking past June 23. The feds would ask that the clock be deemed to have begun only when Saskatchewan passed the accord on September 23, 1990. However, said Murray, this last-ditch action would be taken only if Newfoundland voted in favour of the accord.

"Everything now depends on the free vote in the Newfoundland House of Assembly this afternoon," said Murray. "There is a majority government in Newfoundland and sufficient time to hold the free vote."

Carstairs was furious. "We are tired of being played with, and that is what this prime minister has done to us for three solid years," she said. "We've had it. We are tired of it. We don't want it any more. We don't want him any more. Last night [Lowell Murray] was on a speaker phone with all three of us telling us this, this and this—and today he says, 'Just kidding.' "

Native leaders were equally angry.

"We will use every tactic, we will develop strategies to make sure that aboriginal people are heard," said Harper. "We will make sure that aboriginal people are full and equal partners at future constitutional talks."

"I don't understand why they want this country to be, throughout the summer, in turmoil," said Georges Erasmus. "It sounds like they are desperate men trying to save their own skin."

"It should not be tolerated," decried Fontaine. "It should not be accepted, and we are going to fight it all the way."

An emergency meeting of the chiefs was called for that afternoon. "For the first time I saw frustration in the eyes of the chiefs," says London. "They were being denied their legitimate place in history. [The federal government] had robbed the chiefs and Harper of the responsibility which they were happy to take on in Manitoba."

While the chiefs met, Wells recessed the Newfoundland legislature in order to speak with Opposition House Leader and Tory MP John Crosbie. Wells wanted to adjourn debate without taking a vote, and he told Crosbie that the numbers were against the accord. Crosbie left to consult with Murray and the prime minister, and he returned with a message: "The federal government would agree to Newfoundland adjourning without a vote providing that Wells would thereafter speak in favour of the accord."

Wells was incredulous. If the federal government was serious about testing its rolling-deadline proposal in the courts, the only hope for the accord was to let Newfoundland adjourn without a vote. If the Supreme Court ruled in the government's favour, Manitoba would have time to complete its process, and Newfoundland could find itself isolated yet again. Such pressure might drag enough MLAS on side, but the federal government knew that the Supreme Court idea was a long shot. It was pressuring Newfoundland to vote, even though everyone had been told it would fail.

"Crosbie knew it would be defeated, even though afterwards he made the argument that the only reason we didn't go to a vote was because we were afraid it would be accepted," says Wells.

"Crosbie was told by [opposition leader] Tom Rideout and by [opposition House leader] Len Simms that it would not pass in the Newfoundland legislature. I sat in the room and listened to them tell John Crosbie that."

The Newfoundland legislature adjourned without voting. To this day, Wells remains dismayed by the federal government's move.

"My only conclusion is that the federal government wanted Newfoundland to be in a position where we rejected it," says Wells. "They were desperate for a fall guy, and Elijah Harper was not an easy fall guy because he is an aboriginal. They could pretend it was a rejection by Newfoundland of Quebec, and it wasn't any such thing."

That night and for years thereafter, Mulroney and his allies would point at Wells's signature on the final document and declare that Wells had reneged on a promise to see the accord through his legislature. Each time they did so, they denied aboriginal people their due: it was they, not Wells, who had taken the prize from the federal government.

Despite their frustrations, native leaders in Manitoba celebrated that Friday night.

"All along we said, this was about respect—respect for our people—and that is what this victory is all about, gaining the respect of Canadians," said Ovide Mercredi. "And it is about healing as well. It is very important."

"Well, I am feeling actually great—enthused," said Harper. "This is one victory that Canada cannot deny to aboriginal people."

The next night, a candlelight vigil was held on the lawn of the Manitoba legislature as midnight struck and the accord officially faded into history. Elijah Harper was not there. For the first time in weeks, he was getting a good night's sleep.

Epilogue

LOOKING AHEAD

Elijah stands over the carcass of a roasted beaver and concentrates on applying his carving knife to the fatty, rich-tasting meat. He puts a slice on a plate and serves the evening's honoured guest, 1992 Nobel Peace Prize winner and Guatemalan indigenous activist Rigoberta Menchu.

The setting for the traditional aboriginal feast of caribou pie, roasted beaver, goose and trout—and the not-so-traditional dessert of apple pie and ice cream—is Konrad Sioui's home in Aylmer, Quebec, just a few miles north of Ottawa.

It is November 11, 1992, Remembrance Day, a fitting time for Harper to muse about where life has taken him and where it will lead in the months and years to come.

"Dealing with the demise of Meech Lake, being part of the process, is the highlight of my political career," he says in a rare moment of shared introspection. "Being involved in changing history and awakening Canada and the Canadian people in terms of aboriginal people is something that I will never forget."

Since the accord's defeat, Elijah has told the story and explored its meaning with thousands of natives and non-natives across Canada, the United States and Europe. Each time, Harper talks about native people's lives in Canada. Unfortunately, their lives are much the same as he described them in his maiden speech in the Manitoba legislature long years ago.

From the day Harper said his final no to Meech Lake, he believes it became his responsibility to share with aboriginal people the sense of empowerment he experienced. "I feel a personal obligation to talk to the people, to continue the feeling I had in Winnipeg, which was a feeling of unity, togetherness and solidarity. I am trying to share that feeling of what you can accomplish if you speak with one mind, if you speak with one voice."

"All it takes is one person if you have the backing. With the support of the people, the impossible can become possible." This is the message that Elijah has carried to small and large gatherings. It was there just weeks after Meech Lake died, when Harper emerged like an apparition from the pine forest in Oka, Quebec, to speak with surprised Mohawk warriors. The armed Mohawks, protesting incursions by the town onto an ancestral burial ground, were behind the barricades for seventy-seven days, while the Canadian army taunted them from the other side. Harper says he went to Oka because he was asked to show his support. He knew that his arrival would cause a stir and get media coverage. The message, he says, was that native Canadians were united. Before returning home, Harper agreed to deliver a letter, written by two aboriginal children, to the prime minister's residence. A picture of Harper walking up to the locked gates of 24 Sussex Drive, the children at his side, travelled across the news wires.

Some native leaders believe that the federal and Quebec governments' aggressive stance during the Oka confrontation was directly due to Quebec's residual anger at the aboriginal victory over Meech Lake. Konrad Sioui, then with the Assembly of First Nations, had an angry face-to-face confrontation with Quebec Premier Robert Bourassa and others a few days after the accord's demise. Captured by television cameras and broadcast widely in Quebec, the incident left Sioui convinced that the Quebec government would try to get back at aboriginal people. Two weeks later, Oka erupted.

Harper says he has not been close enough to the politics of Quebec to draw conclusions about the roots of Oka. His role, he says, is to serve where asked.

He got that chance again in October 1992. After weeks of canvassing chiefs and elders across the country—and weeks of agonizing that he might be forever labelled a naysayer—he had concluded that native people needed more time to explore the ramifications of the so-called Charlottetown Accord. If the time could not be made, then Harper recommended that people vote no. He took this stand even though the Charlottetown deal was supported by former anti-Meech ally and now leading national aboriginal leader, Assembly of First Nations Grand Chief Ovide Mercredi.

"We blew it as Canadians," charged an angry Mercredi the day after the referendum vote. "Canada has said no to us. We are sick of it," he added, a veiled threat in his tone. "We can't wait for you to accept us." Days later, voting results showed that the majority of aboriginal voters—like most other Canadians—had rejected the Charlottetown deal. Mercredi and those native leaders who had joined in his angry denunciation of all Canadians were forced to retreat.

Harper's stand on the referendum did not so much influence the outcome of the referendum, he says, as reflect what he had heard from the grassroots. The problem with the 'yes' side of the campaign was that they were not listening. "Aboriginal issues will be dealt with again," Harper said at the time, responding to Mercredi's charge that native issues had now been set back indefinitely. "They are supported by Canadians."

Harper's overriding message of empowerment seems to have taken hold in many small ways within aboriginal communities. It is there in the deportment of native people on the streets of Winnipeg. Where they once passed by with heads and eyes cast down, many now walk tall, heads up and stride long. It is also there in the eyes of native high-school students who speak of how they never thought there was any hope for aboriginal people in Canada, but do now. "If that is the only thing that Elijah accomplishes," says a Winnipeg woman who has noted the change, "I think it is enough."

Being a leader whose opinion is sought is an honour for Harper, and a position that he cherishes; but not everyone has been impressed with his new stature. His time away from the Manitoba legislature, travelling to speaking engagements, was noted by members of the House and the Manitoba press. One afternoon, Harper walked into the House late and heard Premier Filmon quip, "Another fee in his pocket."

"A lot of people think I should react. But why should I respond? I just ignore it," he says, as always trying to appear as if such criticisms do not bother him. Finally he adds, "Sometimes they get nasty."

The day of Filmon's remark, Harper had flown in from a chiefs' meeting in New Brunswick, for which he did not charge a fee. But his speaker's fees—ranging from zero to $3000 depending on the source of the request—are a new focus for Harper critics. The money is used to cover his expenses as he flies around the country. He cannot understand why people object.

Along with this curiosity about fees has come a renewed interest in Harper's affairs, financial and otherwise. In July 1992, a *Winnipeg Free Press* reporter obtained a partial text of Harper's divorce papers. According to the newspaper account, Harper's annual income was almost $77,000 ($44,000 of that was his MLA's salary); yet Harper's former wife, Elizabeth, told a reporter she was on welfare and forced to sell furniture to survive.

Harper is reluctant to discuss his relations with his former wife. He says simply that the affidavit had been filed two years earlier. At that time, he had been paying a minimum of $600 a month in support, an amount mutually agreed to after negotiations between the couple's lawyers. By the time the story appeared, Elizabeth's payments had been increased to $1200. There was also a $3000 lump sum payment and some pension money. The settlement is periodically reviewed in light of Harper's salary and Elizabeth's financial situation.

The *Free Press* story led to another article. Harper's earnings statement included $7500 from the Red Sucker Lake band for consulting services. Critics said it was unethical for Harper to accept money from a band within his constituency. The news story, written by reporter Dan Lett, was given further impetus when Manitoba NDP leader Gary Doer appeared to disagree with Harper's decision. "Legally, Elijah is covered," Doer said. "But it's now a question of ethics."

Harper says he was not upset by Doer's criticism. "He is always like that, trying to play it safe," says Elijah. "The more you talk the more the press can pick out things. I've been doing it long enough to know."

Harper says he was approached by the Red Sucker Lake band to do research on how they might get out of a management agreement and to help with their finances—neither job was part of his MLA duties. Before accepting the contract, Harper obtained a legal opinion from the legislative council of the Manitoba assembly. Was he breaking conflict-of-interest rules? The opinion was that he was not.

Harper says the reporter was not interested in the legal opinion exonerating him. "I finally told Dan that if he scrutinized me like that, then they should scrutinize other MLAs the same way. If I wanted to hide it, I wouldn't report it," he says of the consulting fee. "Every MLA has to report outside income and gifts. I am just more open about it."

More than a year later, in September 1993, Air Canada sued Harper for $13,800 in unpaid bills. Harper told a reporter the account was supposed to have been taken care of several weeks earlier. About half the account was connected to business expenses incurred by Harper's then girlfriend, who had been setting up a business. Harper had asked her to work out a payment schedule. Two months later, he discovered nothing had been done.

This tendency to trust others with money matters caused Harper trouble during the summer of 1990. Elijah approached his long-time mentor Lloyd Girman for advice on what to do about speaking requests and other business propositions.

As well as helping Elijah to organize his speaking engagements, Girman helped Harper to establish Cha-Cha-Canoe, a company with a home office in Red Sucker Lake, to take advantage of tax exemptions available to registered Indians. Harper's tax status is another source of much curiosity. As a registered Indian, he is exempt from paying taxes on products or services purchased for use on a reserve. Harper was taxed as any other MLA, but he applied for rebates of between 30 and 50 per cent at the end of the tax year for time and money spent on reserves.

About the same time that Cha-Cha-Canoe was established, Harper signed a contract and loan guarantee for a business established by some friends called "Friends of Rupertsland." The plan was to sell T-shirts, buttons and posters with Harper's likeness, the profits would be used to pay outstanding constituency debts. The riding was carrying a deficit from the 1988 election, and Harper's name, as guarantor, was on an election-expense loan. (Candidates often provide early financing for their campaigns and try to make the money back through fund-raisers).

Elijah never saw any money from memorabilia sales. "I got a cheque once for $1000 but it bounced," says Harper. He still has the constituency debt, plus the loan guaranteed to produce the memorabilia—about $4000—and an additional $10,000 for items purchased. "The collection agency calls me and says I am responsible," says Harper of the $10,000 purchase. "But I really didn't have anything to do with that."

This may be, but Harper is the high-profile name attached to the venture and people automatically target him for the debt—as was the case for a fund-raising dinner held in his honour: it ended $2000 in the red, and he is now paying off that as well. "They get after me because it was held in my honour," says Harper.

While the ongoing questions about his finances are troubling, Harper does not plan to change his approach nor is he any more concerned about his reputation than he was years ago. Harper has lived most of his life in both the white and native worlds and there are times when he must adhere to rules he does not particularly share. In the end, however, it is the native world that guides him, he says. "As long as I fight in the white man's world, I will always have support [in the native world]. And at the end of all this, I will still have a home, even if I don't have any money." Moreover, he says, he always pays eventually. "Nobody ever loses."

Public incursions into his personal life have been steady since Meech. Immediately following the accord's demise, Harper found it difficult to walk anywhere without being stopped. "Is that Elijah Harper?" Invariably, the speaker would step forward to shake his hand and often ask to have a picture taken with Harper. On one trip across the country, the pilot announced over the intercom that Elijah was on board. Applause and autograph seekers followed.

When he is under stress, Harper often wishes he could disappear. "I get so uncomfortable," he says. "It is embarrassing. Sometimes, you want to hide." But while the lack of privacy and the notoriety were difficult at first, he now, more often than not, enjoys the recognition.

Two years of travelling almost non-stop have taken a physical toll on Harper. He has been slowed by several bouts of the flu. Once a light smoker, he is now rarely seen without a pack of Export "A"s close to hand; he jokes that he is simply offering up more traditional native thanks by burning tobacco to the Creator. Rumours and news reports that he has been suffering from stomach ulcers or anything more serious than fatigue are untrue, he says.

Since Meech, Harper has been honoured by natives and non-natives alike. There have been words of praise, awards and a myriad of gifts, including traditional native clothing, blankets, paintings, jewellery and one of his most prized possessions—a talking stick, which gives the person holding it the authority to speak.

Born with only an English name, Elijah now has several native ones, each steeped in tradition. The titles show respect and thanks for what he has done. He was granted the title "Soaring Eagle" by a man in East Selkirk, Manitoba. "Buffalo Cloud" was bestowed on him during a powwow in Alberta by Lazarus Wesley. "It means the clouds come over the mountains, and then great things happen," the man who gave the honour told Harper. Someone in British Columbia named him Nuu-Chan-Nulth-Shilth or "Becomes Distinguished When He Comes to Our Nation." "Do-Kwa-Yas"—"Has Risen above the Rest"—was offered by a Campbell River, B.C., resident who wrote, "The name belonged to my grandfather." Elijah has also been given the honorary title of permanent chief of Red Sucker Lake.

On this November day in 1992, Elijah Harper says he knows only one thing for certain—in about two weeks' time, he will leave provincial politics. A few months earlier he had been fairly clear about what he would do next—he was going to run for a seat in the next federal election for the NDP, probably in urban Winnipeg North Centre. But now he no longer knows.

The Meech Lake Accord had barely been put to rest before friends began suggesting that Harper should run for a federal seat. The idea struck Elaine Cowan as she watched Harper walk down the legislature steps during the Meech Lake protest. Others were not far behind.

"We have to start plotting a move," Girman told Harper. "You can't just run around the country." He made three suggestions. Two were tongue in cheek—senator and lieutenant-governor. The serious proposition was that Harper consider running federally.

"I know exactly where you should run," Girman told Harper. "Stanley Knowles's seat, a historic seat." (Knowles, an icon of the New Democratic Party, held the Winnipeg North Centre seat from 1942—with a one-term interruption—until 1984, when a stroke forced him to retire. He has been allocated a permanent seat in Parliament and is still in the House most days watching the proceedings.) "You could move into that seat and be there the rest of your life. You'll be sitting next to Stanley."

But Harper had doubts about federal politics. "I'm not sure I can really do anything," he told Girman. Elijah's decade in provincial politics had not been easy. He never fit into white politics, despite his efforts. "I constantly struggled to be a part of it, whether it was caucus or cabinet. Somehow I was always viewed as an outsider. I could just feel it—even after Meech," he says.

As well, the demands of being a politician had left little room for a normal private life. His career as an MLA had robbed him and his family of several important things, he felt. "When I looked back, I realized it had been really hard for them," he says of Elizabeth and their four children. "I have paid a great price in terms of my own life, my time and my family—of being together."

Moreover, a federal seat would mean another ten-year commitment, and there were times when Elijah was not sure he was ready for that.

Still, Harper believed he had accomplished what he could in the provincial arena. The burden of being the sole political representative of native people was lifted in September 1992, when three more aboriginal men were elected to the Manitoba legislature—George Hickes, from Point Douglas, Oscar Lathlin, from The Pas, and Greg Dewar, from Selkirk.

The election of Hickes, Lathlin and Dewar was well timed for Harper's new role as native leader at large.

"My constituency appears to be Canada now," says Harper. "I got mail from across the country, people asking me to help them." More often than not, the problems were outside his provincial jurisdiction. Often, all he could do was help people contact someone else. "As an opposition MLA, you just don't have the resources to do anything else."

Harper explained to Girman that these requests for help, together with the other expectations of him, were more than enough responsibility for the time being. "There is so much pressure," Harper told his friend and advisor. "Especially children. When I speak to them all over the country, the expectation is hard on me. You are a role model and you don't want to trip. It is a personal and heavy responsibility to keep up that image. And the pace, physically, is immense."

Undaunted, Girman and others continued their efforts, and by the end of 1991 Harper was coming around. He began to cast about for options, a search that would be the beginning of the end of Harper's relationship with the New Democratic Party.

"I want to run in Churchill," Harper told Girman in late 1991. "That is where my people are." Churchill is the fourth-largest federal electoral district in Canada. It includes the provincial riding of Rupertsland, as well as many of the industrial towns of northern Manitoba. It has elected primarily NDP MPs, although there have been a few guest appearances by the other parties, usually the Tories.

Harper's comments caused a ripple through the federal NDP: incumbent NDP MP Rod Murphy, who had held the northern seat since 1979, had no plans to step down.

Girman again suggested that Harper consider Winnipeg North Centre. "It is a seat you can walk into," claimed Girman. The incumbent, Liberal David Walker, would not have a chance against Harper, Girman declared. "It is a natural."

It seemed far from natural to Harper. True, the native population in Winnipeg North Centre is high, but the urban setting was not familiar territory for Elijah. As well, several high-profile NDP politicians familiar in the riding—former MP Cyril Keeper and former MLA Maureen Hemphill—were considering the nomination. Harper would have a tough nomination battle, which he might not win.

The North was where he had always been and it was where he wanted to stay. He considered challenging Murphy for the NDP nomination or running against him as an independent. At this point, efforts were made to find a way to keep Harper "the hell out of Churchill," as one senior federal NDP staffer scribbled on an internal memo.

In December 1991, Harper flew to Ottawa to speak with federal NDP leader Audrey McLaughlin about the issue and about some ideas he had. He was pleased with the outcome. "I would be happy if you would agree to chair an aboriginal search committee," stated McLaughlin in a letter to Harper a few weeks later. "I believe that we should have an Aboriginal Policy and Platform Conference and that recommendations should go to the Platform Committee and conventions."

Internal NDP memos and interviews with NDP staff also indicate that the threat of Harper running independently were diverted during the meeting. "After meeting with Audrey at Christmas, Elijah reconsidered and is now looking at Winnipeg North Centre," indicates a confidential NDP memo dated January 20, 1992.

Harper says he cannot recall if McLaughlin mentioned the Winnipeg seat as an alternative, but her message was clear: stay off Rod Murphy's turf. "She told me they had a better riding in mind for me," says Harper about the exchange.

Still, Harper was pleased. He thought he could attract some high-profile native candidates, especially if the party committed itself to running them in winnable seats. Second, he thought a conference on aboriginal issues would help formulate NDP policy in time for the election. And he had suggested that a fund be established to support aboriginal candidates.

Harper followed the original correspondence with more details of his plans, including a budget. It was not long after that the party became concerned that it might be boxed in by the policy and platform conference Harper had suggested, and backpedalling began. "[I] suggest weasel words for platform and policy conference," advised a senior officer in another confidential memo.

Further correspondence to Harper suggested that party officials feared that the conference would cost too much and that the NDP election-planning committee would not be able to control the outcome.

In early February 1992, Harper received a letter indicating he had been reduced to co-chair of the aboriginal candidate search committee by the NDP strategy and election-planning committee. (The other co-chair had not been chosen.) Two weeks later, things grew positively icy when, at the suggestion of Sharon Clarke, director of organization for the NDP, Harper claimed expenses of $2302.79 for a second trip he had made to meet McLaughlin and other incidentals connected with preliminary work as chair of the search committee. Harper also suggested that Rosalind Caldwell-Moore be appointed co-ordinator of the committee. (At the time, Rosalind and Harper were dating.) Elijah received a letter from NDP Federal Secretary Dick Proctor in which Proctor, referring to the co-ordinator's position, said that "none of this has ever been agreed to."

"I backed off after that," says Harper, and the subjects of the search committee and the conference were not discussed again.

Harper's relations with the New Democratic Party had often been bumpy. He had seen repeated challenges to his nomination bids in Rupertsland, near-defeat just before Meech Lake, and a general feeling of impatience towards him by party officials. "They were always trying to put me out," says Harper. "I always felt like I wasn't good enough, that I should not be the one to represent Rupertsland. It has always been there."

"The NDP is known, traditionally, for not going out of their way for any person, no matter who it is," says Elaine Cowan.

Harper found himself on the outside again during the debate surrounding the Charlottetown Accord. In October 1992, Harper attended a national NDP policy meeting in Saskatchewan, after weeks of canvassing chiefs across the country. He wanted to pass on native leaders' discomfort with the accord to McLaughlin.

"I have problems with the referendum," Harper told McLaughlin, a Charlottetown supporter, during the policy meeting.

"I know you have problems with the referendum," came the reply. "We have problems with it too."

"And that was it," says Harper. "She never bothered to sit down and talk to me about it. I could have told her my feelings, my sense that it was not going to go anywhere. I was very disappointed. I felt that my advice, my intuition, was not valuable, and that was when I began to think seriously about where I was at. I felt I was being alienated from the whole process."

Harper decided to move ahead with his plans to resign his seat in the Manitoba legislature, reassured by a faith that even if he could not yet see them, opportunities would present themselves. "I decided to leave the doors the way they were," says Harper. "Doors would close, and doors would open."

By November 1992, the only remaining question was when Elijah would resign. NDP leader Gary Doer wanted him to wait until the end of the legislative session scheduled to begin November 26. But Harper was exhausted and needed a break, especially if he was going to run federally. He decided to make his announcement a few days before the session began.

Harper is especially pleased to be at Konrad Sioui's feast with Rigoberta Menchu, who has led the fight for indigenous rights in her own country since she was forced into exile as a teen-ager after the murder of her parents. While continents apart, she and Elijah share a great deal. At dinner, Harper tells Menchu the story of Meech Lake. In turn, she tells the guests of the day in October 1992 that she discovered she had won the Nobel Peace Prize.

In Guatemala, Menchu explains, indigenous peoples comprise 65 to 70 per cent of the population, yet they are the underclass. In the days leading up to the peace-prize announcement, there was an outpouring of emotion and support. Two days before the announcement, indigenous people and their supporters marched in the streets. With tears in her eyes, Menchu describes to her listeners the sense of empowerment that came from hearing the thousands chanting her name. "The feeling from the people was wonderful, unbelievable."

There are lighter moments during the evening as well. Host Konrad Sioui tells Menchu about the qualities of the beaver, including the animal's abundance of fat, which helps the northern Crees survive in cold climates. "You need a strong stomach to be a politician," says Elijah, patting his round stomach. "This is my political muscle," he says, as the laughter increases. "Any bigger, and I could be prime minister."

The announcement that Elijah Harper's provincial political career was over was made on November 30, 1992. The press conference had been delayed for about ten days to allow Harper to cope with the unexpected death of his mother. Upon flying home for the funeral, Harper had found the last vestiges of energy sapped from him.

"It is time for me to rest up," he said on resignation day, but he made it clear that he was not necessarily saying farewell to politics. "It is time for me to consider other political and social issues. I want to consider other opportunities and contributions I can make."

The usual accolades for a retiring politician were delivered, most referring to Meech Lake. Premier Gary Filmon, however, was less than generous. "His efforts weren't particularly directive or effective in the legislature," Filmon told reporters. "The only time he was known to have done something that was significant, of course, was in saying no to the debate on Meech Lake."

The federal NDP seemed to take no notice of Harper's announcement and no overture about Winnipeg North Centre was forthcoming. Several people urged him to announce his intention to run, but Harper stalled. "I wasn't sure if there was any commitment [from the NDP]," says Harper.

Several weeks later Harper heard through a friend that the Winnipeg North Centre nomination date had been set for March 31, 1993. The decision had been made a week earlier, but no one in the party had informed him. Soon afterward, Maureen Hemphill called Elijah in Red Sucker Lake to say she was running and had about seventy people working for her. Harper called friends to ask their advice. The consensus was that he could not win the nomination, especially in a five-way battle. A few days later, Harper announced that he would not seek the Winnipeg North Centre nomination. "But I didn't say I wouldn't seek any federal nomination," Elijah says.

While he had not expected Audrey McLaughlin or anyone else in the party to eliminate the competition, Harper had expected some hint that it was the party's wish that he run in the riding of Winnipeg North Centre. The episode forced him to look again at his eleven years with the NDP. His initial choice of parties had been easy due to the fact that the NDP had a progressive approach to indigenous rights. Throughout his years with the NDP, fellow MLAS say, Harper was always a team player, loyal to the party and to his colleagues. Since the Meech Lake Accord, Harper had responded to numerous requests from party officials, signing a fund-raising letter calling on First Nations people to support the federal party and travelling across the country knocking on doors with NDP candidates. But nothing he did, he says, seemed to be enough. "I had been in it for almost eleven years and had been really loyal to our party," says Elijah. "But whether they had been loyal to me was another question."

By February 1993, feelers were being put out by the Liberals, Mel Hurtig's new National Party of Canada and even the Tories. Then Harper crossed paths with Larry Hogan, former president of Liberal MP Lloyd Axworthy's Winnipeg riding. (The two had met a few months earlier when Hogan did some architectural work on the Red Sucker Lake nursing station.) Hogan listened to Harper's frustrations with the NDP and asked if Harper had ever considered running for the Liberals.

The thought had not crossed Harper's mind. Since the Meech Lake saga, Harper had become aboriginal spokesman at large. He had accepted the new challenge simply as part of his work to advance indigenous peoples' rights. So far, that work had been carried out with the NDP. Could he, after so many years, change parties?

Harper and many other native people see political parties as the creations of white politicians. "This is the first generation of Indian people who have ever talked about political parties, about political philosophy, and of having some say in the political process in this country," says Harper. He had spent many election campaigns trying to explain to his northern constituents, usually in vain, the differences between parties.

Politically, Harper did not see that the Liberals were much different from the NDP, especially when viewed from the native perspective. Regardless of which white political entity he worked for, he would remain an outsider working on behalf of aboriginal people. Why run for *any* party? Why not run as an independent? Because to effect change, says Harper, "you have to work with the system that's in place, the political system."

Opinion polls in early 1993 indicated that the Liberals were poised to become the government in the next federal election. While this was not his reason for switching, says Elijah, he felt that as a member of the governing party he could have a serious impact on aboriginal policies.

As always, he canvassed for opinions. Phil Fontaine was cautious but not openly negative. Harper's long-time critic Lloyd Stevenson was not opposed, but he said that Elijah must examine whether he believed in what he was doing because those who did not know him could view the move as opportunistic. Elijah talked with his father and his friends; he checked with the chiefs in Island Lake.

He then cast his net out farther. Since Meech Lake, Harper's bank of advisors had grown to include native leaders across the country. He contacted Saul Terry of the Union of B.C. Indian Chiefs and Chief Billy Diamond of the Quebec Cree. "They were all 100 per cent in support of my running for the Liberals." (While supporting him in face-to-face discussions, some aboriginal friends would say privately that they were not sure Elijah was making the right decision.)

He was less sure how long-time friends Lloyd Girman and Elaine and Jay Cowan would react. Harper decided to approach Elaine first. He visited her at work to tell her of his plans. "The whole thing made me feel quite ill" says Elaine.

"We should talk about this," she told him. That night, Elaine and Jay Cowan met with Harper and his assistant, Jennifer Wood. Harper's friends listened to his reasoning. They were upset. Jay, his tone level, was angry, says Wood. "I will campaign against you," said Jay. "And you won't win."

Harper says that Jay's reaction bothered him but that, in the end, his decisions had to be dictated by the needs of native people. "They will always be my friends," he says of the Cowans and other former NDP colleagues, "if they are true friends."

He never did talk to Girman about it, either before or after making his decision. Girman says he is neither surprised nor disappointed that he was not consulted and has not heard from Harper for months. "It is not a matter of party politics, but of aboriginal politics," he surmises.

Elaine Cowan and Lloyd Girman believe Harper's decision was the result of a number of factors, personal and political, but both suggest that the treatment he received from the federal and provincial NDP probably gave him the final push to the Liberals. "I think that there could have been some special measures, and they were not there," says Elaine. "There could have been better communication."

She says her recent lack of contact with Elijah is due to the fact that they are now in different political circles, not that the friendship has ended. "Politics is about a different opinion on how to strategize [for social change]," she says. "But beyond that, we are all human beings. He will always be a friend."

Jay Cowan is reluctant to comment. "One has to respect the choice that he made," Cowan says. He and Girman both think that Harper will have a tough time in traditional NDP territory. "I believe, for the most part, ridings are based on parties and not individuals, although that doesn't negate the possibility that someone can break through," says Cowan. "I hope I'm wrong," says Girman, "but he has to take those big white communities up there."

In Harper's discussions with the Liberals, his only condition was that he not be viewed as a token Indian. (In 1993, there were three aboriginal MPs in the House, two Liberals and a Tory). If he joined the Liberals, Harper wanted his action to be viewed as a signal to Canadians that the party was serious about aboriginal issues and planned to introduce major aboriginal initiatives after the election. He says he got the assurance he sought.

On March 16, 1993, Harper announced that he would seek the Churchill nomination for the Liberal Party. "How can you change your principles just like that?" asked a reporter. "I don't think I am changing or violating any principles I believe in," replied Harper. "As an aboriginal person, we have principles that enrich all the political parties."

A few weeks later, while travelling through the airport terminal in Winnipeg, Harper bumped into Rod Murphy. "There goes Chrétien's man," mumbled Murphy as Harper passed.

The political jibes were tough, but an unexpected one gave Harper a great deal of pleasure. Brian Mulroney declared that the Liberals had let in Quebec's number one enemy, the author of the Meech Lake Accord's death. The prime minister's desire to direct a dig at the Liberals had overcome his traditional reluctance to give native leaders credit for the demise of the accord.

Harper's announcement was not greeted with unanimous warmth in the Liberal ranks. He had been warned by his Liberal confidants that several Quebec MPs were unhappy; as a result, Chrétien would not publicly endorse his candidacy. (Chrétien would travel in Manitoba with Harper a few months later and ask that Harper be patient with tensions within the Quebec wing of the party.) Harper still finds it frustrating that, despite exhaustive attempts by aboriginal leaders throughout the three-year Meech Lake battle to emphasize their support for Quebec's aspirations, the message never got through.

Initially, there was also dissatisfaction about Harper's candidacy within the Churchill Liberal Association. The riding association had been run by a small elite for many years, and they were not happy about dealing with an outsider. But all grumbling ended after Harper, in just two days, sold more memberships than anyone else vying for the nomination. Harper was acclaimed on April 13.

In late spring, Harper says he was asked by a prominent party member to cancel a speaking engagement in Montreal for fear of negative press the day before Chrétien planned to launch his campaign. Harper agreed: it is simply a price you pay in white politics, he says.

At a Liberal party function in Ottawa in early summer, Liberal MPs gave Harper a wide berth, while new candidates eagerly sought him out. When asked if the party's lukewarm reception bothers him, he just shrugs.

Despite the criticisms levelled at him and the uphill battle he will face to win the riding of Churchill in the next election, Harper says he is ready. The challenge, he says, will be to motivate the native population to vote. Although aboriginal people make up about 70 per cent of the Churchill population, historically they do not turn out to vote in large numbers. But Harper believes that there is a growing awareness since the Meech Lake Accord.

"We have never exercised that right [to vote] to the extent where we were able to determine election results in certain ridings," he says. "But I think that is just coming to the forefront now. We can be more effectively involved and use it to our advantage."

Harper says he is in the election race to win. However, if he does not, he has no doubt that he will have other options—work at the international level, a job back on his reserve or other possibilities that he is confident will show themselves. While he has accomplished much already, he believes he will "probably be fighting for aboriginal rights until my last breath."

When Elijah Harper first whispered "no" in the Manitoba legislature in June 1990, he paralysed the federal government and thrust native issues into the limelight. But Harper's negative response to the accord will go down in history as far more than a simple no to a constitutional document; it was a no to hundreds of years of being ignored and to centuries of patiently waiting to be treated fairly by people welcomed to this country by the original inhabitants. Harper said throughout the Meech Lake saga that native people "want to build a better Canada, for aboriginal people and all of Canada."

What Meech Lake did for Elijah Harper and native leaders was give them a larger audience, an audience now more enlightened than ever before about aboriginal people and their issues. After years of travelling and repeating that message, Elijah Harper says he has become even more convinced that when he asks the question "Can native people continue to be ignored?" there can now be only one possible answer.

SOURCES

This book is based in large part on one-on-one interviews, usually taped, with many of the major players surrounding the Meech Lake Accord. Several people agreed to extensive and sometimes repeated interviews: Elijah Harper, Phil Fontaine, Ovide Mercredi, Gary Doer, Sharon Carstairs, Clyde Wells, Howard Pawley, Lloyd Girman, Paul Joffe, Jack London and Gordon MacIntosh, to name a few. Many others who were interviewed, including MLAs and senior officials in the provincial and federal offices of the Conservative and New Democratic parties, specifically asked not to be named. Others are not named since they are not quoted directly.

Other information is garnered from Elijah Harper's personal papers—speeches, letters, and newspaper and magazine clippings. Other documents, including handwritten notes taken at the time of events cited, were also provided by the Assembly of Manitoba Chiefs and by Jack London, the organization's legal counsel during the final weeks of the accord, as well as by Elijah Harper's legal advisor during the Meech Lake episode, Gordon MacIntosh.

Extensive use was also made of original documents held in the Hudson's Bay Archives in Winnipeg; parliamentary guides for the years 1950 to 1993; *Hansard* reports of legislative proceedings in Manitoba, Alberta, Newfoundland and Ottawa; newspaper clippings from the *Winnipeg Free Press*, the *Globe and Mail*, the *Toronto Star*, the *Winnipeg Sun*, the *Montreal Gazette* and the *Toronto Sun*; and radio and television interviews, most notably those done by the CBC.

BIBLIOGRAPHY

Brown, Jennifer S. H., and Robert Brightman. *The Order of the Dreamed: George Nelson on Cree and Northern Ojibwa Myth*. Manitoba: University of Manitoba Press, 1988.

Cohen, Andrew. *A Deal Undone: The Making and Breaking of the Meech Lake Accord*. Vancouver: Douglas & McIntyre, 1990.

——. "That Bastard Trudeau: Behind Closed Doors at Meech," *Saturday Night*, June 1990.

Comeau, Pauline. "Elijah Harper: The Man Who Said No," *The Canadian Forum*, July/August 1990.

Comeau, Pauline, and Aldo Santin. *The First Canadians: A Profile of Canada's Native People Today*. Toronto: James Lorimer & Company, 1990.

Comeau, Pauline. "Canadian Micmac used the UN machinery to change the law," *For the Record: Indigenous Peoples and Slavery in the United Nations*, August 1991.

Coyne, Deborah. *Roll of the Dice: Working with Clyde Wells during the Meech Lake Negotiations*. Toronto: James Lorimer & Company, 1992.

Dickason, Olive Patricia. *Canada's First Nations: A History of Founding Peoples from Earliest Times*. Toronto: McClelland and Stewart, 1992.

Fiddler, Chief Thomas, and James R. Stevens. *Killing the Shaman*. Moonbeam, Ontario: Penumbra Press, 1985.

"The Group of Seven: A Gathering of Westerners Confronting the Question of Canada's Future," *West*, March 1991.

Herstein, H. H., L. J. Hughes and R. C. Kirbyson. *Challenge and Survival: The History of Canada*. Scarborough: Prentice-Hall Canada Ltd., 1970.

MacDonald, Jake. "One Little Indian," *West*, September 1990.

Manitoba Task Force on Meech Lake. *Report on the 1987 Constitutional Accord.* October 21, 1989.

Reid, J. H. Stewart, Kenneth McNaught and Harry S. Crowe. *A Source Book of Canadian History.* Toronto: Longmans, Green & Company, 1959.

Richardson, Boyce, editor. *Drumbeat: Anger and Renewal in Indian Country.* Toronto: Summerhill Press, 1989.

Wherrett, George Jasper. *The History of Tuberculosis in Canada.* Toronto: University of Toronto Press, 1977.

Yates, Sarah. "Elijah Harper: The Man and the Mission," *Positive Vibrations*, January/February 1991.

INDEX